Wainwright's Way

FRANCES LINCOLN

WAINWRIGHT'S WAY

A long-distance walk through Alfred Wainwright's life from Blackburn to Haystacks

Nick Burton

Frances Lincoln Limited
www.franceslincoln.com

Printed and bound in China

A CIP catalogue record is available for this book from the British Library.

ISBN 978-0-7112-3321-8

9 8 7 6 5 4 3 2 1

HALF TITLE PAGE: Beetham parish church and war memorial
TITLE PAGE: Windermere – the view from Orrest Head

Contents

BUTTERMERE
Patterdale
Rosthwaite
CUMBRIA
Grasmere
Troutbeck Bridge
KENDAL
River Kent
Holme
boundary
county
Wray
Morecambe Bay
River Lune
Dunsop Bridge
LANCASHIRE
River Ribble
Whalley
BLACKBURN

Introduction

The life journey of Alfred Wainwright was shaped by the Industrial Revolution. His parents arrived in the manufacturing town of Blackburn in search of work and ended up living at the top of a long terraced road that seemed to go on for miles. He grew up in a teeming population crying out for fresh air and escape from the mind-numbing constraints of factory life. The passion he developed for the high fells was born of his years spent amid the working-class poverty of industrial Lancashire, and his Blackburn roots were a significant factor in the creation of the *Pictorial Guides to the Lakeland Fells.* These were never going to be written by a countryman: his writing represents the voice of a class of urban people who for generations had lost all contact with the countryside.

In this respect, the work of Alfred Wainwright – hereinafter referred to as AW – continued the tradition of the nineteenth-century 'weaver-poets'. These were poor industrial workers, often unemployed weavers, who sought solace in the hills, where they were inspired to write about the natural scene as a form of escapism. AW never really found his creative voice until he visited the Lake District for the first time. Why was he so affected by his first view of Lakeland from Orrest Head? Simply put, it was a reaction to the grimness of mill town Blackburn.

This 126-mile walk reflects Wainwright's life journey. Heading in a south–north direction, it starts in the industrial town where he was born and ends in the wild high fells to which he escaped. In distance terms it may not be on the grand scale of Hannibal crossing the Alps, but there can be little doubt that AW had an interesting life – a life that spanned virtually the whole of the twentieth century – and many of the features of this walk demonstrate that.

The basis of this book is that the walker can traverse the countryside of northern England in the company of AW's sketches and writings, even outside the Lake District. He didn't just sketch Lakeland. AW is a bit like Robin Hood: he turns up all over the northern counties. His imprint can be found in the Peak District, the Dales, the North York Moors, Border country and, of course, Lancashire and the Lakes. This walk cannot take in all of AW's north-country ramblings, however. It has a definite objective: to link his place of birth to the place where he was laid to rest – surely a pilgrimage any AW fan would like to make.

AW's *A Ribble Sketchbook* records the landscape of his youth and includes scenes of Whalley, less than a day's walk from the terraced house where he was born. From here the walk goes through the landscapes of AW's *A Bowland Sketchbook* and *A Lune Sketchbook* before entering the more familiar territory of his beloved lost county of Westmorland. He recorded this picturesque fringe of the Lake District in painstaking detail, parish by parish, in *Westmorland Heritage* and the River Kent can be followed, from its estuary to the heart of Kendal, in the company of *Three Westmorland Rivers.* The walk then encounters some of *The Outlying Fells of Lakeland,* the most significant of which in the Wainwright story is Orrest Head. All this, even before it taps into the rich seam of the *Pictorial Guides to the Lakeland Fells* and *A Coast to Coast Walk.*

With the book's particular objective, it has been impossible to incorporate visits to mountain summits in every one of AW's seven *Pictorial Guides.* The Northern Fells, the North Western Fells and the Southern Fells take a back seat on this walk; but though their summits are not climbed they are viewed from a distance. The walk does, however, visit the summits of fells in the other four volumes of AW's *Pictorial Guides.*

Unless you are unfortunate enough to experience the weather AW endured while walking the Pennine Way in 1967 and 1968, this walk should be an expedition of delight from beginning to end, through some of the north's most varied and beautiful scenery. The first few miles of the walk are through the streets of urban Blackburn, but do not be tempted to avoid this, for if you do so you will miss an essential part of the Wainwright story.

Each chapter of this book reflects a different stage of AW's life. His birth, life and death are presented as a series of biographical sketches. The definitive biography of Wainwright has, of course, already been written by Hunter Davies, and this masterful work, together with Davies's edited collection of *The Wainwright Letters*, is wholeheartedly recommended to readers wanting to learn more about AW.

On a practical note, each stage of the walk has been planned to end at a settlement where overnight accommodation is available in one form or another. Sections of the walk crossing the Lake District's mountains may be considered strenuous, although I have outlined alternative routes where possible. The walk is intended to be an expedition not to be rushed and well within the capabilities of the experienced walker.

The sketch maps accompanying the walk route are intended to compliment the relevant OS Explorer Maps that should be used on the walk. It is certainly not advisable to rely on the sketch maps when walking in mountainous and remote areas like the Lake District and Bowland. You will need the following OS Explorer Maps to cover the entire walk route:

Explorer 287 West Pennine Moors
Explorer OL41 Forest of Bowland and Ribblesdale
Explorer OL7 English Lakes (south-east)
Explorer OL5 English Lakes (north-east)
Explorer OL6 English Lakes (south-west)
Explorer OL4 English Lakes (north-west)

WAINWRIGHT'S BLACKBURN

'We were a close-knit and insular community, with few interests outside the town's boundaries.'
Ex-Fellwanderer

This 2-mile preamble through the centre of Blackburn takes us back to AW's youth. He spent both his childhood and early adulthood almost entirely in east Lancashire – more particularly, within the few square miles between his parents' house just off Accrington Road on the east side of the town and the Town Hall, his place of work. This circular town centre trail sets the scene and is a little appetizer before we follow AW's footsteps out of town. The walk starts and ends at the train station – also the start point of the 126-mile Wainwright's Way and highlights some of the buildings and street scenes that were familiar to AW as a child during the Edwardian era and as he grew up in the turbulent period of history between the wars.

Escaping the Mill

In January 1907 *The Blackburn Times* reported:

> DEATH OF MRS PERCY DEAN – Mr. Percy T. Dean, of 73 Alexandra Road, will have the sincere sympathy of his many friends and acquaintances in the sad bereavement which has befallen him this week. Only 11 months after his marriage he has lost his wife, who passed away after confinement on Thursday last. The baby boy lives. Several specialists were called in but nothing could be done to save the life of the young mother whose death is greatly deplored. Before her marriage Mrs Dean was Miss Mabel Margaret Ratcliffe of Didsbury and formerly of Liverpool.

On the same day that Mrs Dean's life journey ended abruptly in a bay-windowed villa overlooking a leafy park on 17 January 1907 – possibly even during the same hour – another life began in a terraced house in a poorer part of Blackburn a few miles away. Alfred Wainwright was born in 331 Audley Range. This event went unrecorded in the local press, although *The Blackburn Times* did report that just outside AW's house on the same day a corn miller's horse bolted and galloped down adjacent Cherry Street and Furthergate, before crashing into the windows of the Daisyfield Co-operative Society. Badly wounded, the horse incredibly survived its ordeal.

Born in a winter when deadly influenza was rife, in a week when eleven infants were interred at Blackburn Cemetery, AW successfully negotiated an Edwardian home birth. He went on to live the next thirty-four years of his life in Blackburn before moving to Kendal in 1941. That's virtually half a lifetime to most people.

Life in Blackburn's densely packed urban jungle – it was a town of 130,000 people – was one of grime, coal dust and cotton fibres on your lungs, clanking trams and the all-too-real northern cliché of the mill hooter and the clatter of clogs. It was a life of hard toil and destitution in equal measures in a world where, in the Victorian tradition, a man's social status was still denoted by his hat.

In his half-memoir *Ex-Fellwanderer,* published in 1988 and one of the last of his collaborations with the *Westmorland Gazette,* AW covered his upbringing and early working life in Blackburn in just a couple of chapters. Unlike the intricately fine detail of his landscape drawings, he uses only broad brushstrokes to characterize the sketches of his early life in words. His family consisted of his parents, Albert and Emily, and his older siblings, Alice, Frank and Annie. He was born into poverty – his father was an unreliable drunk and his mother took in washing – and escaped the hardships of the mill by taking exams and working his way up the local government grades. Perhaps AW felt his working-class life was of little interest to fans of his *Pictorial Guides.*

Thankfully, another Blackburn lad of AW's generation wrote a classic memoir of mill-town life between the wars. William Woodruff (1916–2008) was brought up in the town's weaving community and chronicled working-class life during the Great Depression in his bestselling *The Road to Nab End*. Woodruff was unusual in that his life led him from the backstreets of Lancashire to Florida via Harvard. In reading Woodruff's grim memoir, one senses that AW may have downplayed his own achievement in escaping the normal cycle of Blackburn life.

AW's morning walk to work, just over a mile in length, took him from regimented lines of terraced cottages to the twin lines of the canal and railway, along which ran a big fat belt of cotton mills, iron foundries and breweries. For most of AW's neighbours, coming out of their front doors at the same time every morning to a chorus of coughing, sneezing and wheezing, the walk to work stopped right here. Fortunately for AW, his clerical employment took him another quarter of a mile into the throbbing commercial core of one of the chief manufacturing towns of the British Empire.

Blackburn was then the cotton weaving capital of the world. Cotton goods dominated the export trade and fuelled the economy that maintained Britain's position as an Edwardian superpower. The opening of the Leeds and Liverpool Canal in 1810 had provided the first impetus to growth, bringing coal – tons and tons of the stuff – into Blackburn. The canal became a new focus for urban growth in what was then little more than a village of medieval streets huddled in the shadow of the old parish church, close to where a Roman road forded the River Blakewater.

As with other Lancashire mill towns, it was the railway 'mania' of the 1840s that really transformed Blackburn. The Blackburn–Preston Railway opened in 1846 and soon became part of the mammoth LYR, the Lancashire and Yorkshire Railway. The railway was the main catalyst for rapid urban and industrial development

Right: Ordnance Survey Map of Blackburn (1910)

Boat House
Furthergate
Chemical Works
Tanks
Tank
(Covered)
Kenyon Street
Esther Street
Hill Street
Castle Street
Heyes Street
Crabtree Street
Burnley Road
Reservoir
683
·838
Furthergate
Mill
(Cotton)
Blacklead
Works
Furthergate
Frederick Row
Barnes St.
St. Clement St.
Bates Street
Accrington Road
Hozier Street
Didsbury Street
Hole House
Bentley St.
Longton Street
Patten St.
Winmarleigh St.
Ice Works
682
·393
Reservoir
St. Thomas's Wescoe
Memorial Hall
Tallow Works
BLACKBURN
St. Clement Street
Audley Range
Brick Works
AW's birthplace:
331 Audley Range
Parkside Mill
(Cotton)
676
3·448
677
3·603
675
3·583
F.P.

and was responsible for Blackburn's physical expansion in the latter half of the nineteenth century.

AW's parents wouldn't have arrived in Blackburn if it hadn't been for the railway. His father, Albert Wainwright, was a travelling stonemason from Yorkshire who moved to Blackburn in search of work on railway arches. And without the railway, the Wainwrights' house on Audley Range would not have been built. The sprawling working-class residential district of Audley where AW was born mushroomed into being on the back of the new opportunities that the railway brought to the town. The railway brought factories, factories brought workers, workers needed houses. New houses were laid out in a grid-iron pattern of terraces on farmland released for development.

The external appearance of the present Blackburn station, opened in 1886, would have been familiar to AW. Its Victorian architectural splendours only become apparent when viewed from the far side of the bus station: four tall chimneys, Venetian windows, a station clock adorned with the initials of the LYR and a pillared canopy of wood and glass. Although it is well known that AW's early excursions to the Lake District were by bus, he used the train in his younger days. In *Ex-Fellwanderer* he records taking it from Blackburn to Manchester to sit his professional accountancy examinations in the 1920s.

Blackburn's bus station still occupies the same triangular piece of land it occupied in AW's youth. This is the romantically named Boulevard, the public transport hub of the town since Victorian times and the point of arrival and departure for just about everything from horse and cart to motor bus. AW would have experienced the hustle and bustle of the Boulevard at its height, with an assortment of electric trams – double-deckers, single-deckers, open-topped and closed – running the line between rows of charabancs and taxi cabs. The trams were still there when AW left Blackburn, the last one not going out of service until 1949.

AW grew up just as the great age of the motor bus was beginning. In the 1920s, fast motor cars remained the expensive indulgence of the foolhardy playboy sons of the upper classes.

For most Blackburnians, travelling by tram or bus was the norm. The bus became a homely, convenient and relatively cheap mode of transport for longer journeys and was, of course, to be AW's normal way of travelling when he did all the fieldwork for his seven *Pictorial Guides* in the 1950s and 1960s.

Beyond the bus station, the Cathedral Yard remains much as it was when AW walked through town. During his time at the Borough Treasurer's Department the parish church of St Mary's gained cathedral status and AW would have witnessed the beginnings of the building work to extend the church in the 1930s. The squat family tombs of Blackburn's great and good – the Petres, Peels and Feildens – still stand, neglected, in the old graveyard. To the teeming poverty-stricken masses of AW's generation they were a reminder of where the town's real wealth and power lay: with the old aristocratic families and the new textile barons.

Blackburn's biggest landowners were the Feilden family, who were cotton magnates. It was the Feildens, along with the other major landowner, the Church, who were responsible for opening up the town for development in the nineteenth century by disposing of large parcels of land for sale and rent. When AW was born, however, the Feilden family's influence was on the wane. As a small boy AW witnessed local men marching off to their doom in the Great War, the cataclysmic conflict that also brought the curtain down on the golden days of the Edwardian aristocracy.

AW worked in a vibrant town centre where you could buy just about anything. The old thoroughfares of the pre-industrial town, such as Church Street, Darwen Street and Northgate, were lined with shop windows and gaudy advertising signs. Traditional family shopkeepers – cloggers, grocers, milliners, bakers, tobacconists and drapers – vied for customers with the newly emerging department and chain stores like Liptons, Marks and Spencer and Boots the Chemist.

One of Blackburn's earliest shopping malls was the fashionable Fleming Square, where half a century before AW was born there lived an impoverished writer in an upper garret who, inspired by nature, went on long rambles through the Peak District and North Wales. This was John Critchley Prince (1808–66), who wrote poems about mountains. Prince, a journeyman reed maker, was one of a long line of radical 'weaver-poets' from the mill towns of Lancashire. Poverty-stricken, his life was a grim one and he walked through most of Lancashire and Yorkshire in search of employment for his dying craft. But when he experienced the raw beauty of a mountain landscape, he wrote passionately about it, just as AW did a few generations later.

AW happened to be born in the town where, from their premises at 40 Northgate, pioneering film-makers Sagar Mitchell (1866–1952) and James Kenyon (1850–1925) became two of the country's biggest film producers. They started in 1897 with a private showing of some jerky footage filmed in Blackburn Market and went on to exploit the novelty of the cinematograph by filming local people and events. 'See Yourselves as Others See You!' was the Mitchell and Kenyon mantra. They captured on film a largely forgotten slice of ordinary life in the 1900s. They were there to film the unveiling of the Queen Victoria statue overlooking the Boulevard in 1905 and from 1909 to 1913 their film production was increasingly concentrated on local events in the town. It is surely only a matter of time before through painstaking examination of the restored Mitchell and Kenyon archive an observant scholar identifies a tiny blur in the bottom corner of the screen as little Alfred Wainwright.

Sagar Mitchell, who was one of the first people in Blackburn to own a motor car, also maintained a photographic shop at the 40 Northgate premises once the heady pioneering days of cinema were over and worked here virtually up until his death. Mitchell was no stranger to the Lakes himself, having once been strapped to the front of a railway engine to make a panoramic moving film of the Lake District between Ulverston and Lakeside.

On celluloid Mitchell and Kenyon captured Blackburn at its most confident. Around the time Wainwright was playing hopscotch on the flags outside his house grand new buildings and institutions were still being erected in the town centre. On Darwen Street, the huge Central Post Office rose up just in time for AW's birth. On the boggy open space of Blakey Moor – a scruffy patch used for travelling fairs and cattle markets – an ambitious civic plan came to fruition around 1913. Here a new police station, courtroom and three public halls were constructed side by side to form a dazzling classically Greek frontage. The Blakey Moor improvement scheme also included a state-of-the-art school with an underground swimming pool. This institution brought AW into the town centre on an almost daily basis from the age of twelve.

The Blakey Moor Higher Elementary School was built on the waste ground behind the planned new civic buildings. It had an entrance on Duke Street, facing the town's Technical School and a cotton-weaving mill. The large red-brick building remains intact today. When it opened it was one of a new type of senior schools offering advanced instruction for pupils over the age of eleven. But in AW's day education beyond this age was not compulsory. The norm in Blackburn was to go and work half time in the mill and then full time at the age of thirteen. In Ex-*Fellwanderer,* AW admits that on reaching the age of twelve (and leaving his previous school on Accrington Road) he had no desire to start work in the cotton mills but neither had he considered continuing his education in the new school in the centre of town. He dreamed of being an office boy.

His teachers and mother knew best and to the new school he went. AW was naturally bright and in his first academic year (1919–20) at Blakey Moor School he topped his class.

Also in his year was a girl two months older than AW called Jessica Lofthouse (1906–88), worthy of mention since by strange coincidence she also grew up to write a series of north-country guidebooks which included her own pen-and-ink drawings. While still at school she submitted stories to newspapers, and her first book was published in 1938 – some seventeen years before the appearance of Book One of AW's *Pictorial Guides. The Rediscovery of the North* was printed and published by a newspaper, just as AW's first book was – in Lofthouse's case *The Blackburn Times.* A collection of country explorations and walks, it included chapters entitled 'Four Days' Tramp in the Lake District' and 'Motor Tour in the Lake District'.

It took a good half an hour for AW to walk to the school from the top end of Audley Range and the return home was uphill. In Ex-*Fellwanderer*, he recalls the worry of the expense of tram fares to school on wet days and it was the lack of money at home that shaped AW's next decision. While Lofthouse went on to be Blakey Moor's head girl, AW left school after just one year. He ignored the advice of his teacher this time and, aged thirteen, got his dream job of office boy at the Town Hall, a stone's throw away.

While in the employ of Blackburn Corporation, on one Thursday afternoon in May 1923 AW would have heard an 83-foot mill chimney a few streets away crashing down. As the Duke Street Mill, facing AW's old school, was felled, dust-covered Blakey Moor pupils cheered. The closure of this cotton mill marked the beginning of the long slow painful decline of Blackburn's staple industry.

Hunter Davies's biography gives an excellent account of AW's formative years at Blackburn Town Hall. He began his career there as an office boy in the Borough Engineer's Department on a wage of 15 shillings a week and ended it almost exactly twenty-one years later as a professional accountancy assistant in the Borough Treasurer's Department, earning a salary of £350 a year. In the next decade he studied hard, catching up on all he was missing at school, and taking correspondence courses and evening classes, which culminated in his becoming a qualified municipal accountant in 1931.

Through his teenage years and early twenties AW had very little social life outside the office. Spending his evenings immersed in study was good preparation for the solitary nights he would spend thirty years later in his Kendal home (where he enjoyed even less social life) compiling his *Pictorial Guides*. Working at home alone came naturally to him and helped turn him into a shy, slightly withdrawn character.

But within the confines of the Town Hall AW became perilously close to gregarious, as behind the high wooden desks and heavy ledger books he enjoyed the camaraderie of his male work colleagues. While working in a world of internal audits, balance sheets, statements of accounts and committee minutes AW also sketched cartoons and planned hiking trips.

Ledger books were filled with page after page of red columns, figures in blue ink, and signatures and counter-signatures in black ink as the honest men in the Accountancy Section tried to balance the revenue and expenditure of the labyrinthine departments of Blackburn Corporation. Together with the impeccable handwriting he had learnt at school, there is no doubt that the nature of AW's work at the Town Hall was later responsible for the unique style of the *Pictorial Guides*. He says so himself in *Fellwanderer*: 'Accountancy was my line. I was a pen-and-ink man. I was trained to believe that accountancy is an art . . . I remember being told that every page of my ledgers should be fit for framing.'

The presence of a large public square outside the front entrance of the palazzo-style Town Hall meant that it is likely that AW witnessed all the civic events, parades and fairs that took place there over the two decades he spent in the job, even if he did have to strain his neck out of a side window (his office was along the right-hand side of the building) at the discretion of Mr Pye, the earnest Borough Treasurer. A lifelong Rovers fan, AW would surely have jumped from his desk to the window when Blackburn Rovers returned with the FA Cup one Monday in April

Early AW doodle of ten council employees in a line

1928. The huge crowds of 150,000 lining the town streets meant the winning team had to sneak in a rear door of the Town Hall to reach their civic reception with the Mayor. For the record, Rovers beat Huddersfield Town 3–1 at Wembley.

On a routine day, AW would have stepped out of the Town Hall into the hustle and bustle of the purpose-built Market Place with its indoor Market House, 72-foot-high clock tower and 300 covered stalls which formed the retail heart of Victorian and Edwardian Blackburn. He could cut through the market on his way home to Audley via the canal at Eanam. If he stopped to buy an apple from the 'fruit and veg' man in the shadow of the Town Hall, he would have bought it from Fred Harty. Hanging round Fred's stall might have been a chatty little boy in short trousers: Fred's son, Russell. Imagine AW and Russell Harty (1934–88) – who both became TV personalities in the 1980s – meeting in Blackburn Market *circa* 1939. It could have happened.

Much has changed since AW's day, as the post-war planners shattered the Victorian jewels of the Market Place and clock tower and redeveloped the site. On the north side of the Town Hall, however, fragments of Georgian Blackburn remain just as AW would have seen them, around cobbled James Street and the Byzantine-domed St John's Church. This was the church of the town's growing merchant middle class, the men who originally sparked Blackburn into life. Among them is the tomb of master brewer Daniel Thwaites (1777–1843).

If the Wainwright family arrived in Blackburn at the tail end of the Industrial Revolution, then Daniel Thwaites came in near the beginning. He was born in a farm above Threlkeld in the wilds of Cumberland and scraped out a meagre living as a shepherd until he moved to the land of opportunity – Lancashire. In moving from the Lakes to industrial Blackburn, Thwaites did AW's journey in reverse.

He arrived on horseback in Blackburn around 1805, as an Excise Officer collecting duties on beer. He had the good fortune to marry the daughter of a prominent Blackburn brewer and the seeds of the Thwaites empire were sown. Within the space of one generation, the son of this Cumberland shepherd, also Daniel Thwaites (1817–88), had become one of the richest men in town, a Blackburn MP with his own country estate.

On his walk home to Audley Range AW would have walked by the Thwaites Brewery and countless of its pubs via Eanam. The Eanam district was a thin wedge packed with thick industry that squeezed along the railway and the canal between Blackburn town centre and the workers' terraces of Audley. AW's quickest way home would have taken him up Cicely Lane, through the manufacturing heart of the town that sprouted when the Leeds and Liverpool Canal opened in 1810 and brought coal to the new wharves at Eanam. From the canal bridge at the top of Cicely Lane AW would have looked down and surveyed belching mill chimneys, beyond which rose a wave of terraces stretching up to wooded ridges and moorland.

This industrial townscape would have been the dominant image of AW's early years. The countryside was hidden by steam and brick; there was constant noise from sunrise till dusk; there was no fresh air. Not surprising, then, that the blissful but all too brief Lakeland holidays that punctuated AW's mill-town life in the 1930s became so important to him.

The watershed in this life is noted almost as a footnote in the minutes of Blackburn Borough Council's Finance Committee dated Wednesday 26 November 1941: 'The Borough Treasurer submitted the resignation of Mr A. Wainwright, an Accountancy Assistant in his Department, on securing an appointment with the Kendal Borough Council, and reported that the Chairman and Vice-Chairman had given authority for a temporary re-organization of the accountancy work in his office to be effected.'

And with that, the official endorsement by a gathering of aldermen and councillors, AW debunked to Kendal.

THE ROUTE

Start outside Blackburn train station, facing the bus shelters, and turn left to cross Bridge Street and reach a zebra crossing.

The turreted building on the corner of Bridge Street with a blue plaque was once part of the town's first power station, which generated electricity for the town. Facing this building on the far side of Jubilee Street once stood two variety theatres – the Palace (1899) and the Grand (1906), formerly the Prince's Theatre. The escapologist Houdini once appeared at the Palace. AW would have known it as the picture house to which it was converted in the 1930s.

Cross Jubilee Street and walk down the paved area on the left-hand side of the bus station past Queen Victoria's statue.

The River Blakewater runs underground here. This is the river – during the nineteenth century a stinking foul sewer and now largely built over – that gave the town its name – 'Blake-burn', the Blake valley. Queen Victoria's statue was unveiled two years before AW was born and the statue of Gladstone now sited at Blakey Moor was also here when AW was a lad.

Enter the Cathedral Yard on the left. Follow the paved path through the yard, passing the old tombs of prominent families and landowners on the left.

The tombs include memorials to the Feildens, and seven generations of the Peel family. The Peel tomb once lay flat along the middle aisle in the nave of the old parish church, which was demolished in 1820. The present St Mary's was built on a realigned site. The Blackburn branch of the Peel family, who became cotton barons, produced the Tory Prime Minister Robert Peel.

The path leads out of the Cathedral Yard to a pedestrian area facing the old Lloyds Bank.

The ornate bank, dating from 1878, symbolized the prosperity and confidence of Victorian Blackburn. When AW was a lad this junction where Church Street and Darwen Street meet was one of the busiest parts of the town centre and had been since medieval times, when it was the old Market Place, overlooked by the ancient Old Bull Inn. Looking left down Darwen Street you will see a blue plaque on the Radio Lancashire building that records an 1842 'Plug Plot' skirmish, when three textile workers protesting against wage cuts were shot by troops. The Central Post Office with which AW would have been familiar is now a Wetherspoons pub. To the right of the Old Bank, the town centre has been redeveloped beyond AW's recognition by the Mall shopping centre. He would have been able to cut through to the Town Hall from near the top end of Church Street via the shops of the ornate Thwaites Arcade, demolished in 1971.

Cross Darwen Street and enter Fleming Square immediately to the left of the Old Bank. This leads to the Exchange Arcade on the left.

This is a surviving example of a Victorian arcade, built in 1849, in a Georgian square, laid out in the 1820s by a local cloth merchant, John Fleming.

At the road junction on the far side of Fleming Square turn right, and cross over with care by the entrance ramp to a car park. Continue straight ahead down Corporation Street.

In the eighteenth century, Robert Peel, father of the Robert Peel who was Prime Minister in the 1830s and 1840s, lived in a farmhouse just to the left of here. Robert senior became an MP himself and also a peer of the realm, thanks to the hugely

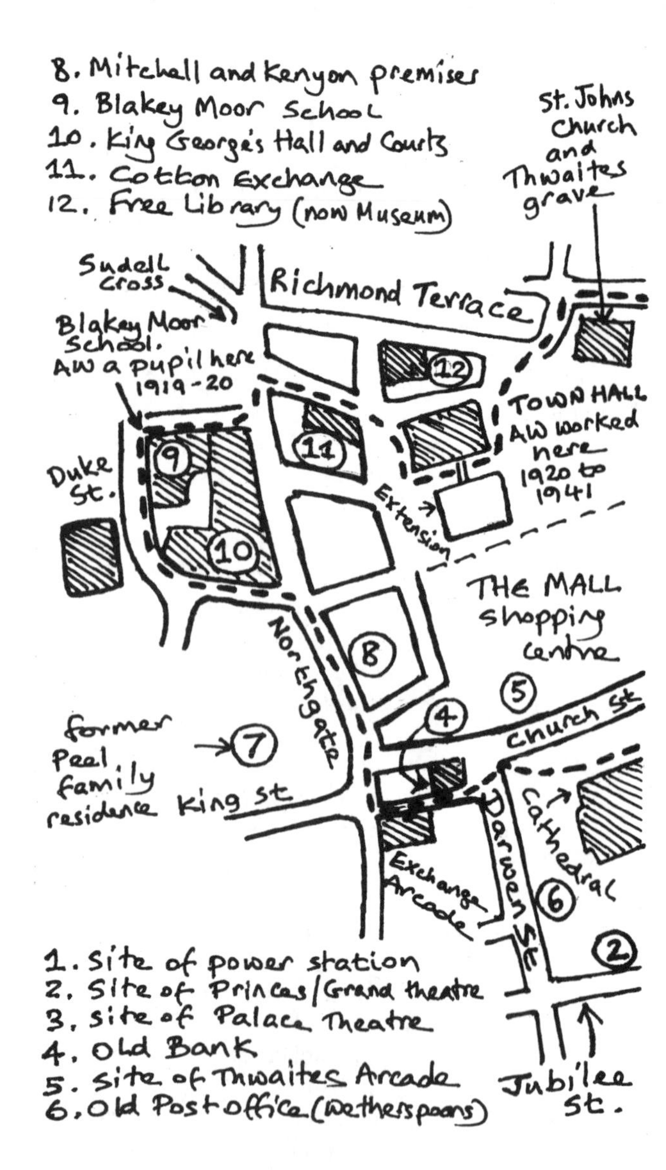
8. Mitchell and Kenyon premises
9. Blakey Moor School
10. King George's Hall and Courts
11. Cotton Exchange
12. Free Library (now Museum)
St. Johns Church and Thwaites grave
Sudell Cross
Richmond Terrace
Blakey Moor School. AW a pupil here 1919-20
TOWN HALL AW worked here 1920 to 1941
Duke St.
Extension
THE MALL shopping centre
Northgate
former Peel family residence
King St
Church St
Cathedral
Exchange Arcade
Darwen St
Jubilee St.
1. Site of power station
2. Site of Princes/Grand theatre
3. site of Palace Theatre
4. Old Bank
5. site of Thwaites Arcade
6. Old Post office (Wetherspoons)

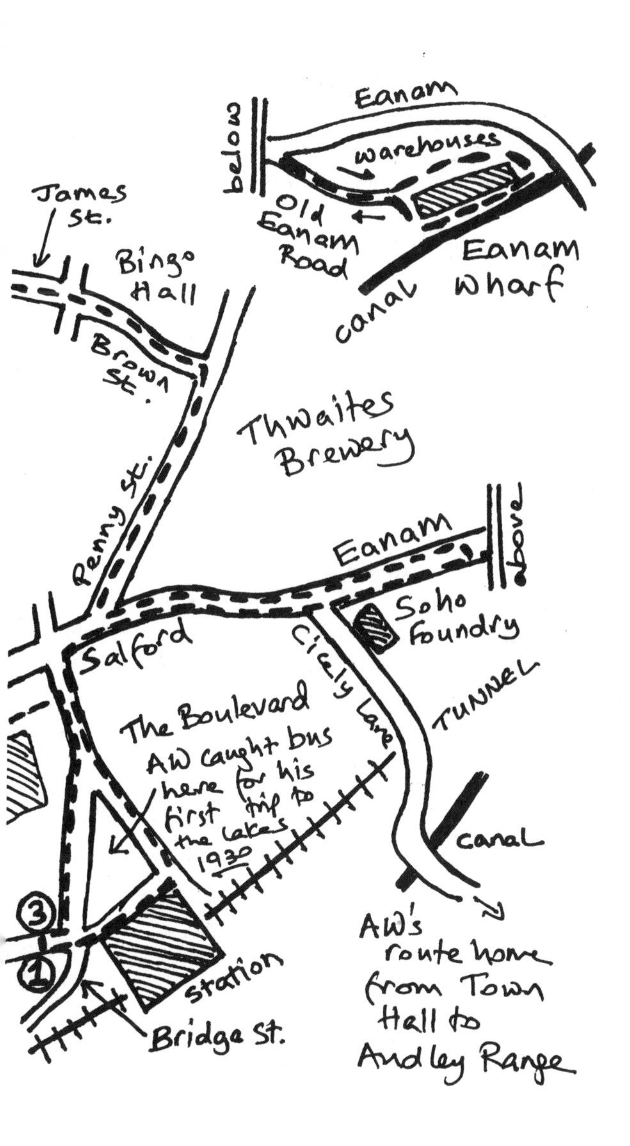
Eanam
below
warehouses
Old Eanam Road
Eanam Wharf
canal
James St.
Bingo Hall
Brown St.
Thwaites Brewery
Penny St.
Eanam
above
Soho foundry
Salford
Cicely Lane
TUNNEL
The Boulevard
AW caught bus here for his first trip to the Lakes 1930
canal
3
1
station
Bridge St.
AW's route home from Town Hall to Audley Range

successful cotton-spinning firm of Peel & Yates he established on the banks of the River Irwell at Bury in the early days of the Industrial Revolution.

Bear slightly right and continue straight ahead along Northgate. Walk along this pedestrian route towards the statue of William Ewart Gladstone gesticulating towards King George's Hall.

Only the shops have changed here as Northgate, mercifully spared post-war annihilation, still merrily winds its way along the route it followed in pre-industrial days, when it was the main north road out of the town. On the right look out for the plaque on the wall of 40 Northgate marking the premises of Mitchell & Kenyon's film production company here 1897–1901. AW would have known this as a photographic shop, though he may not have realized the shop was run by Sagar Mitchell.

On the left of Northgate slightly further up is a blue plaque marking the site of a pub in which the Italian violinist Paganini stayed in 1833. Gladstone's statue was along the Boulevard in AW's day and was moved here recently. It is reputedly the first public monument unveiled in honour of the Liberal statesman, erected in 1899, just a year after his death. To the right of Gladstone's statue, a bit further along Northgate, is a pub that was once the offices of the town's main weekly newspaper when AW was growing up, the *Blackburn Times*. Having begun in 1855, and also printed in Northgate, in the 1930s and 1940s it included a weekly rambling column written by Jessica Lofthouse, who went to AW's school.

Cross at the zebra crossing and walk straight ahead past the front entrance of King George's Hall. Turn right into Duke Street, facing the ornate terracotta Technical School building, opened in 1891, on the opposite side. Follow the pavement to the next junction alongside a large red-brick building.

This building was formerly the Blakey Moor Higher Elementary School, opened in 1910, where AW was briefly a pupil between 1919 and 1920.

Turn right along the continuation of Duke Street to rejoin Northgate at the corner of the magistrates' court.

The ambitious civic improvement scheme that included Blakey Moor School also led to the building of King George's Hall, the police station and the sessions court from 1912 onwards. George V laid the date stone for King George's Hall in 1913 but it was not completed until 1921.

Turn left along Northgate as far as the modern sculpture at Sudell Cross, and then first right into King William Street. This street opens out into the Town Hall Square.

Three Victorian buildings here remain as AW would have known them. To the left is the former public library, now Blackburn Museum, opened in 1874 along Library Street, now Museum Street. Opposite the Town Hall is the Cotton Exchange, opened in 1865, the weekly meeting place for cotton traders, which was also used for concerts and lectures; AW would have known it as the Majestic Cinema. Then there is the Italianate-style Town Hall, where AW spent most of his waking hours for over twenty years. Squat, sombre and functional, it was completed in 1856 after the rapidly expanding town had received its Charter of Incorporation five years earlier.

Walk to the statue of William Henry Hornby, to the right of the Town Hall's main entrance.

Hornby was the Borough Council's first mayor and one of the town's Victorian cotton barons. His Brookhouse Mills enterprise employed a workforce of some 1,400 people. He was a Conservative MP for the town for ten years until he was unseated in 1867 on a charge of voter intimidation. His statue was not here in AW's day. The Borough Treasurer's Department was on the first floor of the Town Hall with windows looking out on to what is now the Mall shopping centre and the overhead walkway to the Town Hall extension. In AW's day the windows looked out on to the covered market stalls and the clock tower, which was built in 1848 and demolished in the 1960s.

Walk along the right-hand side of the Town Hall under the overhead walkway and then turn left along Tackett Street at the back of the building. Cross over Exchange Street and follow the pavement as it swings right towards St John's Church, passing the fine town houses of Richmond Terrace on the left.

These Georgian properties were built in the 1820s and 1830s on what was then known as West Street. Richmond Terrace was originally the home of gentlemen and their servants but soon developed into the town's office quarter once the professional classes fled to the new suburbs opened up by the railway.

Cross over to St John's Church and turn left at the church entrance, following the side of the churchyard to the corner of cobbled James Street.

St John's Church, consecrated in 1789, was the resting place for 'new'-moneyed people, the town's prosperous middle classes, as revealed by the epitaphs on the gravestones. The overgrown patch of this once elegant churchyard on the corner of James Street hides a large memorial stone to the Thwaites family, including the founding brewer, Daniel Thwaites, along with his wife and several of his children.

Turn right along James Street and continue straight ahead until the road junction by the Gala Bingo Hall. Turn right and first left into Brown Street to the next road junction. Turn right into Penny Street.

Penny Street was one of the main tram routes into town from the north when AW lived here. It was laid out in the 1790s, when land here was opened up for development by the Church, this being glebe land, as was the Audley estate, where the Wainwright family house was built. The name of Penny Street derives from the rental charge of one penny per square yard on the development land. AW would have been very familiar with the sights and smells of Thwaites' Brewery, which has evolved over 200 years on its town centre site between Penny Street and Eanam Wharf. At the time of writing, the brewery so synonymous with Blackburn has announced its intention to move out of the town centre and build a more modern cost-effective plant.

Cross over to the opposite side of Penny Street and walk to the traffic lights at the next road junction. Turn left at the lights, following the road known as Salford.

This junction was in AW's day a busy town crossroads overlooked by coaching inns, where roads and tram routes from all directions converged at Salford Bridge, the medieval crossing point of the River Blakewater.

Continue slightly uphill on the left-hand side of the road. Cross over with care to the old Soho Foundry and the archway entrance to the Thwaites' estate buildings.

AW's quickest way on foot to and from the Town Hall would have been this way, from Salford Bridge up to Eanam in the shadow of the Thwaites' Brewery and the Soho Foundry. He would have turned up Cicely Lane, crossed the canal and railway, before disappearing into the terraced streets of Audley. The original Eanam Brewery which Daniel Thwaites joined as a business partner in 1807 had its entrance on the opposite side of the road to the surviving old estate office and stables. AW would have seen the dray horses pulling their wagons of beer barrels out of here.

Turn right into Old Eanam Road, which winds uphill to the cobbles of Eanam Wharf. Join the towpath on the right here to view the Leeds and Liverpool Canal, adjacent to the surviving coal warehouses, which are now a business centre and pub.

The cobbled setts and listed buildings here are a reminder of the days when Eanam Wharf was the industrial heart of the town. The canal opened in 1810 and in the first week of its operation, some 380 tons of coal arrived at Blackburn by barge. Not surprisingly, the Eanam Brewery and countless other factories took advantage of this prime site and set up on the canal's banks. The hustle and bustle of freight-carrying barges would have been a familiar sight to AW, who grew up less than half a mile from the Leeds and Liverpool Canal.

Turn left along the towpath to the far end of the warehouses and then left to complete a little circular loop around the old buildings. Rejoin Old Eanam Road and retrace the route back down to the main road at Eanam. Cross over the bottom of Cicely Lane and continue straight ahead towards the traffic lights and road junction at Salford. Turn left into Railway Road and follow the pavement back to the train station entrance, with the bus station over to the right.

Stage One
BLACKBURN STATION TO WHALLEY ABBEY
(11 miles)

'Ill shod and ill clothed, with jam butties in my pocket and no money for tram fares, I often tramped twenty miles in a day's walk, interested in all I saw; I liked looking around corners at fresh scenes.'
Ex-Fellwanderer

This first stage takes you from Blackburn to the rural Ribble Valley. It passes the house where AW was born and the sites of his early schools, before joining the towpath of the Leeds and Liverpool Canal and heading east out of the town. The route climbs to the broad ridge of Billington Moor, where there are extensive views north on a good day. The route follows paths AW explored in his twenties on his local excursions into the Lancashire countryside and reaches the ancient village of Whalley, with its abbey ruins overlooking the River Calder. AW returned to this timeless place in later life to collect scenes for *A Ribble Sketchbook*.

Youthful Ramblings

All great journeys begin with the romance of a railway station. So does this one, although strictly speaking AW's journey began with the romance of the bus stop facing the railway station, for the bus, not the train, was his gateway to the Lakes on that fabled first trip north in 1930 when his love affair with the mountains began.

The likelihood is that the bus went only as far as Preston, where he would have got on the Ribble bus service which ran every two hours from Manchester to Ambleside via Kendal. Fortunately for AW, he made his first trip to the Lakes just at the time the Ribble Bus Company's fleet of Leyland buses was expanding rapidly in a spider's web of routes from Lancashire northwards to Yorkshire and Scotland: Ribble had acquired an existing Lakeland bus operator, Lancashire and Westmorland Motor Services Limited, in 1928 and started a regular service from Manchester to the Lakes.

When as a child AW crawled and toddled over the front step of Number 331 Audley Range, he would have seen half a dozen cotton mills lining the long straight road downhill towards town. The 1910 Ordnance Survey map of Blackburn (see page 13) reveals this industrial landscape in all its glory. There was the Parkside Mill, Alexandra Mill, Audley Range Mill, Audley Hall Mills, Audley Bridge Mill and Higher Audley Street Mills, the last of which sat squat on the banks of the Leeds and Liverpool Canal.

Directly opposite AW's front door were the chimneys of the Audley Range Brick Works. Here were churned out, by the million, the bricks that built Number 331 and the thousands of identical two-up, two-down terraced houses that surrounded it.

Only fifty years before AW was born, the Audley district was still a farmland estate, owned by the church, at the centre of which was Audley Hall. Recorded as early as 1166, the hall was a sixteenth-century nunnery and was still occupied, in a dilapidated state, by a farmer as late as 1877. By this time it was surrounded not by fields of potatoes and oats but by the terraced houses of Edith Street on the south side of Audley Range. The hall was demolished in 1888. Following the arrival of the railway in Blackburn, the Ecclesiastical Commissioners started selling off plots of the Audley Hall estate for development in the 1860s. And so a new working-class residential district was created, with its overstretched wind-blown spine, Audley Range, laid out in 1872, heading eastwards from the Leeds and Liverpool Canal to the Accrington Road toll bar.

The walk up to AW's house at the top end of Audley Range follows the old tram route from the Boulevard in the town centre towards Queen's Park. The trams turned off Audley Range a third of the way up, turning right down Queen's Park Road and terminating at the park gates. Opposite the gates was the café (now a shop) where AW and his first wife, Ruth Holden, held their wedding reception when they married in 1931. Queen's Park itself, less than a mile from AW's house, was a municipal park created for the townsfolk and is undoubtedly where AW had his first encounter with trees and a lake. The tram route to the park closed in 1935 but trams were still running in the town when he left it in 1941.

The Audley district has changed much since AW lived here. The canal-side mills are now a land of budget carpets, tiles, bathrooms and wallpaper. Residential Audley is now a mix of Asian and white working class and much of the Victorian street pattern laid out on the north side of Audley Range has been replaced by a less rigid network of residential avenues and cul-de-sacs. But Audley Range is still the same terraced highway stretching towards infinity and beyond. AW's oldest sister, Alice, and her husband, John Fish, lived just a few doors down from her parents at 323 Audley Range. At 331, where AW lived the first twenty-four years of his life until he married, there is now a blue plaque that reads:

THE BIRTHPLACE OF
ALFRED WAINWRIGHT
AUTHOR AND FELL WALKER
(1907–1991)

Barrett's Directory of Blackburn and District 1909 notes that baby AW's next-door neighbours were a Mr Wilkinson, an overlooker, at Number 329 and a Mr Panton, a cloth-looker, at Number 333. These were occupations in the cotton industry and all down Audley Range and neighbouring Cherry Street the residents were predominantly employed by the cotton mills.

From Number 331, the Wainwrights could turn left out of their front door and walk downhill for a few minutes to reach the junction with Accrington Road. Along this old highway ran the tram route between Blackburn and Accrington. In Ex-*Fellwanderer* AW mentions catching the tram to Accrington to watch the 'pictures'. The working-class district of Furthergate and 'Accy Road', the gateway to Blackburn from the east, played a big part in his early life.

Overlooking the road junction at the top end of Audley Range was Accrington Road Elementary School, where AW attended up to the age of eleven and where he developed his fine handwriting. Turning left at the same junction back towards town, much of the area that AW knew has been redeveloped. Beyond Tesco, the Furthergate Congregational Church and School, where the Wainwright family worshipped and where AW and his siblings were first educated, now lies under a garage. The church was also where AW married Ruth Holden in 1931. Here too was his first marital home on the now demolished Artillery Street.

AW habitually came back to Blackburn twice a year to watch the Rovers and lived to see the demise of 'Accy' Road School and Furthergate Church, and the construction of Tesco. His correspondence with old friends from Blackburn records that he found it depressing that Furthergate had developed into a concrete wasteland. AW visited the area for the last time in 1990, when he was filmed outside his house on Audley Range in the company of a TV crew and broadcaster Eric Robson.

In fact, AW resided at a total of four different addresses in Blackburn, all in this part of town. After Artillery Street his rising status as a married man and municipal clerk in the 1930s led him to 11 Hamer Avenue, a council semi with a garden, where his son, Peter, was born in 1933. Then he bought a semi-detached residence, 90 Shadsworth Road. These two houses still exist but are not visited on this walk.

AW conducted most of his early escapes to the country on the cheap, on foot, from his Blackburn home. Throughout his teenage years and his early twenties, the local countryside was a vital green lung for him and countless other mill-town dwellers. In this sense he continued the tradition of the Victorian urban working class, who escaped to the moors for exercise, education and inspiration. AW climbed to the local viewpoint of Darwen

Tower, perhaps unaware that in the 1890s, after a mass trespass by the people of Darwen, this monument was erected to celebrate the hard-won freedom of access to these moors. These were the hills that, several generations earlier, 'weaver-poets' had roamed in solitary fashion, writing about simple scenes of nature as an antidote to the alien sight of factories in the valley towns below.

As AW acknowledges in *Ex-Fellwanderer*, his journey out of Blackburn really began when he was given a tatty map of Lancashire. With this he discovered he could escape the grime of the mill town by following the roads up to the moors that encircled his home town. His twin passion for both lonely uplands and maps was born in these early adventures. His explorations of the West Pennine Moors, Ribble Valley and Pendle flourished when AW went to work at the Town Hall and met like-minded office colleagues.

Chief among these was Lawrence Wolstenholme (1909–2000), one of his closest friends, two years younger than AW and with a similar upbringing. Lawrence had also gone to Blakey Moor School but unlike AW he stuck it out, not joining the Borough Treasurer's Department until 1925, where he discovered Alf Wainwright with his feet already firmly under the table. Lawrence went on to be Blackburn Borough Treasurer from 1953 to 1971. He and AW hit it off straight away through the combined interests of work, walking and women. In the 1920s, both single and barely out of their teens, both working all week with little spare cash, they spent many Sundays walking from their doorsteps. They even used a guidebook.

Still in the possession of Lawrence Wolstenholme's family is a book, *Rambles by Highway, Lane and Field-path* written by Blackburn journalist Harry H. Green and published in 1920. It is a collection of local rambles taken from the *Blackburn Weekly Telegraph*, encouraging readers in its introduction: 'Shaking the dust of the town from your heels you may, without much exertion, soon foot it jauntily over the white road, breathing the inspiriting air of the open fields and breezy hills.' According to Lawrence's son-in-law, Paul Holden, Lawrence and AW together completed all the rambles in this book around 1928; Lawrence has even ticked off in pencil each walk on the contents page, presumably after they had completed each one. So step forward into the limelight Harry H. Green, the writer who originally guided Wainwright.

Harry Green's rambles cover the countryside on the outskirts of Blackburn, particularly on the north side of the town, where the steep-sided suburbs gave way to a series of broad moorland ridges, beyond which lay a landscape of hedged meadows and woodland rolling down to the banks of the River Ribble. This countryside had been popular with weekend day-trippers from the town since Victorian and Edwardian times.

From the edge of Blackburn AW would have got his first glimpse of Lakeland. It was probably a view of Black Combe, the most visible and distinctive of the hills north of Morecambe Bay to be seen from the moorland tops above AW's home town. Black Combe, just under 2,000 feet, is a prominent spur at the south-western edge of the Lakes, described by AW in *The Outlying Fells of Lakeland* as 'like a huge whale stranded on a beach'.

Harry Green's rambles entitled 'A Glimpse of Lakeland Near Home' and 'Through York and Over the Nab to Whalley' would have taken Lawrence and AW through a delightful chunk of undulating countryside between the north-eastern edge of Blackburn and the ancient village of Whalley on the banks of the River Calder. Less than a few miles from Audley Range, AW discovered a landscape of gorse, meadows, scrubby cloughs, battered old farms and drystone walls, where the calls of the curlew and oystercatcher could be heard and flashing glimpses of deer and hare could be seen.

Following Harry Green's guidebook – which includes a few photos and rather crude hand-drawn sketch maps – AW and Lawrence would have passed by Dean Clough Reservoir, nestling in a fold in the hills carved by Dean Brook between Harwood Moor and Wilpshire Moor. They would also have followed some of the old packhorse and pilgrim routes along the broad ridge formed by these moors to the village of Whalley, the site of one of the great Cistercian abbeys of northern England (the others being Furness, Fountains and Kirkstall). The ridge offers views to two other prominent hills AW explored in his youth, Longridge Fell to the north and Pendle Hill to the east.

Hunter Davies's biography provides two accounts of AW climbing Pendle Hill which, at just below 2,000 feet, was the closest he would get to a mountain experience in east Lancashire. Both ascents were motivated by women. In the 1920s a lovelorn AW followed Betty Ditchfield, one of the few women in his office, up to the summit of Pendle Hill, possibly with the intention of proposing to her. If he did, she turned him down. Then in 1941, boosted by the wartime influx of young women into the office, he helped form the Pendle Club, a very short-lived office rambling group (he moved to Kendal later that year) which at least managed a climb up Pendle Hill. Lawrence Wolstenholme (appointed chairman of the club) was accompanied by his wife, Margery, on the outing but AW did not bring his wife, Ruth. However, he did manage to coax along several single office girls.

The slopes of scrubby pasture that form Wilpshire, Harwood and Billington Moors actually take root in the town of Blackburn, climbing gradually as a broad ridge to the summit of Pendle Hill. The one major interruption to this upland mass is the meandering River Calder, which cuts a route through the hills, which has resulted in the steep-sided bluff known as the Nab. This prominent hill and the village of Whalley below it have been popular haunts of Blackburnians since the railway arrived here in 1851. Several of Harry Green's rambles end at Whalley, so there can be little doubt that AW visited the village in his youth.

Take away the present-day traffic and Whalley remains much as AW would have seen it in the 1920s. From the old tracks over the Nab there are long-distance views of the hills rising beyond the valleys of the 'Three Rivers', the name given to this area in the title of a 1952 book by Jessica Lofthouse. She settled in the hamlet of York, just over the hill from Dean Clough, and wrote prolifically about this fascinating district where the rivers Ribble, Hodder and Calder meet. Whalley is at the heart of 'Three Rivers' country, its thirteenth-century parish church and the ruined abbey sitting side by side on the north bank of the Calder. The other distinctive feature of the village that would have been familiar to AW is the impressive Whalley Viaduct, its forty-eight red-brick arches carrying the railway from Blackburn to Clitheroe over the river.

AW sketched the parish church, the abbey, the arches and the village's main street when he returned to Whalley in his retirement while composing *A Ribble Sketchbook*: drawing numbers 52 to 55 in that book cover Whalley village. He may not have realized then that Whalley was the one-time home of a fellow Lancastrian who created the Pennine Way. AW praises the creator of that pioneering long-distance trail in the introduction of *Pennine Way Companion*, published by the *Westmorland Gazette* in 1968.

That man was Tom Stephenson (1893–1987), born in Chorley

The Calder Valley

but living with his parents and numerous younger siblings in Princess Street, Whalley, at the time AW was born in nearby Blackburn. He became a colossal figure in the twentieth-century countryside movement. He was secretary of the Ramblers' Association for twenty-one years and a tireless campaigner for access to mountains and moorlands. His 1930s dream of a trail for walkers along the backbone of England finally became a reality in 1965, when the Pennine Way was designated Britain's first official long-distance footpath.

Like AW, Tom Stephenson was brought up in a weaving community but unlike AW he became a teenage apprentice in a calico printer's. His own youthful awakening to the glorious countryside of the north came in 1912, when a Saturday afternoon ramble took him on to Pendle Hill and revealed the extensive view to the Three Peaks, Bowland and the Ribble Valley. It is perhaps no coincidence that the textile districts of Lancashire gave birth not just to AW, the author of the *Pictorial Guides*, but also to the creator of the Pennine Way.

THE ROUTE

Blackburn Station to Harwood Moor (6½ miles)

From the train station entrance facing the bus station, turn left and then first left along Bridge Street, continuing along George Street, crossing the River Blakewater, to reach the junction with Darwen Street.

Just as AW began his first journey to the Lake District in 1930 at the bus station, public transport depositing him at Windermere several hours later, the walker starting this journey here is also heading for Windermere and should arrive there on foot in about six days' time. The River Blakewater runs underground through most of the town centre but is revealed in all its grotty glory where it runs beneath George Street. Rest assured there are many more delightful rivers to come.

Turn left along Darwen Street, crossing under the railway bridge, to reach the traffic lights at a busy road junction. Turn left and join Lower Audley Street by a metal sculpture in the pavement marking the site of the Atlas Iron Works. Look straight across the road junction here for a view of Wainwright Bridge with its distinctive arches.

AW would have been very familiar with the Darwen Street Bridge, carrying the railway over the road. It was built by the Lancashire and Yorkshire Railway in 1884. He would also have known the Atlas Iron Works which, until it was finally demolished in 2000, occupied the site between the railway bridge and Lower Audley Street for well over a century. It made steam engines for the cotton mills and, during the Second World War, tank parts and guns. AW would not have been familiar with the bridge that bears his name, a road bridge crossing the railway that was opened in 2008. Naming it the Wainwright Bridge, after a competition run by the *Lancashire Evening Telegraph*, saw Blackburn finally getting around to honouring publicly one of its most famous sons.

Walk straight up the left-hand side of Lower Audley Street as it runs gradually uphill to the junction at the top, where it crosses over the Leeds and Liverpool Canal. Use the pedestrian crossings to join the bottom end of Audley Range, which continues straight ahead from this busy road junction.

Although this was not the quickest way home for AW from the Town Hall, he would invariably have used this route to and from his parents' home. It was also the tram route from the Boulevard to Queen's Park. Audley Range begins at the junction overlooking the canal and there were two cotton mills here. The Higher Audley Street Mill occupied the site that is now a conference centre and car park overlooking the canal on the left. The brick premises which once housed the Audley Bridge Mill still survive on the right-hand side of the junction.

Walk up the right-hand side of Audley Range to the traffic lights at the junction with Queen's Park Road.

So begins the long trudge up the street that AW traversed countless times. When this area was still farmland in the 1850s, crumbling Audley Hall stood on a site to the right of Audley Range, just before you reach Queen's Park Road. At the junction of Queen's Park Road the tram from town turned right here and followed this thoroughfare to the park gates facing the café where AW had his wedding reception. Queen's Park opened in 1887 and as it is ten minutes' walk from AW's house, the chances are that he would have spent time here in his childhood watching the locals promenading around the boating lake in their Sunday best.

Continue along Audley Range beyond this junction. Beyond the little roundabout at the junction with North Road cross over to see the blue plaque next to Number 331, Wainwright's house.

Please respect the privacy of the current residents here. At the higher end of Audley Range, and along adjacent Cherry Street, most of the original Victorian terraces remain intact. The grassy open space directly opposite AW's house was the site of the Audley Range Brick Works. North Road then led uphill between open hedged fields. AW lived at Number 331 with his family from 1907 to 1931 – from when he was born to when he married Ruth Holden. The terraces of Audley Range were uniformly two-up, two-down houses with a backyard containing a privy. The rear of AW's house overlooked the alley and the backs of the houses on adjoining Cherry Street. AW revisited this area and stood outside the house in 1990, only a few months before he died.

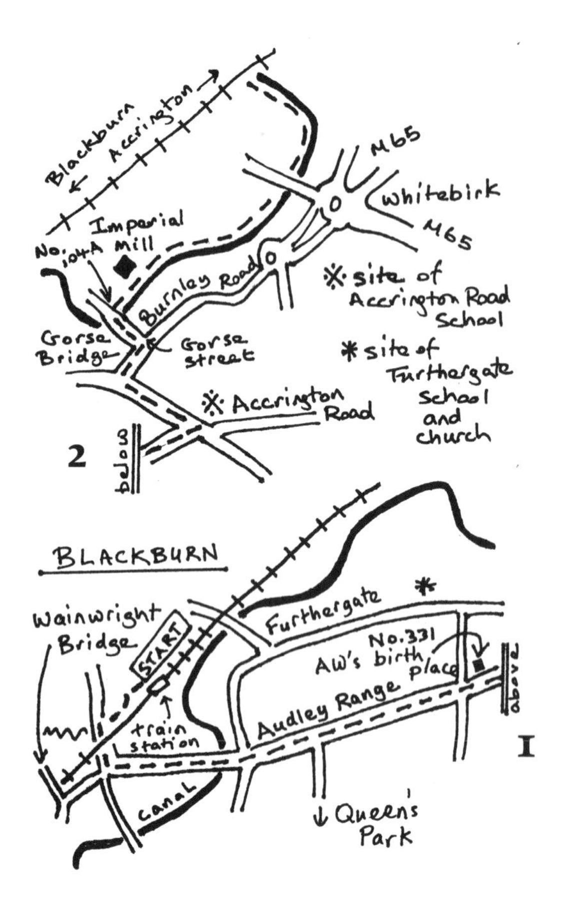

Continue to the end of Audley Range, which starts to drop downhill beyond AW's house. At the traffic lights turn left into Accrington Road.

Facing this junction is the Accrington Road Day Centre, built on the site of one of AW's primary schools. Along Accrington Road another tramline ran from Blackburn to Accrington.

Walk along the left-hand side of Accrington Road to the next set of traffic lights and cross over the junction to join Burnley Road. Look left beyond Tesco towards the petrol station on Furthergate.

At this road junction Accrington Road becomes Furthergate, heading downhill to Blackburn town centre only a mile away. Furthergate was a thriving community when AW was a lad, with its own shops, post office, pubs, school and churches. The roadside site now occupied by a petrol station, car wash and scrubby grassland just beyond Tesco was where AW's first school – Furthergate Congregational School – stood.

The Furthergate School and its adjoining church were Victorian institutions that developed as this part of Blackburn became increasingly populated. The school passed from the church to the Blackburn School Board and, between 1905 and 1918, had at the helm the Reverend William Harrow, a popular and active pastor. He had long gone by the time AW got married in the church. After the wedding AW moved into his wife's house (where her sister also lived) on Artillery Street, which faced the church. This street stood just beyond the present-day petrol station, on a site now partly occupied by the Furthergate Business Park.

Follow the left-hand side of Burnley Road downhill as far as Gorse Street on the left. Turn left here to reach Gorse Bridge, where the road crosses over the canal.

To the left on the far side of the canal are the ruins of Gorse Bridge Mill, one of the many cotton mills that once lined the canal bank between here and Eanam Wharf. The Blackburn of AW's youth is gradually being bulldozed away year by year in piecemeal fashion.

Join the canal towpath to the right of Gorse Bridge (bridge number 104A). Follow the towpath to the huge Imperial Mill on the left.

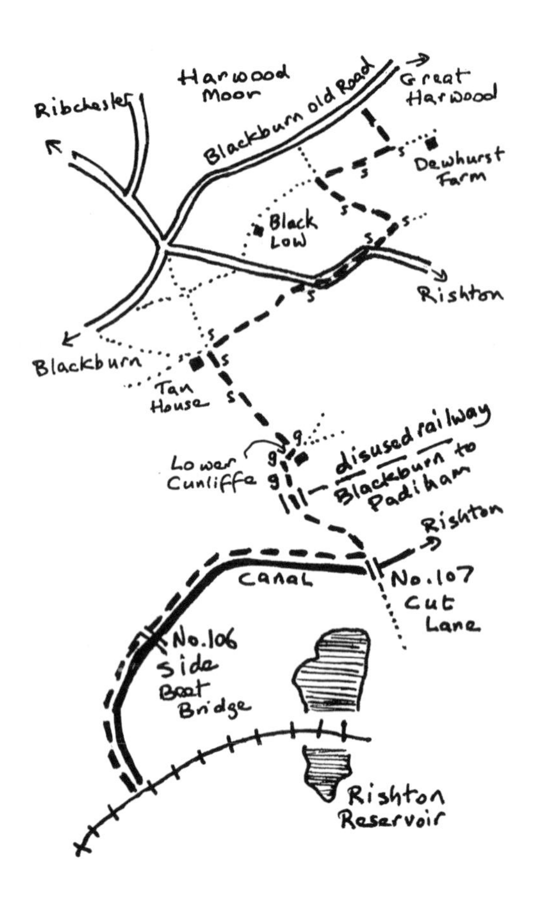

This vast enterprise, the only listed mill building in Blackburn, was a brand-new state-of-the-art spinning complex when AW was born. Opened in 1901, the Imperial Mill was a project aimed at reviving the decaying cotton-spinning industry in Blackburn. At its height it employed 300 people and the mill's construction was a symbol of the enduring confidence in Lancashire's textile industry that still persisted then. Unfortunately, the confidence was misplaced, for as early as 1929 the Imperial Mill, and indeed the whole of Lancashire's declining cotton industry, had to be rescued by the Bank of England. It soldiered on until 1958.

If the Imperial Mill physically symbolizes industrial Blackburn's last hurrah, then geographically it does the same. It is the very last of the long line of mills strung along the canal from the town centre a mile to the west.

Continue straight ahead along the towpath and follow this for the next 2 miles in the direction of Burnley and Leeds. Leave the canal at bridge number 107.

Built between 1770 and 1816, the 127¼-mile-long Leeds and Liverpool Canal is the longest canal in Britain. Its immense size, the fact it linked so many industrial towns on either side of the Pennines and the wide variety of its trades meant it successfully competed against the railways and was still a major commercial route when AW was growing up in Blackburn.

Where the canal skirts by the busy roundabout at Junction 6 of the M65 it leaves the Borough of Blackburn with Darwen and enters the Borough of Hyndburn. It passes under the Blackburn–Accrington–Burnley railway line and enters a surprisingly rural section as Blackburn is left behind.

Do not go under Bridge 107 but leave the towpath here via steps on the left. Turn left and follow the track, Cut Lane, towards Lower Cunliffe Farm. The track crosses a stone bridge, underneath which once ran a railway line from Blackburn to Padiham. Go straight ahead, through the gate to the left of the farm buildings and then sharp right behind the farm through another field gate. Then go through the field gate immediately on the left to climb the first real hill of the day. The path goes steeply uphill to the left of a little gorse-lined clough that marks the right-hand boundary of the field. Cross a stile in the boggy top right corner of this field where it meets the spring running down the clough and go straight ahead towards the farm, Tan House, on the top of the hill. Aim for the right-hand side of the farm buildings.

Enjoy the extensive view southwards across the industrial Calder Valley. To the left of sprawling Blackburn is a cluster of east Lancashire towns – Rishton, Great Harwood, Clayton-le-Moors and Accrington – beyond which rise the moors that separate them from Rossendale and the cotton towns of north Manchester. It is this landscape of mill towns and bleak moorland heights that shaped AW's teens when he first started to explore this area with map in hand. Try to blot out the M65, as in AW's teens it was not there.

Go through the wall gaps between the farm and shed to reach a track. Swing right here, following the track away from the farm and keeping a stone wall on the right. When the track soon forks into two, keep to the right alongside the wall that follows the top of the ridge. A peep over the wall will reveal a final view of Blackburn. The route now heads eastwards with a view straight ahead to Pendle Hill. Keep to the wall-side track past a pond, skirt around a wall end and enter another field. Continue in the same direction and head for a line of trees by the wall on the right. Cross a stile in the right-hand field corner and join a road.

Follow the road downhill for a short distance and cross over to the left-hand side of the road before the sharp right-hand bend. At this bend leave the road via a stile on the left, signed as a footpath. Go straight ahead to cross a little footbridge and stile; then turn sharp left and head uphill through the field, aiming for gates at the top end. Cross the stile and follow the left fence line uphill to the top field corner. Turn right here and follow the top field edge to go through another gate and continue straight ahead. Turn left along the driveway of Dewhurst Farm to meet Blackburn Old Road.

This ridge-top road marks a watershed between industrial Lancashire to the south and rural Lancashire to the north. Goodbye Blackburn, hello Ribble Valley.

Harwood Moor to Whalley Abbey (4½ miles)

Cross Blackburn Old Road with care. Go through the kissing gate on the opposite side, signed as a footpath to York Lane, and join a sunken track leading across rough pasture.

Suddenly at the top of the hill as you look down on Dean Clough Reservoir the scene has been transformed from a landscape of mill

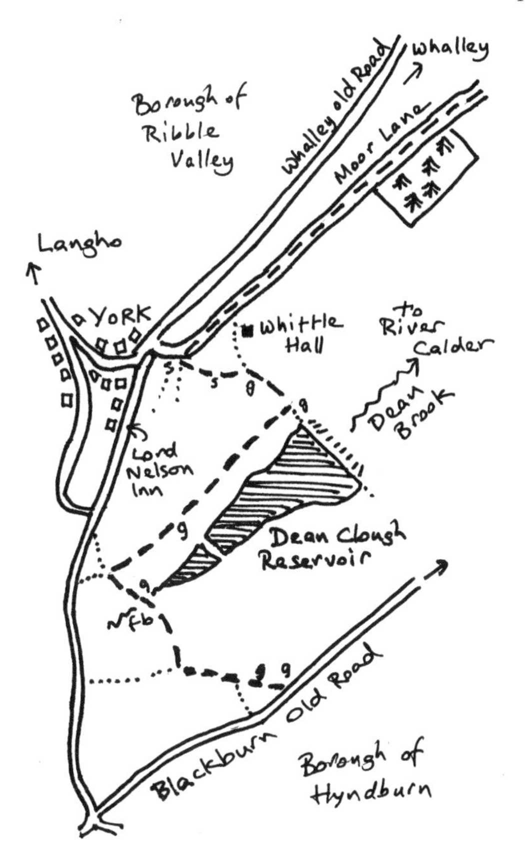

towns to a much fairer landscape of ridges and valleys. On a good day the view will stretch from the Ribble Estuary, Fylde coast and Blackpool Tower in the west to Pendle Hill in the east. Looking north, beyond Dean Clough and the nearby heights of Wilpshire Moor and Whalley Nab, a series of ridge tops leads the eye to the summits of Yorkshire's Three Peaks and to Longridge Fell and Bowland. The good news is that the walk is heading this way!

Follow the sunken track above Dean Clough for about ¼ mile and then leave it by turning sharp right along a footpath running steeply downhill along a reed-lined drain. The start of this path is indicated by a large patch of rubble on the right of the track. Keep to the right-hand side of the drain down to the inlet of Dean Clough Reservoir. Cross the little footbridge and go through a kissing gate. The path starts to climb uphill, heading to the left of a line of hawthorn trees. Just below the trees there is a gateway between fences. Ignore this and just continue uphill between the fence on the left and the hawthorn trees on the right. The path becomes steeper but soon meets a grass track running left to right alongside a wall.

AW and Lawrence Wolstenholme explored the upper valley of Dean Clough when they completed a ramble in Harry Green's guidebook entitled 'A Glimpse of Lakeland near Home', the title referring to the reservoirs of Parsonage and Dean Clough. The latter dates from 1879 and was built to supply water to the growing industrial town of Accrington.

Turn right along the grassy track, which heads gradually downhill towards woodland and the reservoir. Follow it for the next ¾ mile along the length of the reservoir. It eventually reaches a kissing gate above the dam.

Dean Clough Reservoir was formed by damming the waters at the head of Dean Brook. This stream trickles out of the reservoir and gets a brief chance to shine – forming a lovely wooded clough alive with bluebells in the spring – before it joins the River Calder on the outskirts of Whalley.

Go through the kissing gate and turn left uphill. Go through the gate at the top of the hill; this marks the administrative boundary between the Boroughs of Hyndburn and the Ribble Valley. Turn diagonally left to a stile in a wooden fence on the far side. Continue in the same direction, skirting a rock outcrop where there is a good view of the Ribble Valley below. Drop down from the outcrop to a stile at a junction of paths and join Moor Lane.

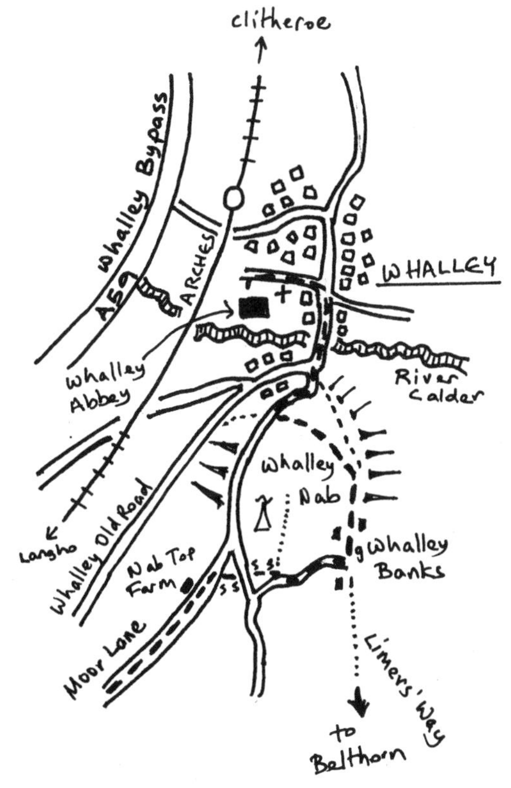

Here is the first proper view of the Ribble Valley since leaving Blackburn. Beyond the stile is the roadside hamlet of York, where AW's contemporary Jessica Lofthouse once lived. AW and Lawrence Wolstenholme would have explored this area when they walked Harry Green's ramble entitled 'Through York and Over the Nab to Whalley'. In the company of Harry Green, they would have walked along Moor Lane, formerly the Old Nab Road, which links York with Whalley. Our walk heads the same way, following the old highway that AW would have wandered along in his youth.

Turn right along Moor Lane and follow it straight ahead for the next 1½ miles along the top of the ridge that ends dramatically in the Nab. You finally leave the tarmac after passing Nab Top Farm on the left. After the farm cross a stile on the right and follow the field edge to cross another stile and join a lane. Cross the ladder stile opposite with the radio mast, near the highest point of the Nab, over to the left. Walk directly ahead over the top of a little hillock and cross another stile to rejoin a lane. Ignore the footpath signed left over the cattle grid and keep to the lane as it winds downhill to reach houses at a path junction.

The view south across the Calder Valley from here includes the redundant arches of the Martholme Viaduct which once carried the Blackburn–Padiham Railway over the river. At the path junction by the houses the route joins an old packhorse road running left to right. This is the Limers' Way, which ran from the weaving and mining village of Belthorn, on the moors above Blackburn, to Clitheroe in the Ribble Valley. Along this route ponies carried limestone to the east Lancashire mill towns and coal towards the market towns of the Ribble Valley.

Turn left at the path junction, following the Limers' Way in the Clitheroe direction. Pass several houses and continue straight ahead through a gate. Pass Whalley Banks, after which the track becomes a driveway. It runs slightly uphill and passes on the left a well-kept rockery sheltering a stone memorial to the Bracewell family. Ignore the old packhorse road forking right down the steep north side of the Nab but instead keep to the driveway that swings left around the hillside. Cross a cattle grid and a spectacular panorama unfolds.

Beyond the cattle grid the 'Three Rivers' landscape, shaped by the confluence of the rivers Ribble, Hodder and Calder, is revealed in all its glory. Above the valley floor rises a ring of fells – Longridge Fell, Totridge and the Bowland Fells, Middle Knoll, Birkett Fell, Browsholme Moor, Waddington Fell, Grindleton Fell and Beacon Hill. Then beyond the Ribble Valley rise Penyghent, Whernside and Settle Moor. Close by to the east lies the limestone knoll of Worsaw Hill, then Pendle Hill, Wiswell Moor (with a radio mast on it), Read Heights and Spring Wood sloping down to the banks of the River Calder. The village of Whalley straddles the river directly below, with the old church and abbey largely hidden by trees for most of the year.

Continue straight ahead along the driveway to cross another cattle grid and rejoin Moor Lane winding down the side of the Nab. Stand by the gate on the opposite side of the lane for a good view of the River Calder beneath the Whalley Arches.

This point is just above where AW sketched his view of the railway viaduct for *A Ribble Sketchbook*. He stood on the roadside to the right of the Judge Walmsley Inn.

Turn right and follow the lane steeply downhill. The lane joins the main road at the bridge crossing over the River Calder.

The river marks the boundary between the adjoining parishes of Billington and Langho (south side) and Whalley (north side), and the road bridge has medieval origins. Looking upstream, to the right of the bridge, the slopes of the Nab descend steeply to the floodplain on the south bank of the river and hide from view a little knoll, Turn Hill, also known as Abbot's Mound. It was here that in 1537 the body of the last Abbot of Whalley Abbey, John Paslew, was brought back from Lancaster Castle, where he had been executed for the part he played in the uprising known as the Pilgrimage of Grace. Paslew's body was gibbeted on Turn Hill and possibly his head was placed on a spike here before his body parts were put on show in a field on the edge of the village.

Cross the road bridge and walk into Whalley down the main street, known as King Street. You will soon pass the adjoining Princess Street on the right.

In the 1900s, a house on Princess Street was the home of Tom Stephenson, the founder of the Pennine Way, who lived here with his parents. He was an apprentice block printer who, like AW, went on long walks as an escape and actually got some of his own walks published. He had left Whalley long before AW came here in his twenties. As a conscientious objector in the First World War, Tom Stephenson was arrested by the Whalley village policeman in 1917 for ignoring his call-up. His penalty was twelve months' hard labour in Wormwood Scrubs.

Continue along the left-hand side of King Street as far as the De Lacy Arms.

In *A Ribble Sketchbook* AW includes a scene of Whalley's main street, taken from the pavement opposite the De Lacy Arms. He shows little traffic, possibly because he didn't like cars spoiling his picture or possibly because he produced this book some ten years after the A59 Whalley bypass had opened. Before then, Whalley had become a bit of a bottleneck for traffic, as the village high street was on the main west–east route between Preston and Skipton.

Main Street, Whalley

At the corner by the De Lacy Arms turn left down Church Lane. This leads to the historic parish church of St Mary the Virgin on the left. Continue along Church Lane as it winds around to the gatehouse entrance to Whalley Abbey.

Between the River Calder and Church Lane, the thirteenth-century church and the largely fourteenth-century abbey form the medieval heart of Whalley. They remain much the same today as they did when AW visited them on a Harry Green ramble in 1928 and when he returned to photograph them for sketches in *A Ribble Sketchbook*.

The ancient parish church pre-dates the neighbouring abbey and was founded on the site of a wooden Saxon church, where baptisms took place in the adjacent river. A wander around the churchyard reveals three pre-Conquest preaching crosses. This

Whalley Church

church had great significance in the Middle Ages, when it was the religious focus of a vast parish covering most of central Lancashire and stretching eastwards into Yorkshire.

The site for Whalley Abbey was granted by the Earl of Lincoln, Henry de Lacy, in 1296 after some 'White Monks' earmarked the bountiful banks and fruitful woodlands of the River Calder for their new monastery. It was to replace their failed monastic venture on the marshy mudflats of the tidal River Mersey at Stanlow. The abbey took about 150 years to complete – at a cost of £3,000 – and throughout the fourteenth and fifteenth centuries it became a powerhouse of the north. The wealth of the abbey put other local landowners to shame, the monks here providing warmth and hospitality in this otherwise barren part of the world. The Lancashire moors

Ruins of Whalley Abbey

are dotted with tracks, wayside crosses and wells that marked the routes journeying pilgrims took to arrive at this 'Locus Benedictus' or 'Blessed Place'. Abbot Paslew, an extravagant man who was reputed to have gone on a London shopping trip and spent £5 on a new habit (that's £5 in the 1520s!), was one of the most important men in Lancashire.

These good times came to an end with the Dissolution of the Monasteries in the sixteenth century. But the town's ancient history, legends and pastoral setting still provide romance, just as they did for AW and countless Blackburnians who arrived here on Sunday day trips, escaping from the harsh realities of life in the industrial town.

Stage Two
WHALLEY ABBEY TO DUNSOP BRIDGE
(16 miles)

'Born wild and brought to gentle maturity in a rural Arcadia the Ribble is a river of delight.'
A Ribble Sketchbook

This stage of the walk takes you from the flat pastures of the Ribble Valley to the heart of the Forest of Bowland. Encountering two Roman roads and crossing both the majestic River Ribble and the enchanting River Hodder, the route explores the countryside of AW's youth before he discovered the Lake District. It is a magical patchwork of woods, streams, meadows and manor houses, a land of forgotten ferry boats and farmer-ferrymen that inspired, among others, J.R.R. Tolkien. Between the two rivers, the walk climbs a hill AW conquered as a boy on an expedition from Blackburn – Longridge Fell, the most southerly fell in Britain. AW's scenes from *A Ribble Sketchbook* and *A Bowland Sketchbook* accompany us along the way.

The Sketchbook Years: Part One

In his early twenties, AW explored the Ribble and Hodder Valleys in the company of Lawrence Wolstenholme using Harry Green's *Rambles by Highway, Lane and Field-path.* Green, writing for the *Blackburn Weekly Telegraph,* knew how popular this area of countryside was with the people of the town. Villages like Whalley and Hurst Green abounded with refreshment rooms catering for ramblers, cyclists and the day trippers who arrived via train and charabanc. Throughout AW's Blackburn years, two little ferry boats operated across the Ribble at Dinckley and Hacking Boat. Ticking off the rambles in Harry Green's book as they completed them – 'Dinckley and Sale Wheel', 'Hacking Boat to Dinckley Old Hall', 'Hacking Boat to Higher Hodder Bridge', 'Ribchester, Dutton and Hurst Green' – AW and Lawrence would have become very familiar with the middle stretch of the River Ribble from Clitheroe downstream to Ribchester, from Whalley in the south to Hurst Green and Stonyhurst in the north.

These landscapes also inspired AW's later sketchbooks. AW's marriage to Betty McNally in March 1970, following his divorce from Ruth in 1968 marked the beginning of a remarkably fruitful period of writing when AW, probably the happiest and most contented he had been all his life, grabbed the challenge of retirement and his new lease of life with Betty, firmly with both hands. From 1970 to 1988 he produced some forty books for the *Westmorland Gazette*, averaging about two a year, though in 1980 he published four, including *A Ribble Sketchbook*. Admittedly most of these were simply sketchbooks of drawings with captions, requiring little research or time spent away from home, but AW was still putting in a nine- or ten-hour a day, even in his seventies. It makes the comment he made about his retirement in Ex-*Fellwanderer* seem rather an understatement: 'I had planned a very full literary programme for my years of retirement.' He was not kidding.

There are also several other factors that explain his extraordinary output in his later years. First, his work was facilitated by Betty, who brought a car, and the ability to drive it, into their marriage. With the need to travel across northern England, Scotland and Wales to take photos for his various projects, Betty and her car were invaluable. So much so that she even succeeded in persuading AW to buy her a new car in which to drive him around. Second, AW was indulged by his publisher, the *Westmorland Gazette*, and given free rein to pursue whatever projects he liked. He was their cash cow; if he wanted to potter around sketching local rivers, projects that involved little inconvenience to AW, then that was fine. Third, AW needed the money from book royalties to realize the dream he shared with Betty of raising funds for Animal Rescue Cumbria to build a shelter for stray cats and dogs.

AW commenced his retirement compiling books covering his favourite walking areas outside the Lakes – namely, the Yorkshire

Dales, the Howgill fells and the Scottish mountains. Added to that were books about Kendal and Westmorland, and the phenomenally successful guidebook of his own long-distance route, *A Coast to Coast Walk*, published in 1973. Then towards the end of the 1970s he turned his gaze to Lancashire. It was somewhere he had explored already, so it required little research. Perhaps the biggest plus point was that it wouldn't involve tiresome overnight stays from his home in Kendal.

So it was that at the depressing tail end of the 1970s AW found himself in the passenger seat of Betty's car driving the entire length of the River Ribble to collect photos for *A Ribble Sketchbook*. In fact, he may well have sat in the back seat, giving him more room to spread his map out and smoke his pipe. In 1978 and 1979 he had published two books covering Lancashire's Furness Peninsula; now he turned his attention to the northern rivers. His exploration of the Ribble was one of three river sketchbooks published in 1980, the others being *A Lune Sketchbook* and *An Eden Sketchbook*.

Surveying the River Ribble from its Yorkshire beginning on Gayle Moor to its meeting with the Irish Sea beyond Preston Docks was an easy task for AW. Even at its source, just off the B6255 road near the Ribblehead Viaduct, the river was never far away from a road.

AW dedicates the book to a Blackburn woman, Doris Snape, a friend he had known for forty years since the days when he had set up Blackburn Rovers Supporters' Club with her late husband, Tom. He would often stay with the widowed Doris when he returned to Blackburn to watch the Rovers. In the 1979–1980 football season, at the time AW was writing *A Ribble Sketchbook*, his beloved team had just been relegated to the old Third Division of the English League. AW sold the original drawings for *A Ribble Sketchbook* to raise money for Furthergate Church in Blackburn in 1980, the place of worship he had attended as a boy.

AW had a lot of time for the River Ribble. In the sketchbook he refers to it as 'a proud river that has carved a lovely valley' and 'a river much loved'. He also notes that Whalley is a 'delightful and much-loved village' and that Old Langho Church is 'humble, yet lovely'. As a big fan of the limestone country of the Yorkshire Dales his favourite stretch of the river was its upper reaches, the waterfalls, caves, gills and potholes penetrating that soggy moorland around Ribblehead – a landscape he sketched in *Walks in Limestone Country* (1970). Hunter Davies's biography recalls that he even proposed to Betty in Ribblesdale.

This stage of the walk takes you alongside the River Ribble. Of the seventy-eight scenes AW drew for his sketchbook, the walk encounters ten of them – from Whalley, Old Langho and Dinckley on the south side of the river, to Hurst Green and Stonyhurst on the north side.

Apart from the appearance of cars, the rural Ribble has changed little since the days when a young Wainwright wandered here as a boy and with Lawrence Wolstenholme in the late 1920s. One notable exception is the suspension footbridge over the river at Dinckley, which opened in 1951. AW drew this for *A Ribble Sketchbook* while at the same time lamenting the loss of the old ferry boat that it replaced and with which he had grown up.

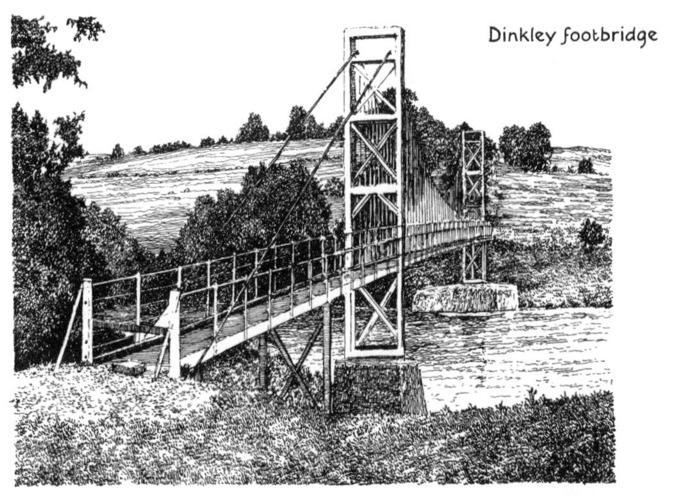

AW would have known the pretty village of Hurst Green and the architectural splendours of Stonyhurst College long before he came to sketch them in 1979. He also knew Longridge Fell from his boyhood, a hill over 1,100 feet, which provides the most spectacular views of this part of the walk. Longridge Fell is a watershed between the valleys of the mature Ribble and its unspoilt youthful tributary, the Hodder. It is also a watershed between Wainwright sketchbooks. In crossing over the fell and continuing north, you enter the landscapes of *A Bowland Sketchbook*, published in 1981.

From the top of Longridge Fell it is a walk of less than 1½ miles before you encounter the scene of AW's next sketch – Doeford Bridge over the River Hodder. AW's half a dozen sketches of this river north from here to Dunsop Bridge accompany you for the rest of this stage.

Once AW had ticked off the Lune, Ribble and Eden, 1980 saw him wandering through Bowland on day trips from home, as well as taking a few short holidays in North Wales to compile sketches for his planned book about Snowdonia. The fruits of his labours were published in 1981: *A Bowland Sketchbook* and *Welsh Mountain Drawings*, the latter being his first foray into Wales. AW was still then going about his business unnoticed, as he had not yet experienced his fleeting brush with TV fame.

The scenes AW sketched of the River Hodder have not changed at all in thirty years. He sketched the stone arched road bridges at Doeford and Burholme, the river at Whitewell and a view of the valley from the lane between Burholme and Chipping. He also sketched two village views of Dunsop Bridge. Not one of these views would have required AW to venture far from Betty's car, but AW would still walk a few miles to get a good photo – some of his Bowland views are taken in fairly remote locations.

When AW first went to work at the Borough Engineers' Office in Blackburn Town Hall in 1920, he probably came across the name of William B. Bryan, the town's Borough Engineer in the

Hodder Valley

1880s. It was he who oversaw the construction of the Blackburn Corporation Waterworks scheme, which extended into the gathering ground of the River Hodder in Victorian times as the burgeoning town of Blackburn's insatiable demand for water increased. A series of weirs, conduits and pipes soaked up the waters of the Bowland valleys north of Dunsop Bridge, and W.B. Bryan planned the route of and built the pipeline that carried the water back to Blackburn.

Towards the end of this part of the walk, this pipeline can be seen crossing over the River Hodder. Further south it goes under the same river east of Doeford Bridge and then skirts around Longridge Fell before being exposed again as it crossed the River Ribble close to the Dinckley Ferry. The pipeline entered Blackburn at Furthergate, not far from AW's house, where via a series of storage reservoirs, water from the Bowland fells poured forth from the taps in the working-class terraces.

Whalley Abbey to Longridge Fell (9½ miles)

From the abbey entrance continue down the Sands, signposted 'Gatehouse ¼ mile'. Follow the road under the Gatehouse.

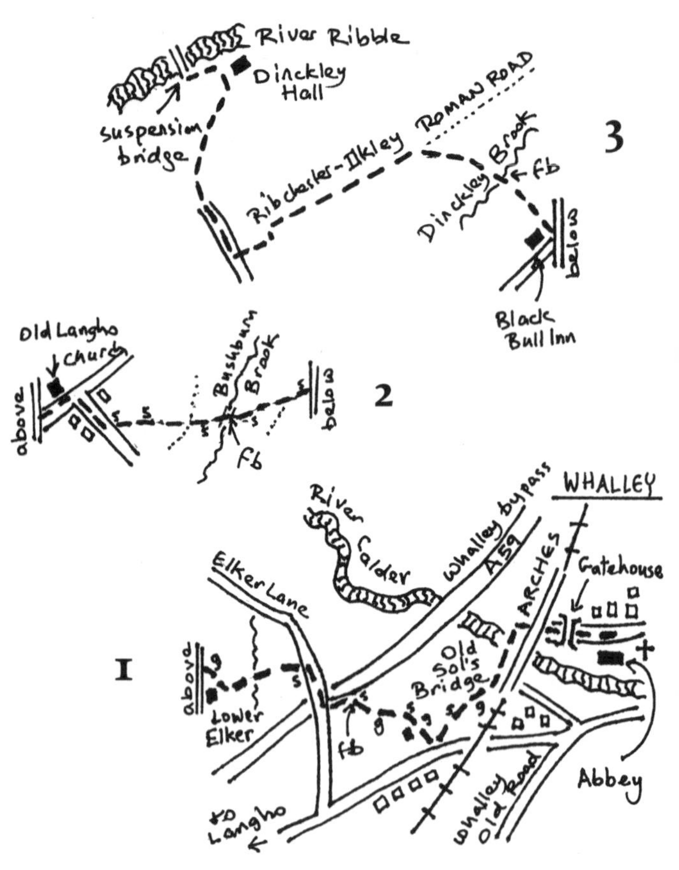

The walk leaves the abbey via the fourteenth-century West Gate. The Roman Catholic Church situated between this and the abbey entrance contains many important and sacred relics. These include a fragment of the baby Jesus's 'swaddling clothes' and the signet ring of Abbot John Paslew. The upper storey of the well-preserved West Gate once housed a chapel and later a school house. Either side of this gatehouse are field earthworks that indicate the site of an Anglo-Saxon fortified settlement at Whalley, recorded as early as AD 664.

Continue straight ahead under the railway arches. Arches 23 and 24 are castellated to fit in with the approach to the abbey. Turn immediately left after the viaduct along a tarmac path. Cross the River Calder over Old Sol's Bridge.

To the left can be seen the ancient road bridge crossing the River Calder, as well as the railway viaduct, the longest and largest in Lancashire, built between 1848 and 1850. To the right can be seen, crossing the river, the A59 bypass, opened in 1970. Old Sol's Bridge is the fourth river crossing here. The present bridge was erected in 1993 to replace one built in 1909 by local mill owner Solomon Longworth. In crossing the River Calder you re-enter the parish of Billington and Langho.

The path enclosed by railings leads to Longworth Road. Bear right towards the corner terrace and then immediately left along a terraced row leading to Sunnyside Avenue. Go through the metal gateway straight ahead to a new housing development. Go through a gate in a hedge on the right and turn left, following the path along the left hedge side. Cross another stile and continue straight ahead along a driveway to reach Neddy Lane. Turn sharp right here and swing right around a barn conversion and farm buildings, crossing a cattle grid to reach another stile. There is a good view straight ahead to the walk's next objective: Stonyhurst College (identified by its domed towers) and the wooded ridge of Longridge Fell. A stile and gate lead to trees at the edge of the A59 bypass. Cross a footbridge, climb steps to a stile and then turn sharp left through the trees along the bypass verge to reach Elker Lane.

Turn right and cross the road bridge over the bypass. Turn left along the next farm road on the left-hand side, which begins at a stile and gate. The footpath starts on the farm road and goes straight ahead across the low hill to the left of the farm road, taking a slightly more direct line towards Lower Elker Farm, seen straight ahead. It rejoins the farm road by trees, where it crosses a little brook, and then follows this track uphill to Lower Elker, which has an 1865 date stone. Skirt around the right-hand side of the farm, following the gated track straight ahead to enter a large field at a stile. Using the two solitary trees in the field as navigational aids, head straight ahead, aiming just left of the right-hand tree. Cross a stile in the next fence boundary and drop to a footbridge over a brook.

Turn left after the footbridge and uphill to cross another stile in a fence next to an oak tree. Go straight ahead here, with a fence to the left, to cross a farm track. Ignore the track and continue straight ahead through the field. The path is not clear but aim slightly left of a line of trees on the next field boundary. Cross a stile at the next hedge boundary; then walk straight ahead to a stile at the next boundary, and join Northcote Road. Turn right and follow the pavement over Skenning Bridge (crossing Bushburn Brook). Reach a road junction by Keeper's Cottage. Turn left along the adjoining road to reach the Church of St Leonard's, Old Langho.

AW sketched this tranquil church from the large copper beech tree that dominates the roadside corner of the churchyard. The church was built using stones, roof timbers and even glass fragments from the remains of Whalley Abbey. The old Langho Church was once the centre of the village, but Langho effectively shifted a mile further south of the Ribble when both the turnpike road and later the railway between Blackburn and

Old Langho Church

Whalley were built in the nineteenth century. When AW drew old Langho Church it was still an occasional place of worship; it was finally declared redundant in 1990.

From the church, walk along the road to the adjacent Black Bull and turn right here along the footpath to the right of the pub that leads to a gate between hedges. Go straight ahead alongside the right field edge. The path swings around a line of trees – keep them on the right – and drops steeply downhill to a footbridge over Dinckley Brook. This stream is heading directly north to the River Ribble. Climb up the steep slope on the north bank of the brook. At the top of the hill go diagonally left across the field towards some cottages. Go through a gate in the left-hand corner of this field and then straight ahead to the cottages.

At the cottages, marked on the OS map as 'Aspinalls', you join a Roman road from Lancashire to Yorkshire. This west–east route headed from nearby Ribchester through the Ribble and Aire Valleys to Ilkley. Just over 1 mile east of Aspinalls was

Dinckley Hall

Potter's Ford, where the Roman road crossed the River Calder near to the Jacobean residence of Hacking Hall. You now follow the route of the Roman road for the next ¼ mile, heading west towards Ribchester.

Pass between the cottages and the track soon becomes a quiet lane. Follow it for ¼ mile to a T-junction. Turn right at the junction and follow the lane downhill towards the River Ribble. At the bottom of the hill pass Dinckley Hall on the right and then turn sharp left. Follow the woodland path, cross a stile and enter a meadow overlooking the graceful Dinckley suspension bridge.

Long before *A Ribble Sketchbook*, Dinckley was familiar to AW as a boy with jam butties in his pocket and as a youthful rambler in the company of Lawrence Wolstenholme in the late 1920s. The distinct chimneys, old windows and garden wall of Dinckley Hall appear much as AW sketched them. Originally dating from the fifteenth century, the hall was once the home of John Talbot, a Royalist who lost his estate during the English Civil War.

You finally reach the River Ribble along its south bank, at the spot where AW sketched the footbridge across it. The current bridge opened in October 1951. AW remembered the ferry boat here linking Dinckley and Hurst Green. Traditionally this had been a craft known as a 'trow' or trough – two hollow troughs joined together which glided backwards and forwards across the river, pulled by ropes. The 'trow' gives its name to nearby Trough House on the north bank of the river.

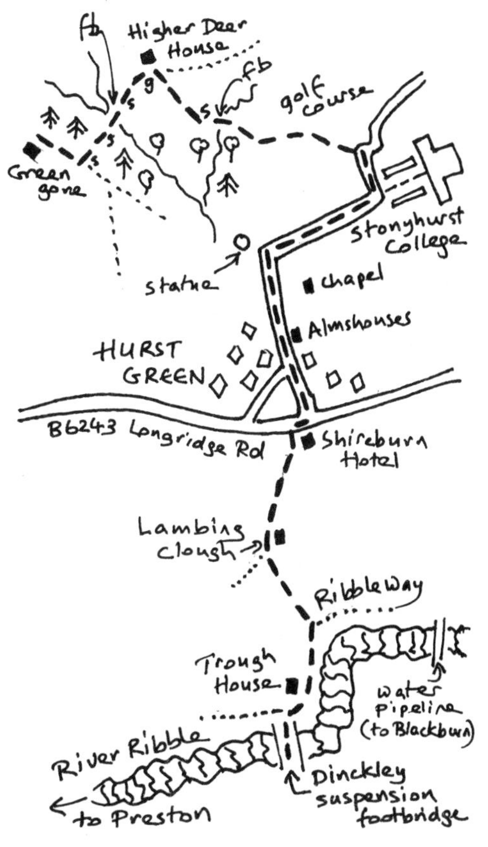

Cross the bridge and follow a fenced path straight ahead between trees. The next stile leads on to a track waymarked as the Ribble Way. Our route now follows a short section of this 80-mile long-distance route from the sea to the river's source towards Hurst Green. Bear right and follow the track as it swings left between the buildings that make up Trough House. Go straight ahead along the farm road. It climbs uphill and passes the old stone farm at Lambing Clough, which gives this lane its name. The lane meets Whalley Road next to the Shireburn Arms Hotel. Cross over to Avenue Row, where two war memorial crosses stand among flower beds.

Hurst Green is part of a large rural parish of hamlets on the north side of the River Ribble collectively known as Aighton, Bailey and Chaigley. Much of this area was part of the manor of the Shireburns, one of Lancashire's most important and prosperous families in Elizabethan and Tudor times. Their crest can be seen on the inn sign outside the Shireburn Arms and above the entrance to the almshouses they built nearby. Harry Green's *Rambles* would have brought AW here in the late 1920s and AW described Hurst Green as a 'sweet village' in *A Ribble Sketchbook*. He sketched cottages in the village and also the nearby Lower Hodder Bridge.

At Hurst Green you also enter the Forest of Bowland Area of Outstanding Natural Beauty, which stretches north from here all the way to the River Lune at Hornby. Almost the next 30 miles of walking will be within this officially designated area.

Continue straight ahead along Avenue Row, the main village street, past the Guild Hall on the right. After passing the Bailey Arms Hotel and the village hall, you reach the Shireburn Almshouses on the same side.

These almshouses were sketched by AW from the street entrance, though strangely, despite having a date stone of 1706, they were not here when he visited Hurst Green in his youth.

They were transplanted in the 1940s from their original location on the hillside at the eastern end of Longridge Fell and rebuilt in the village to provide houses for staff at Stonyhurst College.

Shireburn Almshouses

Continue straight ahead along the lane at the top end of the village. This enters woodland through the gateway to Stonyhurst Park. The lane soon swings sharp right at the statue of Our Lady to reveal a spectacular view of Stonyhurst College. Walk straight ahead along the avenue to the point where it swings sharp left at a white gate leading to the two rectangular ponds.

The Our Lady statue is Victorian but the avenue and the ponds were built around 1696 by Sir Nicholas Shireburn. Stonyhurst College, a Jesuit boarding school, began life as Stonyhurst Hall, the manor house of the staunchly Catholic Shireburns. Though parts of the hall date from 1523, it was Richard Shireburn and his grandson Nicholas who developed it, largely in the years between 1592 and 1717. In 1794 a party of Jesuits fleeing from Liege following the turbulence of the French Revolution were invited to make use of a decaying Stonyhurst Hall by the then owner, Thomas Weld, and the college was born.

When the grand house was half-built, Oliver Cromwell and his troops invited themselves to stay on 16 August 1648. His army of nearly 9,000 men camped in the deer park while their leader slept in full armour on a table in the Great Hall, supposedly to protect himself from assassination by his Papist hosts.

Stonyhurst College now houses a rich treasure trove of religious relics entrusted to the college for safe-keeping. This includes two hats belonging to Sir Thomas More, a thorn allegedly taken from Jesus's Crown of Thorns that once belonged to Mary, Queen of Scots, and the eyeball of a martyred priest executed along with Guy Fawkes. Ex-pupils of the college include Arthur Conan Doyle, Charles Laughton and George Herbert Walker, great-grandfather of President George W. Bush.

Just after AW had moved to Kendal in the 1940s, the author J.R.R. Tolkien became a frequent visitor to Stonyhurst, staying with his family at one of the college lodges while his son John studied here. Tolkien was greatly inspired by this area and wrote part of his great epic *The Lord of the Rings* in one of the college classrooms. The variety of landscapes to be seen on short walks from the college helped him shape his descriptions of the Hobbit land known as 'The Shire'. He even had a ferry boat crossing the fictional River Brandywine – in other words, the River Ribble.

AW sketched Stonyhurst from the parkland to the right of the lane that gradually climbs uphill from the gated driveway towards the golf club.

Stonyhurst College

Keep to the lane turning sharp left at the gateway following it slightly uphill until you reach the entrance to Stonyhurst Park Golf Club on the left. A signed footpath leads through the car park to a memorial to George Herbert Walker.

The American banker was not only the ancestor of two US presidents but also helped create the golfing competition known as the Walker Cup. The nine-hole Stonyhurst golf course was a late Victorian addition to the deer park. Various notices in the car park state club rules and regulations. Hopefully passing ramblers are exempt from the rule stating that shorts must be tailored.

Be vigilant when crossing the golf course. The footpath follows a generally westerly course but the waymarkers are not easy to spot. Start at the track to the right of the clubhouse and cross fairways heading towards woodland on the far side of the golf course. Keep well below the distinctive copse enclosed by a wall on a hill to the right. On reaching the woodland edge turn right and follow the fence along the edge of the fairway until you soon meet a track forking left down into the wood. This drops steeply down to a footbridge over a beck. Follow the path up the bank on the other side and leave the wood at a stile and gate. Go straight uphill, heading for the farm, Higher Deer House, at the top of the field. Join the track directly in front of the farm and turn left through field gates between barns to enter a field on the left.

Bear slightly left through this field, heading for conifers on the far side. Cross a stile at the edge of the wood. The path drops steeply down through another 'clough' to cross Dean Brook at a footbridge near where two streams meet. On the far side of the bridge bear left, following the path uphill, and when it soon forks take the right path that climbs steeply to cross a ladder stile on the edge of the wood. Go straight ahead through the field to cross another ladder stile in the fence on the right near the boundary wall. Cross a stile across the

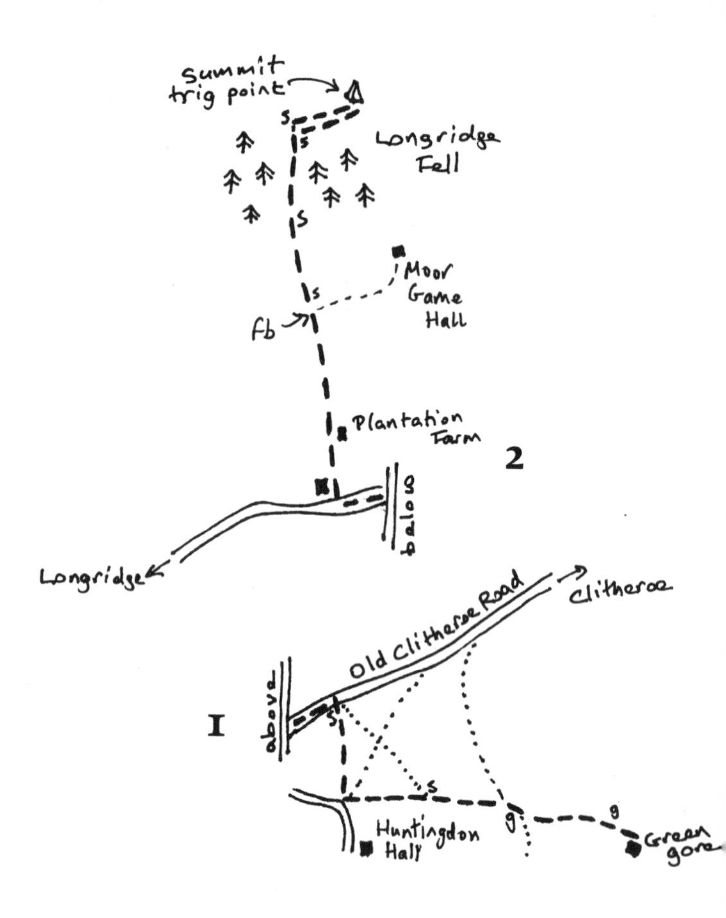

boundary wall to join a bridleway track. Turn right along this and you will soon reach the impressive Greengore, an ancient hunting lodge, on the left.

Continue along the wall-side track straight ahead through several bridle gates. Beyond the woodland on the right the view opens out north towards Longridge Fell. When you reach a junction of tracks beyond a gate, the route leaves the track by going almost straight ahead through a boggy pasture. The path is faint at first but heads gradually uphill, aiming for a ladder stile in the next boundary wall between two copses. Cross the ladder stile and walk straight ahead from here along the bottom end of a field of gorse bushes. Keep to the left wall side and at the opposite end of the field you will see Huntingdon Hall on the lane down to the left. When you reach the stile leading on to the road, do not cross it but turn at right angles in the same field and head uphill with the fence on the left. At the top left corner of this field cross a stile to reach Old Clitheroe Road.

The broad ridge of Longridge Fell is now to be crossed. This takes us right back to AW's youth, as it was one of the first hills he climbed as a boy.

Turn left along the Longridge–Clitheroe road and follow it slightly downhill only as far as the next junction on the right, signed to the Dutton Dog House Kennels and Cattery. Turn right here and follow the farm road uphill. Now begins a steady climb for the next mile to the summit of Longridge Fell. When the farm road swings right towards the cattery, leave it and go straight ahead over a railway-sleeper footbridge on a path between fences, crossing a stile at the sign marking the boundary of open country. A boggy moorland path through heather crosses further stiles in a wall and fence to meet a track running left to right at the edge of conifers. Cross this and go straight ahead along a track between the conifers. This shady path can be very boggy but the path soon emerges from the trees on the top of the fell. Cross a stile and turn right along a narrow path through heather between a wall and the conifers. The summit triangulation pillar can be seen on the other side of the wall straight ahead. Reach this by crossing the wall stile on the left at the top of the hill.

The best view can be seen by walking a few yards down from the summit pillar to the steep-sided edge looking north. The panorama revealed is almost the perfect view, the rolling hedged meadows and woodland copses of the Hodder Valley giving way to the bleak open moors of Bowland further north. That is the way the walk is heading – into a remote northern wilderness. The densely wooded stretch of the Hodder Valley at Whitewell, visible in the middle distance, is the next objective.

On a good day looking north, the view from west to east (from left to right) should encompass Blackpool Tower, Beacon Fell, the Vale of Chipping with the village itself below the prominent spur of Parlick, the southern aspect of the Bowland fells (sketched by AW in *A Bowland Sketchbook*) including Totridge, the Hodder Valley guarded by the distinctive Middle Knoll with Salter Fell behind it, Beatrix Fell, Waddington Fell, Grindleton Fell and Yorkshire's Three Peaks behind them, together with Settle Moor and Barden Fell.

Longridge Fell to Dunsop Bridge (7 miles)

Walk downhill from the trig point in the same direction as before but now along the wall-side track, with the wall on the left. When you reach the next wall stile on the left, turn sharp right along a narrow path through heather. This descends the hillside very steeply at first along a sunken track with a view directly north towards Bowland. The track quickly swings right and runs downhill, overlooking three farms strung out along the road below. The route is heading for the left of the three farms, marked on the OS map as 'Bradley Hall'.

Just above the intake wall below, the track swings sharp left and continues downhill to a gate in the wall. Go through this gate, leaving open access country behind. The field path heads downhill directly towards the farm buildings. Keep to the left of a very boggy spring at the bottom end of the field and cross a stile in the fence. The path continues straight downhill through an area of boggy springs, crossing stiles and going through gates to arrive at the Longridge–Clitheroe road opposite Bradley Hall. The descent of Longridge Fell is certainly a lot quicker than the long ascent from Hurst Green.

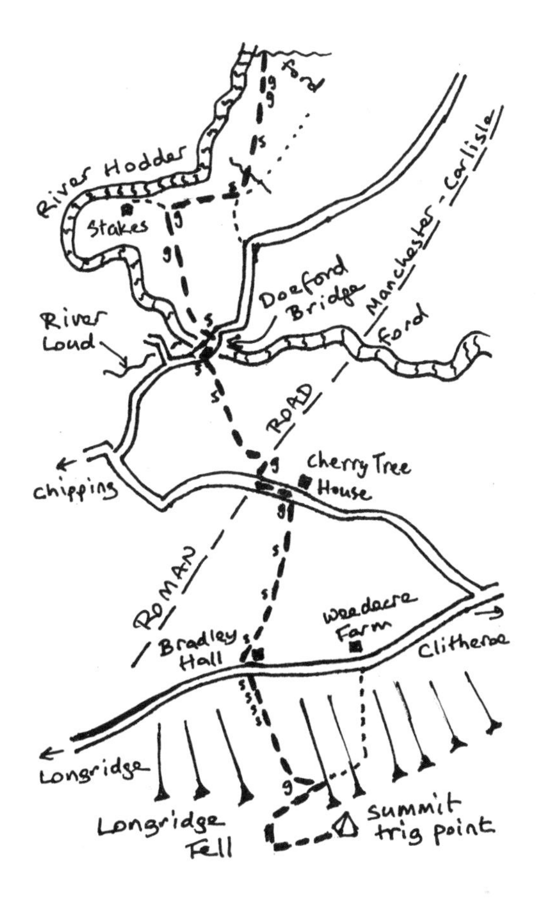

Join the footpath opposite, which goes straight up the driveway of Bradley Court, a residential development attached to the old hall. The waymarked path turns right after garages and leads around the side of the houses to cross a stile into a paddock, and then another stile on the left, over which you enter a large field sloping downhill. Bear diagonally right through this field, aiming for farm buildings beyond the next few fields. Cross a stream that forms the right field boundary at a stile and then continue in the same direction, heading

for the farm. Cross two more fields to reach the Chipping–Clitheroe road opposite Cherry Tree House. Turn left along this road for a short distance until you reach a footpath signpost on the right. Turn right along this path, which starts as a farm track leading to a barn.

This is actually a Roman road, as marked on the OS map, part of an important military highway running south to north from Manchester and Ribchester to Hadrian's Wall at Carlisle. It crosses the Bowland fells between the rivers Ribble and Lune. The very brief stretch of the road encountered here is part of the straight alignment between the western end of Longridge Fell and the crossing of the River Hodder, just downstream of Doeford Bridge. The walk route leaves the Roman road here at the barn, but we will rejoin it on the high Bowland hills on stage three of the walk.

After passing the barn, turn left through the second field gate on the same side. Follow the field path directly ahead, slightly downhill with a hedge side to the left. Pass through other fields until you reach the woodland directly ahead. At the bottom field corner, look out on the left for a small footbridge and stile in the trees on the left. Cross these and go straight ahead through the next field. Do not drop to the River Hodder but keep to the higher ground and cross a ladder stile to reach a road. Turn right along this and cross Doeford Bridge over a lovely stretch of the river.

This bridge, with the River Hodder below it, has always formed a significant boundary. Crossing the bridge takes you into what was, prior to 1974, the West Riding of Yorkshire as the river here formed the old county boundary with Lancashire. The roadside sign north of the bridge indicates that you are now entering land owned by the Duchy of Lancaster – in other words, the Queen of England.

Doeford Bridge is also the first introduction to AW's *A Bowland Sketchbook*. His sketch of the road crossing over the River Hodder is taken from the north-east side of the bridge. To the left of the bridge the River Hodder is joined by the River Loud, which drains the Vale of Chipping west of here between Longridge Fell and the Bowland fells.

Cross the stile on the left side of the bridge by the Duchy of Lancaster sign. The river is worth a look here and a good place to stop if time allows. The path runs uphill above the bank on the right-hand side of the river. Keep going straight ahead, aiming for the top right-hand corner of a large pasture. On reaching a waymarker post in a tree line, turn right and follow the line of trees on the left through another large field. When the line of trees soon ends, go through the field gate to the left leading into another field and follow the field edge, with the fence now on the immediate right. The path drops down to a barn. Go through the gate on the right after passing the barn and follow the stony track climbing uphill to join a tarmac farm road. This soon swings sharp right at a junction of paths. Leave it at this point, crossing a stile on the left.

Two footpaths start in the field at this point. Take the path going downhill from the stile along the line of a little gully. This bears right and fords a stream; then it turns left and bears straight ahead to cross

Doeford Bridge

a stile by a tree at the next field boundary. Continue straight ahead here, passing two old stone gateposts to reach a kissing gate in a boggy patch. Go straight ahead along a grassy path to ford another stream, continuing in the same direction with the River Hodder down to the left. Do not drop down to the floodplain but keep to the higher ground, following a faint grassy path slightly uphill with rock outcrops and woodland to the left. Cross a stile and keep the woodland on the left. The woodland boundary changes direction, but keep going straight ahead to reach a stile on to the Whitewell road.

Turn left and join the footpath on the opposite side of the road, starting at a big metal gate. Turn left along the wall side and follow the path through further gates. The path then bears slightly right and uphill along the contour line as the view opens out quite spectacularly ahead to the pastures of the Middle Hodder Valley. Go through another kissing gate at the next field boundary and then follow the left wall side only as far as the next field gate in the wall on the left. Go through this and continue straight ahead as the path starts to swing gradually downhill around the hillside. Keep to the grassy track, which leads to cottages at Seed Hill. Turn left at the cottages and follow the path downhill alongside a burial ground, through a gate and steps to reach a lane. Turn left to reach the hamlet of Whitewell and its famous inn.

The walk from Doeford Bridge to Whitewell has followed the old Yorkshire side of the River Hodder along the western boundary of an enclosed medieval deer park centred on Radholme Laund. This was one of two managed deer parks, the other being on the Lancashire side of the Hodder, within the ancient royal hunting ground known as Bolland Forest. The village of Whitewell played a significant role in the life of the forest, part of the present inn being the old manor house and court once occupied by the Keeper of the Royal Forest, Walter Urswyck. He also built the original chapel, now the enlarged Georgian Church of St Michael's, around 1400 and this little church overlooking the valley is worth a look. Both the chapel and the later eighteenth-century inn were important resting points for travellers crossing the perilous Trough Road over the Bowland fells between Lancaster and Clitheroe. Behind the inn's car park are stepping stones which cross the river.

The most direct way upstream to Burholme Bridge is to follow the road straight ahead, starting at the right-hand side of the inn. After about ½ mile you reach the road bridge.

A Bowland Sketchbook includes four sketches of the Middle Hodder Valley between Doeford and Dunsop Bridge. As well as the two road bridges over the river at Doeford and Burholme, AW sketched the densely wooded limestone gorge at Whitewell just downstream from the inn. He could have taken photos for all of these views more or less by the roadside, although the sketch of the Whitewell gorge would have involved scrambling down the wooded river bank. The fourth scene of the Hodder Valley could almost have been captured without AW getting out of the car – it is the broad view taken from the lane running downhill from the direction of Chipping to Burholme Bridge.

Do not cross the road bridge but leave it on the right, following the footpath along the access road to Burholme Farm. At the second cattle grid the definitive path leaves the farm road on the left, crossing a stile and going straight ahead through rough undergrowth to cross another stile on the riverbank. Turn right there and cross a third stile to rejoin the access road. Follow the road to the farm buildings. Walk past the front of the old farm and then turn left behind it, following a path that leads to a ford and footbridge.

There was a hamlet, chapel and forest court at Burholme long before the development of Whitewell in the 1400s. Quakers settled here in the seventeenth century and the families of Nicholas Waln and his sister Ann, both born at Burholme, were

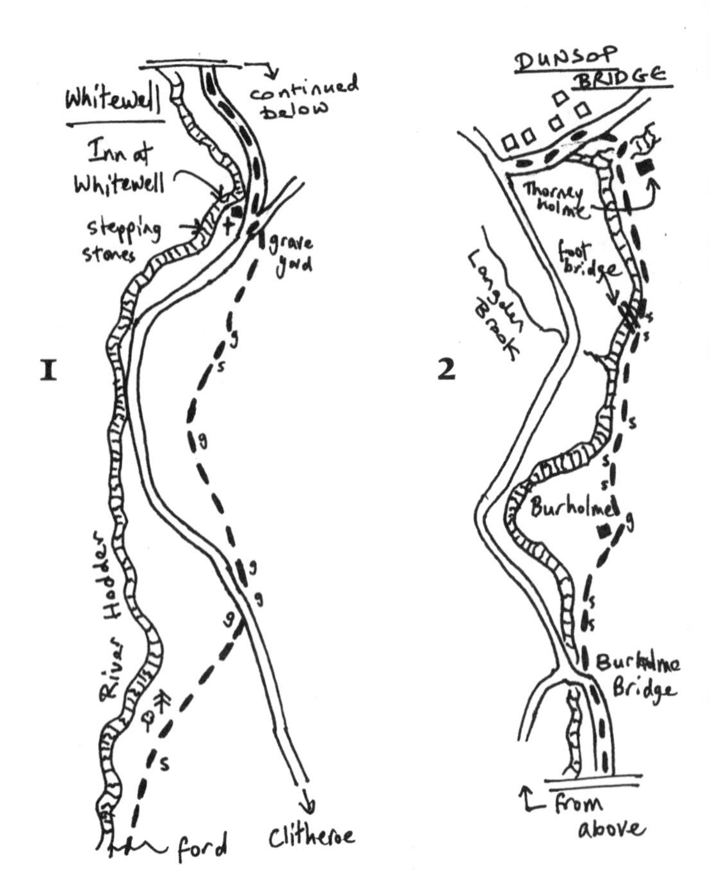

early settlers of Pennsylvania. They sailed there in 1682 on a ship called the *Lamb*, after buying land from founding father William Penn. Burholme-born Nicholas (1650–1721) became a prominent politician in Philadelphia.

Cross the ford or footbridge and enter the field via the gate straight ahead. The path bears slightly left and heads for a gate and stile at the far field boundary. Enter the next field and walk straight ahead towards the right bank of the River Hodder. Cross further stiles along the waymarked path, keeping the river on the near left and the wooded hillside on the right. You pass the tributary of Langden Brook on the left where it joins the River Hodder. Continue straight ahead until you reach the ornate cast-iron footbridge over the river.

The pipe running under the bridge and over the river was constructed in 1882 and has the name of the Borough Engineer W.B. Bryan, stamped on it. As part of the Blackburn Waterworks' operations in Bowland, the pipe carries water collected in the tributary valleys of the River Dunsop over the rivers Hodder and Ribble to Blackburn, some 20 miles to the south-west. The elegant design of this arched bridge was a gesture to the Towneleys, owners of nearby Thorneyholme Hall, who obviously had no desire to stare at something ugly.

Do not cross the footbridge but continue straight ahead along the right bank of the River Hodder. After crossing further stiles, at a junction of paths keep to the one that follows the riverside. This leads through a large field, which eventually joins a track swinging right between the river and farm outbuildings. Keep to the left of the buildings and follow the riverside to the bridge at the entrance to Thorneyholme Hall. Turn left and cross the River Hodder over the bridge, following the driveway with its grand avenue of redwood trees to meet the road.

The River Dunsop, fresh from the soggy fells, can be seen joining the River Hodder on the far side just before you cross the bridge at the entrance to Thorneyholme Hall. Thorneyholme was part of the Bowland Forest estate, purchased by Peregrine Towneley in 1835. Throughout Queen Victoria's reign the wealthy Towneleys, whose main family seat was Towneley Hall in Burnley, were effectively the 'lords of Bowland'. Thorneyholme was the residence of their estate manager, Richard Eastwood, a cattle and racehorse owner who ran the Towneley stud at nearby Root Farm.

It was on these pastures along the River Hodder that Colonel Charles Towneley's racehorse Kettledrum was trained. In 1861 Kettledrum won the Derby, and the race winnings of Eastwood and the Colonel were used to fund the building of the Roman Catholic church of St Hubert in Dunsop Bridge. As for Kettledrum, possibly the only Derby winner to have his image painted on the ceiling of a Roman Catholic church, he was eventually exported to the Austro-Hungarian Empire, where he was put out to stud and died in 1885 aged twenty-seven.

Turn left along the road and enter Dunsop Bridge past the toilets and the phone box on the green.

The village phone box was BT's 100,000th public phone box, opened here in 1992 after the Ordnance Survey recognized this village as being the nearest to the geographical centre of the British Isles. It was unveiled by the explorer Ranulph Fiennes.

Continue straight ahead to reach the road bridge over the River Hodder.

Dunsop Bridge

Stage Three
DUNSOP BRIDGE TO WRAY INSTITUTE
(15 miles)

'And above all are the wild fells. This is the true Bowland, and the best part of it.'
A Bowland Sketchbook

This stage of the walk is a watershed for walkers not just geographically but also in a physical and mental sense. It takes you on a long desolate crossing of the high Bowland fells that separates the catchments of the River Ribble and River Lune. The moorland traverse is book-ended by encounters with two contrasting river valleys whose upper reaches flow in completely different directions but seep from the same peat hags. These are the conifer-clad River Dunsop, flowing south, and the orchard-lined River Roeburn, flowing north. The route is a wander through the landscapes captured in *A Bowland Sketchbook*. The walker who survives the morale-sapping bogs of Upper Whitendale and the lonely crossing of the desolate fells will arrive at Wray village in high spirits. A gentler enchanting countryside awaits and views of the Lakeland fells will already be appearing on the horizon. They are getting closer with every step.

The Sketchbook Years: Part Two

Unlike the Ribble Valley and Longridge Fell, the Bowland fells were just beyond the range of a day's tramp for a small boy from Blackburn. In fact, for most of the twentieth century they were out of the range of all walkers, being private land, prime grouse shooting country, with hardly any legal public access. AW was aware of this, and indeed mentions it in the introduction to *A Bowland Sketchbook*. He dedicates this book to one of his many correspondents, Matthew Leedal, who sent him an unpublished guide to Bowland, which 'influenced an old man to follow in his footsteps and see Bowland for himself'.

By the late nineteenth century the burgeoning town of Blackburn was consuming millions of gallons of water a day. The urgent need to keep the town's reservoirs stocked led Blackburn Corporation to acquire land 20 miles away in what was surely one of the wettest places in the north: Bowland. The town's waterworks scheme was constructed in the late 1870s, initially capturing the water from the fells that seeped into the moorland valleys of the Brennand and Whitendale rivers. Through a series of intakes in these gathering grounds, weirs diverted the water into conduits and pipes and whisked it off down a mains pipe to Blackburn, where by 1882 it was keeping the town's Fishmoor Reservoir nicely topped up. The natural recipient of this water, the River Dunsop, was never the same again.

In the 1920s, long before United Utilities and electronic cash transactions, Blackburn Council Waterworks' employees living and working in the Dunsop Valley would have had their weekly wages delivered. Paul Holden, the son-in-law of AW's Town Hall colleague Lawrence Wolstenholme, recalls Lawrence saying that he and AW, as clerks in the Borough Treasurer's Office, were occasionally given this job. Lawrence remembered delivering wages to the Dunsop employees from about 1925 onwards. This must have been a treat, a welcome break to the routine of Town Hall ledgers.

Council water bailiffs and their families, who lived at Bishop's House, alongside the River Dunsop, were responsible for managing the catchment from the head of the valleys down to the River Hodder at Sandal Holme. A Post Office telegraph was installed at Bishop's House to ensure the waterworks staff had direct communication with the Borough Engineer at Blackburn Town Hall.

When AW returned here in 1980 he made sketches of both the Dunsop Valley and the Whitendale River, and he mentions the waterworks. In typical AW fashion, the few words that accompany his sketches of this area in *A Bowland Sketchbook*, published in 1981, convey the feeling that he is slightly unhappy with the man-made intrusions into the landscape – not just the concrete of the waterworks, but also the conifer plantations on the hillsides and the car park catering for an increasing number of motorists to Dunsop Bridge, a place that was once 'undisturbed by visitors'.

The rise and rise of cars in the countryside was annoying to AW, who had used the bus to write his *Pictorial Guides*. Yet fast forward to 1980 and here is Betty driving him around the northern countryside in a car! AW in his seventies had become a motor tourist.

The comments accompanying his sketches in *A Bowland Sketchbook*, published in 1981, suggest a slight preoccupation with motorists and their picnic parking places. Perhaps because so much of the Bowland fells was out of bounds to walkers, he spent a lot of time taking photos from the roadside. He includes fifteen sketches taken around the main vehicular route through the hills, the Trough of Bowland.

A Bowland Sketchbook, and indeed the earlier studies of the rivers Lune and Ribble, reflects an author in contented retirement. The intrepid explorer who surveyed the grand sweep of the Lakeland fells using only bus and foot was gone. AW and Betty motoring through the Trough and stopping to take snapshots presents a more sedate image. But septuagenarian AW had not quite hung up his walking boots. Some of his Bowland sketches required climbing uphill from the car for a few miles – for example, his views of Salter Fell, Croasdale, Whitendale and the summits of Clougha Pike and Ward's Stone.

Of the seventy drawings in *A Bowland Sketchbook*, we have already encountered those covering the Hodder Valley from Doeford Bridge to Dunsop Bridge. This stage of the walk follows the trail of another twelve AW sketches. It takes the walker from AW's village views of Dunsop Bridge to his views of the Dunsop, Brennand and Whitendale Valleys. It then climbs to the sketches he made of Salter Fell and the County Fence on the old Lancashire–Yorkshire boundary, and to the farm at High Salter, before descending to the north side of the fells in the company of his drawings of Roeburndale and Wray village. Both Dunsop Bridge and Wray remain unchanged from the day AW sketched them over thirty years ago.

In sketching the high places of Bowland, AW used the sparse public rights of way together with permissive paths in agreed open access areas. The summits of Clougha Pike, Grit Fell and Ward's

River Roeburn

Stone, which AW sketched, were all linked by a permissive path recently opened through access agreements. It was only in the 1970s, after years of negotiations between Lancashire County Council and reluctant moorland landowners, that a few square miles of Bowland's fell tops were opened up for walkers. Tom Stephenson, the inspiration for the Pennine Way, fought all his life to see the hundreds of 'Private Keep Out' notices removed from Bowland. He was still involved in 1969, as the recently retired Secretary of the Ramblers' Association, when a rally of outdoor groups was held in Chipping demanding greater access to the fells. Even in the twilight of their years, the generation that included AW and Tom Stephenson never got to wander freely across the extensive heather moors of Bowland.

This stage is wholly in Lancashire, but much of Bowland was once part of the old West Riding of Yorkshire. Prior to 1974, the Lancashire–Yorkshire county border followed natural boundaries like the River Hodder and the high fell tops of Wolfhole Crag, Whins Brow and Fair Snape Fell. After government reorganization more or less the whole of Bowland was lumped into an enlarged Lancashire.

AW refers to the pre-1974 county boundary several times in *A Bowland Sketchbook*. He mentions it in the first sentence of his introduction, where he also includes a little sketch of the county stone marking the old Lancashire–Yorkshire boundary crossing the Trough Road. He mentions it at Doeford Bridge on the River Hodder. He also sketches the County Fence on Salter Fell, passed on this stage of the walk.

AW had an affection for Yorkshire. Although his parents moved to Blackburn in search of work, they came from Penistone, near Barnsley, where two of AW's older siblings were born. By the time AW came to sketch Yorkshire Bowland, the county had already come under his radar in *Pennine Way Companion*, and it went on to feature heavily in his 1970s guidebooks.

Once AW had familiarized himself with Bowland, a year later this area featured again in his sketches of the source of Lancashire's River Wyre in *A Wyre Sketchbook*, which completed his survey of the major rivers flowing into the Irish Sea between Preston and Lakeland.

Starting with *A Lakeland Sketchbook* in 1969 and ending with *A Peak District Sketchbook* in 1984, the *Westmorland Gazette* published some thirty books of AW's drawings, including his Lakeland, Scottish and Welsh mountain volumes. Sticking to a simple winning formula, he didn't need to research and write much in the sketchbooks; he just let the drawings speak for themselves.

In his biography of Wainwright, Hunter Davies notes that by 1985 AW had sold in total over 2 million books. By 1984, AW and Betty had finally managed to finance and open the Animal Rescue Cumbria shelter Kapellan, in the village of Grayrigg, 4 miles outside Kendal on the Appleby Road. In 1988, the *Westmorland Gazette* published its last original Wainwright title, *Fellwalking with a Camera*. Surely now AW had achieved all he had set out to and was finally going to retire.

Of course not. The late 1980s saw him as busy as ever, thanks to two new developments. First, he had a lucrative new deal with London publisher Michael Joseph for a series of 'coffee table' illustrated books covering Lakeland, the Pennine Way, Scotland and the Yorkshire Dales. He would pen the words to accompany the photos of Derry Brabbs (and in one instance, Ed Geldard). He could happily sit at home and do this work, albeit with failing eyes, giving Betty a rest from the driving. Second, at the age of seventy-nine, he became a TV star, as we shall see later.

Although this stage visits the locations of some of the sketches he made later in life, its end reminds the walker of the more familiar image of AW as the man who wrote seven classic volumes about the Lakes. Following the old Hornby Road packhorse route over Salter Fell, a distant panorama of the Lakeland mountains is finally revealed for the first time in the walk. It is both inspiring and uplifting. AW's heaven on earth is now within sight.

THE ROUTE

Dunsop Bridge to the County Fence (6½ miles)

Dunsop Bridge was dominated in Victorian times by the Towneley family and is now part of the Duchy of Lancaster estate. It developed at the crossing point of the River Dunsop, lying at the foot of the Trough of Bowland, the moorland pass linking Clitheroe with Lancaster to the north. The Trough Road is at the heart of the history of this area. It was an 'assize road', used by the King's judges as they travelled between the county assizes at York and Lancaster. The infamous Pendle Witches were taken along the Trough Road for trial and execution at Lancaster Castle in 1612.

Along the Trough Road on the outskirts of Dunsop Bridge is St Hubert's Church, built by the Towneleys. Members of the Towneley family, as well as their estate manager, Richard Eastwood, are buried here. AW sketched St Hubert's Church from the Trough Road, half a mile off this walk' route. Closer at hand here are AW's views of Dunsop Bridge itself.

River Dunsop

Join the private road signed as a bridleway between the bridge and Puddleducks Café. Walk straight ahead past the playground with the River Dunsop on the left. Follow this river closely upstream for 1¾ miles to the point where it is formed at the meeting point of the Brennand and Whitendale rivers. The road crosses two gated cattle grids and passes a row of cottages on the right. Follow the road behind the cottages, which continues beyond a stile as a riverside path under trees. Cross a wooden bridge over the river and turn right to follow the access road straight up the valley, with the river now on the right. Pass on the left the estate cottages at Bishop's House before reaching the Foot Holme pumping station.

This walk follows the River Dunsop along its entire short route. You will have first seen it at the end of the previous stage of the walk entering the River Hodder, just west of Thorneyholme Hall. Now, only 2 miles later, you reach its starting point just upstream of the Foot Holme pumping station. The Bishop's House, where Blackburn Waterworks bailiffs once resided, takes its name from an earlier tenant, Richard Roskell (1817–83), who was the Roman Catholic Bishop of Nottingham for over twenty years and attended the First Vatican Council in 1869. He retired to the wilderness of the Dunsop Valley and is buried in the churchyard of St Hubert's.

The big water company United Utilities now dominates this valley, though the legacy of Blackburn Waterworks can be seen in the access road and Victorian buildings like the squat Meter House. The confluence of the Brennand and Whitendale rivers was at the heart of the original waterworks scheme, which had even considered building reservoirs along the two valleys upstream from here.

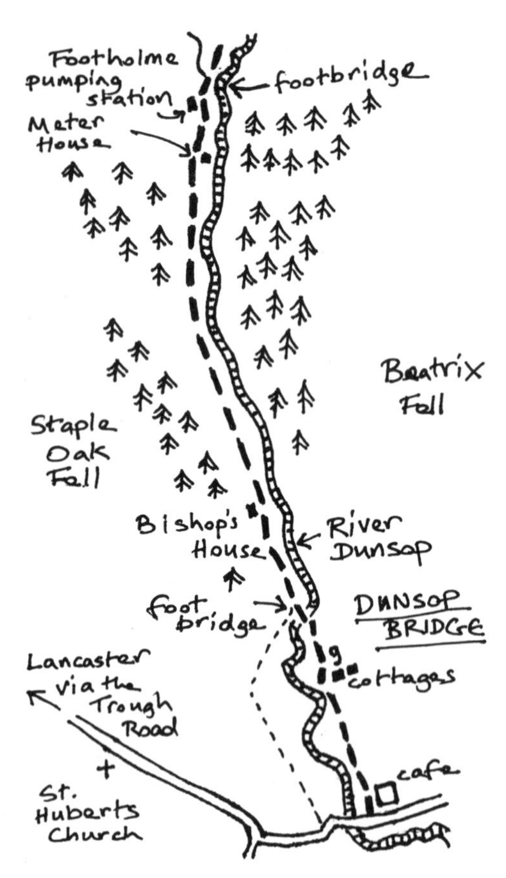

AW sketched the concrete left bank of the River Dunsop just south of the present pumping station. His view looks north to the very distinctive conical-shaped hill of Middle Knoll, which keeps the Brennand and Whitendale rivers apart. He also sketched two views just north of the pumping station, one of the Brennand Valley and one of Whitendale River.

Continue along the access road that crosses a bridge over the Brennand River. Ignore the higher footbridge on the right, which carries a footpath up the Whitendale River. Instead go through the gate by the cattle grid and continue along the road, which swings left uphill around the bottom of Middle Knoll. The surprising view of the perfectly compact Brennand Valley is soon revealed on the left.

AW sketched this valley and its farms from the hillside just to the left of the access road. In the comments that accompany his sketch, he refers to this as 'a vista that haunts the memory long after being seen'.

Whitendale River

When the road forks, take the right fork signed for Whitendale Farm. Continue uphill and the road soon swings left for a spectacular view of the Lower Whitendale Valley looking across to the high moor tops of Burn Fell and Dunsop Head. The road has a lonely Scottish feel to it; it is very remote save for the single line of telegraph poles heading up the valley. The road starts to wind downhill to the river with farms coming into view straight ahead. Cross the river and continue along the access road to the cottages and farm buildings.

The present Whitendale Farm has a date stone of 1854, built when the Towneleys owned this valley. Walkers please note: this is the last encounter with habitation for over 6 miles, so at least make an effort to say hello (or should that be goodbye) to the farmer. Ahead is over two hours' walking with the prospect of not meeting a single soul.

Keep to the left of Whitendale Farm and continue straight ahead along the farm track that begins at a gate. Continuing up the valley the track leads through two more gates. Keep to the lower track with a fence and river on the immediate left. Go through another gate and the track winds gradually uphill towards the moors, heading for two small blocks of conifers. Leave the track on the right when it starts to swing left. A wooden waymarker post signed to Salter Fell indicates the way, across a pasture to a gate in the wall between the two conifer woods.

Cross this boundary wall and the route now enters open access moorland. For the next 1½ miles the path runs through boggy pastures, keeping the Whitendale River down to the left and following it upstream, as it shrinks to the size of a small beck, to reach the wide track of Hornby Road at the head of the valley. The distinct but rough path crosses several cloughs, heading more or less directly north, and is waymarked with yellow-painted wooden posts. In poor visibility navigation can be difficult here until you reach Hornby Road.

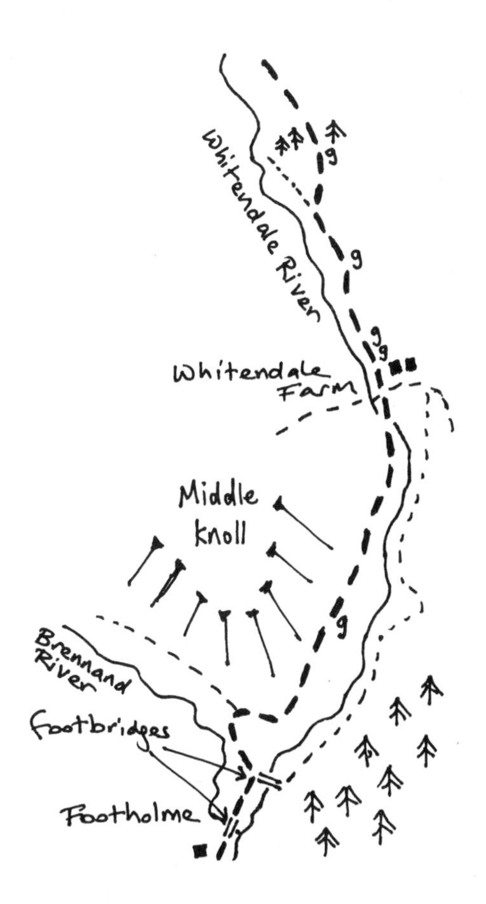

From the boundary wall walk with the line of conifers on the left through an area of boggy springs. Cross a footbridge and then go through a kissing gate, getting close to the river down to the left. Cross another footbridge at Higher Stony Clough; then go through another kissing gate in a wire fence by a prominent cairn. Beyond the second kissing gate cross the inlet of Brim Clough. The path starts to climb uphill, away from the river, which swings left to a morass of stream inlets. Follow the path waymarked by the posts uphill

through heather; it becomes less boggy once the river is left behind. After approximately 1/3 mile uphill from Brim Clough, you reach the firm track of the Hornby Road, running from left to right, at another wooden waymarker signpost.

The boggy trudge uphill from Whitendale Farm is certainly worthwhile if the weather is kind enough to reveal the excellent view back down the unspoilt valley. AW sketched the same view of Whitendale, complete with four grazing sheep in the foreground. This is Bowland at its wildest, much as the Romans would have seen it on their dreary march north from Manchester to Carlisle.

The route known as the Hornby or Salter Fell Road here follows part of the Roman military highway briefly met in the Hodder Valley during the second stage of the walk. This Roman road was the main south–north route on the west side of the Pennines. It linked forts at Ribchester on the River Ribble and Over Burrow on the River Lune, near Kirkby Lonsdale. The Romans built their roads in a series of straight alignments that sometimes suddenly changed direction to avoid natural obstacles like boggy river valleys. The alignment of the road where it follows the Hornby Road across the fells is on a south-east to north-west course.

Hornby Road may well have prehistoric origins but was certainly a medieval packhorse route used long after the Roman legions left Britain around AD 400. It linked the villages of Hornby and Slaidburn on either side of the Bowland fells and was important in the transport of salt from Morecambe Bay. It was also part of a more extensive network of salt routes that linked with Clitheroe and Whalley Abbey further to the south. AW mentions this salt traffic in the comments accompanying his sketch of Salter Fell, which takes its name from this trade, as do the farms of High, Middle and Lower Salter.

Turn left and follow the track as it heads north-west, following the contours of the broad Salter Fell ridge. The track crosses over a little ravine

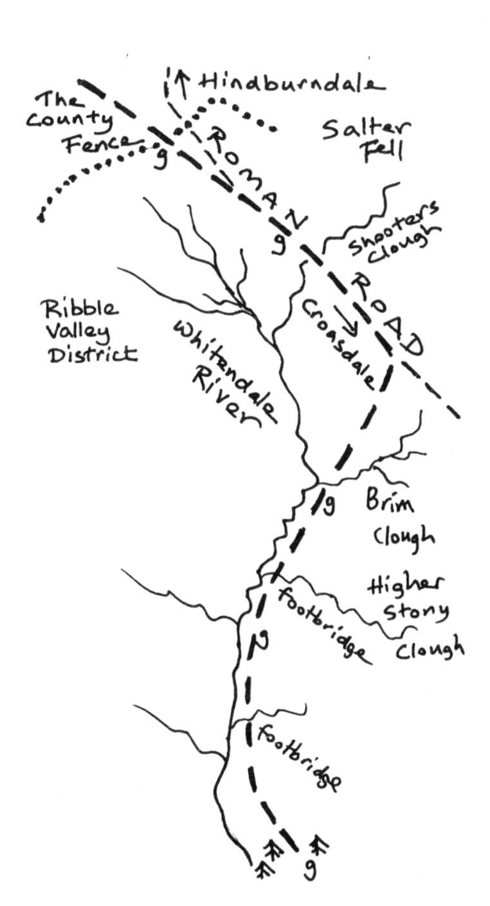

known as Shooter's Clough, goes through a gate, and after a further ½ mile reaches a second gate across the track at a boundary fence.

AW knew the boundary at this gate as the County Fence and sketched it for his book. In the comments accompanying the sketch he points out that this was the county boundary between Yorkshire and Lancashire prior to 1974. His view is taken from the old Lancashire side, looking towards Yorkshire. It is still an administrative boundary but now between two Lancashire authorities. In passing through the gate you officially leave the District of Ribble Valley and enter the District of Lancaster City. AW notes that the County Fence marks the true watershed between the tributaries of the River Hodder (and, eventually, the Ribble) and the River Lune. Shooter's Clough marks the last crossing of a stream flowing south to the River Ribble.

Just before you reach the County Fence, the Roman road bound north for the River Lune forks off to the right. Its course is fairly indistinct here but it leaves the Hornby Road, crosses the old county boundary and heads off over the hill to join the infant River Hindburn on the other side.

The County Fence to Wray Institute (8½ miles)

Go through the gate in the County Fence and continue along the track. Follow this gated old road straight ahead for 3½ miles – over an hour's walk – until you reach the next habitation, the farm at High Salter.

Unlike the Roman road, the old Hornby road runs in a north-west direction across the broad plateau of Salter Fell, aiming for Roeburndale. As you now follow streams heading for the River Lune, you can see the infant River Roeburn rising in a deep gully to the left, fed from a series of springs and cloughs seeping from the deep peaty slopes of Salter Fell, Wolfhole Crag and Mallowdale Fell. The view to the left above the stream is of the desolate Bowland ridge between Wolfhole Crag and Ward's Stone. On the other side of this ridge are the streams that form the source of the River Wyre, another of Lancashire's rivers originating in Bowland.

AW sketched a view of Salter Fell, showing rocky outcrops and a solitary walker tramping along the old Hornby road. Bowland is beautifully bleak. But if the weather is kind, you will be relieved from this stark emptiness by distant views of Ingleborough and Lakeland.

On reaching High Salter, the enticing wooded valley of the River Roeburn can be seen down below. Follow the tarmac road downhill past Middle and Lower Salter Farms.

AW sketched the farm at High Salter and also the River Roeburn just downhill from Middle and Lower Salter. His viewpoint for the river sketch is just off this walk's route, reached from the side road

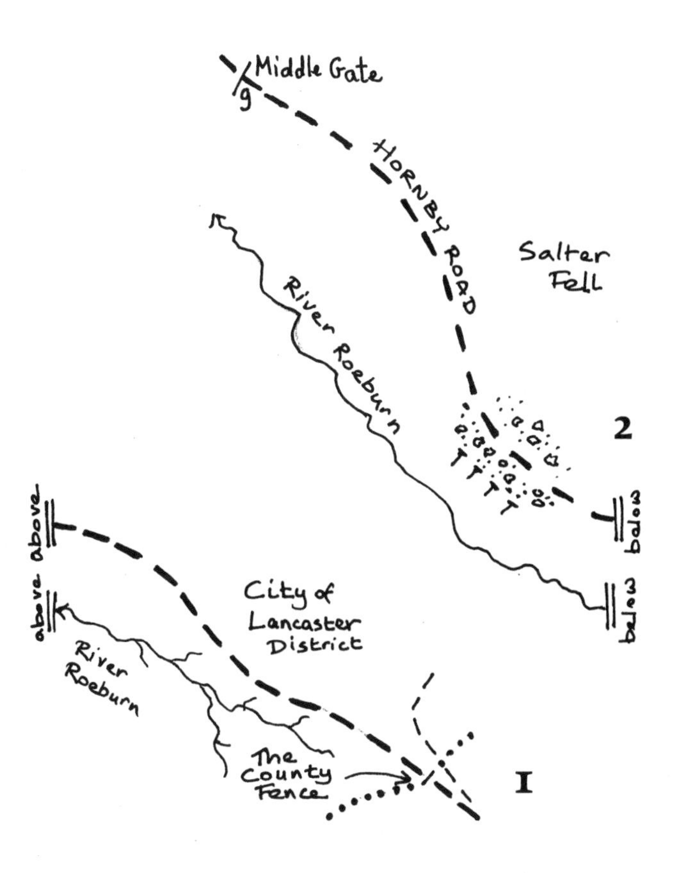

to Littledale, which winds down to the left just before you reach the lonely Methodist chapel at Lower Salter. AW's river scene looks upstream towards Mallowdale Pike, which he described as 'one of the few fells in Bowland with a graceful outline'. He notes the ample car parking space along the river bank, which suggests that he and Betty probably parked up here.

Continue along the road and soon cross the river at Barkin Bridge. Although heading downstream the road now rather inconveniently climbs steeply along the west side of the valley. At the top of the hill there is a good view back up the valley.

AW sketched this same view from the road above Barkin Bridge, looking down to the wooded river with the high fells in the background. He also drew sheep sitting on the road just as they do today.

After crossing a cattle grid, walk along the road for another ¼ mile until you reach the first signed footpath on the right-hand side, pointing down the access track to Back Farm.

This stage of the walk, which started along the banks of the River Dunsop, now ends alongside the River Roeburn and its

Salter Fell

ancient woods and fruit orchards. Any walker who is struggling with bad weather or is frankly just too tired may like to note that there is a quicker alternative way to Wray village: straight down the road for 1½ miles. That said, the route through the dale is really not to be missed.

Turn right and follow the farm track, which leads through a gate towards the farm. There is a good view across the valley to

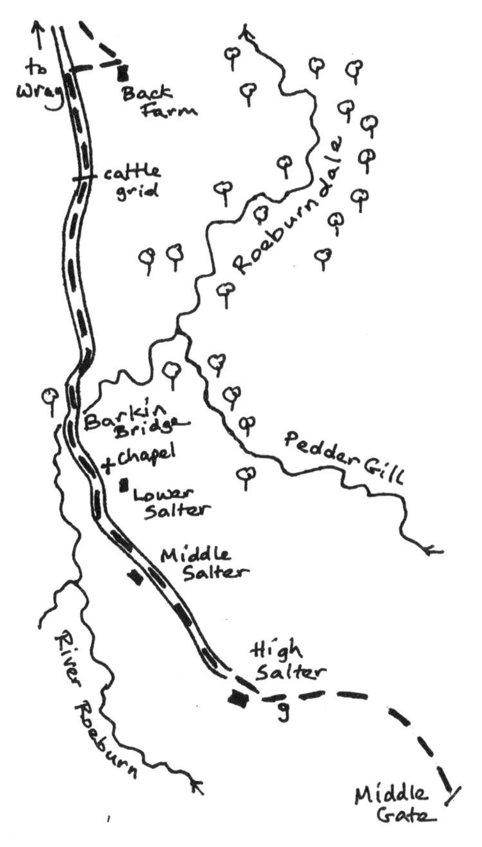

Ingleborough, Penyghent and the Howgill fells. When you reach the farm turn left through a gate. The route now heads for the next farm on the hillside down the valley but does not take a direct route because of the boggy terrain and the need to cross a beck. Head diagonally left through a field to a waymarker post; then drop steeply down to a footbridge crossing the beck. Climb up to another waymarker post and walk through another pasture towards the farm buildings.

To the right of the farm barn cross a wall stile and bear left around the back of the barn to follow the left hedge side. Walk towards the bottom end of the field and cross a stile on the left. Walk straight ahead to the next stile at the woodland edge and cross this. There is a very steep descent through the woodland: take care on the uneven steps, which will be very slippery if wet. The steps swing right at the bottom of the woodland to cross another stile at the woodland edge and enter a rough pasture.

Turn left and go through a gate to enter the ramshackle community of the Middlewood Trust. Pass the study centre on the left and keep to the main track as it swings slightly right to reach a footpath signpost. There is a bench here with a good view across the valley.

The Middlewood Trust is a charity aiming to develop sustainable and natural ways of living. The turf-roofed study centre is powered by a wind turbine and heated by solar panels. Roeburndale Woods, traditionally managed as a coppice wood, is a designated Site of Special Scientific Interest. It is one of the best examples of northern upland deciduous woodland in the country as well as one of the most extensive ancient woodlands in Lancashire.

Take the right forking track, dropping downhill towards the valley below. The track (a permissive bridleway and public footpath) zigzags, swinging sharp right, then sharp left, heading downhill

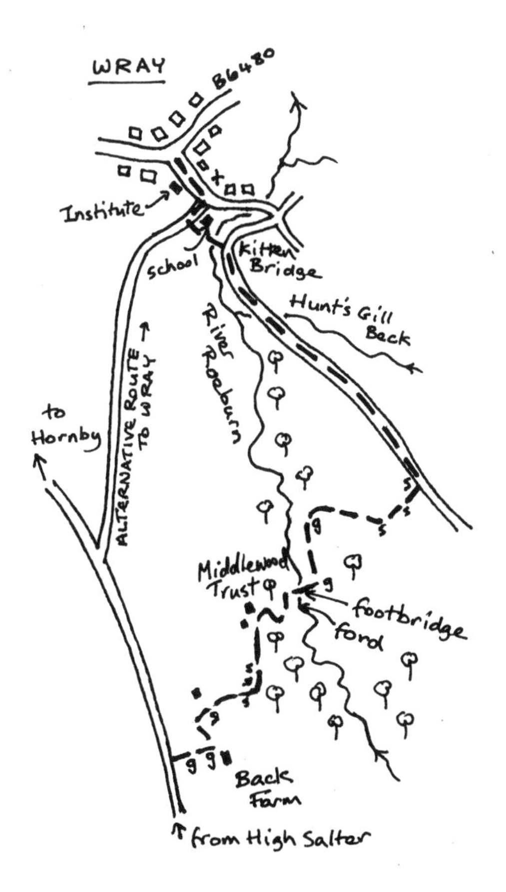

towards the fast-flowing River Roeburn. When the track swings sharp right again just above the river, leave it by going straight ahead along a grassy path between the bracken hillside on the left and the river on the right. This leads to a stile and gate signed to the Woodlands Workshop. Enter the woodland but leave it shortly on the right, at a post signed 'Lunesdale Walk'. A steep set of wooden steps leads down to cross a long footbridge over the River Roeburn.

An orchard has been planted in the meadow on the far side of the bridge. Since the 1980s the Middlewood Trust has been establishing apple, plum, damson and pear orchards in the valley and trying to bring back traditional Lancashire varieties of fruit. If there is time for a late afternoon siesta or snack break, take a right turn on the far side of the bridge across the meadow to a lovely open stretch of the fast-flowing river, which can be forded at low water.

To continue the walk, go straight ahead on the far side of the footbridge along the left field edge. This leads to three gates. Go through the middle gate – the rusty metal one waymarked as a footpath. The path climbs through Outhwaite Wood. Soon it swings right, away from the river, to a gate at the top edge of the wood. Go straight ahead from here through the field to the gate in the wall on the opposite side. The path then follows a more distinct track uphill through the next field and crosses a beck at a hedge gap to enter another field. Continue along the right field edge to a wall stile. Cross this and another little beck, continuing straight ahead to a wall stile leading to a lane.

From these fields looking left down the valley there are extensive views north beyond Hornby Castle to the Lakeland fells, which put a spring in the step. From here it is only a few hours' walk (about 6 miles) to the Cumbria country boundary. Along the lane to Wray village there are also views to the limestone crags of Hutton Roof and the Howgill fells across the Lune Valley.

Turn left along the lane and follow it downhill for the final mile into Wray. The lane crosses Hunt's Gill Beck, a tributary of the River Roeburn, and then passes cottages and the old Wray Mill on the left.

Wray Mill has a long history dating back to the early days of the village. Even in Tudor and Jacobean times Wray established itself as a centre of small-scale industry, of not just textiles but also cloggers, hatters and basket-makers. Wray Mill started as a woollen mill, eventually powered by the water of the River Roeburn. It adapted over the centuries and later produced silk, cotton and bobbins. A big employer in the village in the early nineteenth century, it was still operating in the 1930s.

After passing the mill, walk on for a short distance until there is a gap in the big stone wall on the left. Join a tarmac path here, which is a short cut into the village, crossing the River Roeburn again over the curiously named Kitten Bridge. The path winds between walls and emerges in the village by the side of the primary school.

The path from the bridge to the school is known locally as the Spout. Kitten Bridge was washed away in the infamous flash flood at Wray in August 1967 when a freak storm over the Bowland fells dropped 2 inches of rain in twenty minutes. The River Roeburn burst its banks and houses and cattle were washed away.

The village primary school can trace its history back to 1684, when it was established through a £200 endowment by a local Civil War soldier, Captain Richard Pooley, who had fought with Cromwell at the Battle of Worcester. The school was largely rebuilt in Victorian times but retains some of its original seventeenth-century features. Wray's famous son Bryan Holme (1776–1856) is recorded on a blue plaque at the front of the school he attended as a boy. He went on to be a London lawyer, resident of Brunswick Square and the founder of the Law Society in 1825.

Turn right down School Lane past the front of school, to reach the village's Main Street.

AW made his one sketch of the village looking right down the Main Street towards the commemorative garden built on the site of the cottages washed away in the 1967 flood. He mentions this historic event, noting that 'the Roeburn is docile again and serenity has returned to the 18th Century century village'. As with many of AW's sketches drawn in the 1970s and 1980s, the only difference is that now the village street is lined with parked cars. Only one vehicle is shown on AW's sketch, though perhaps he just didn't include parked cars in his scene as they spoilt the view. Cars apart, time appears to have stood still in Wray.

Turn left along the Main Street and you soon reach Wray Institute on the left, where there is an information board outlining the history of the village.

The institute dates from 1923, a relatively new building amid the fine Jacobean and Georgian architecture to be found in the heart of the village. Like packhorse travellers of old, there is a great sense of satisfaction for the walker who arrives at Wray having survived the perilous crossing of Bowland. There is civilization here, so shake the mud off the boots and take the opportunity to stock up on cake.

Wray village

Stage Four
WRAY INSTITUTE TO HOLME WAR MEMORIAL
(12½ miles)

'While its heritage remains there can be
no requiem for Westmorland.'
Westmorland Heritage

This stage of the walk is in total contrast to the previous day's hike. It enters limestone country beyond the graceful River Lune and crosses from Lancashire into Cumbria or, as AW would prefer it, from Lancashire into Westmorland. The route heads north over rolling green hills, wandering across fields, woods, becks and parkland estates. It starts with the river landscape of AW's *A Lune Sketchbook* and crosses into the territory of the masterwork on his adopted county, *Westmorland Heritage.* The route also uncovers Lancashire's short-lived River Keer, as well as a delightful stretch of the Lancaster Canal.

Westmorland Heritage

Born a Lancastrian to Yorkshire parents, at the age of thirty-four AW adopted a whole new county. He was to live in it, cherish it and explore it in every intimate detail for the remaining half century of his life. This county was of course Westmorland, with the largest town of Kendal at its heart. It was one of the most rural counties in England; its total population in 1941 was little over 65,000, almost half the population of the borough of Blackburn.

As a small boy amusing himself in Audley Range, AW had already meticulously drawn the boundaries and shaded in the area of the county of Westmorland on his hand-drawn maps of the northern counties. His first actual view of it was sitting on that Ribble bus bound for Windermere in 1930. In Ex-*Fellwanderer* he notes that even Lancaster was new to him and he glimpsed the sea for the first time in Morecambe Bay. Beyond Lancaster, 'the landscape was undulating and more varied'. With the Lakeland fells suddenly coming into view he may have been too excited to realize that travelling along the A6 about 5 miles north of Carnforth marked a significant moment in his life. Amid the flat moss lands and coppiced limestone ridges of Hale, he officially crossed the Lancashire border and for the first time entered the Lake District county of Westmorland.

He was still crossing this county boundary right up to the end of his life. But the difference from 1941 onwards was that when he went back down south to Lancashire he was not going home but just visiting. His last visit was in October 1990 when, aged eighty-three, he came back to Blackburn to film a BBC programme with Eric Robson. After a few days, illness forced him back to Kendal and a three-week stay in hospital. He never saw Lancashire again.

During the very productive sketching years of the late 1970s and early 1980s AW spent more time than usual traversing the county boundary, setting off from Kendal in Betty's car on day trips into Lancashire. The result was his *Lune*, *Ribble*, *Bowland* and *Wyre Sketchbooks*. Out of all of these it was *A Lune Sketchbook*, written in 1979 and published in 1980, that required least effort for the Wainwrights in terms of time and petrol. With its source high in the Howgill fells and its exit to the sea beyond the old port of Lancaster at Sunderland Point, the River Lune was largely within half an hour's drive of his Kendal home and therefore easily photographed.

This stage of the walk flirts briefly with the River Lune in late middle age. AW's views of this mature river between the Devil's Bridge at Kirkby Lonsdale and the outskirts of Lancaster at Halton are largely roadside sketches of bridges, castles, villages and churches. These include four sketches around Hornby, including one of the Loyn Bridge crossing the river. *A Lune Sketchbook* is dedicated to the Borrow Beck Action Group, who were opposing the construction of a reservoir in one of the River Lune's tributary valleys.

AW's books had started to tap into the rich seam of Lancashire only towards the end of the 1970s. He spent most of that decade writing,

Main Street, Hornby

photographing and sketching in Lakeland, the Yorkshire Dales and the Scottish Highlands. In that decade he also managed to publish two works that are often put on a par with his *Pictorial Guides* of the 1950s and 1960s. The first was *A Coast to Coast Walk*. The second was his less familiar but unsurpassed *Westmorland Heritage*.

This mammoth publication was unusual not just because if accidentally dropped it could break a toe. It was AW's biggest book, 500 pages in length with nearly 2,000 line drawings. At first glance it seems slightly self-indulgent and of limited appeal. But as AW was the *Westmorland Gazette*'s cash cow, if the ex-Borough Treasurer wanted to spend months and months drawing all 110 parishes of the county, then his publisher wasn't going to stop him.

The *Westmorland Gazette* had already published AW's detailed map of the county, grandly entitled *A Map of The County of Westmorland As it Was on the 31st Day of March in the Year of Our Lord 1974*. This included about twenty sketches along the map's borders and was commissioned by Paul N. Wilson (1908–80), who had the distinction of being the last Lord Lieutenant of Westmorland and the first Lord Lieutenant of Cumbria.

With the help of Betty, his chauffeur and walking companion, AW spent 1974 exploring Westmorland, from its popular high spots to its remotest corners. During the same year, Britain faced two general elections and endured the 'three-day week'. AW was still putting in at least five days a week, though he could be home from his excursions in time to see Ena Sharples slip quietly out of *Coronation Street* for the last time and to follow the Rovers still languishing in the old Third Division.

Westmorland Heritage was duly delivered and published as a limited edition of 1,000 copies, with each book numbered and signed by AW in green ink. The book was intended as a pictorial record of the county of Westmorland as it looked on its official last day of existence – 31 March 1974. The autographed limited edition, sold at the princely sum of £11.50 each, was quickly snapped up. Today, if in good condition, an original signed limited first edition of *Westmorland Heritage* can sell on the Internet for over £1,000. Happy is the man or woman who finds one pristinely preserved in their loft. But the story of this publication does not end there. The *Westmorland Gazette* discovered that there were a lot of people out there with deep roots in Westmorland and, responding to demand, it reissued the book as a 'popular' edition in 1988, minus AW's signature. Perhaps in recognition of the uniqueness of this book, Frances Lincoln, the current publisher of AW's guidebooks, reissued it again in 2004.

Westmorland Heritage is so extensive in its scope that its sketches accompany the walker through six stages of this walk. The first sketches from the book encountered on the route are in the parish of Dalton on the boundary with north Lancashire; the last sketches from the book encountered are in the Langdales: AW's drawing of Sergeant Man's summit and his numerous other views of the more spectacular mountains around the head of Great Langdale.

AW had spent over three decades living and working in Westmorland when, on 1 April 1974, it ceased to exist. Historically, Westmorland was one of the old English counties, created around

1226 from lands that were part of the barony of Kendal and the barony of Westmorland – the latter being centred on the county town of Appleby. Westmorland County Council was formed in 1889, with Kendal as the base for its administrative offices: AW would have passed the offices, which were on Stricklandgate, on his way to the Town Hall each day. The county was subsequently divided into urban and rural districts together with two municipal boroughs of Kendal and Appleby.

After 1974 the new local authorities of South Lakeland District Council and Cumbria County Council both operated in Kendal. The latter was formed by an amalgamation of Cumberland, Westmorland, the Furness peninsula of Lancashire and a little chunk of Yorkshire's West Riding around Sedbergh.

The countryside south of Kendal to the Lancashire border was administratively part of the South Westmorland Rural District Council, set up in 1894 and abolished with local government reorganization in 1974. AW knew this area very well. It was a delightful mix of limestone pavements, grassy drumlins and moss land alongside the estuary of the River Kent.

This stage of the walk takes the walker through three traditional rural Westmorland parishes – Dalton, Burton-in-Kendal and Holme.

Dalton was the most southerly parish in Westmorland and prior to 1896 it was part of Warton parish in Lancashire. Its eastern boundary is in part formed by the River Keer, a river flowing into Morecambe Bay that AW neglected to write a sketchbook about. Hardly surprising, as from its source, below Hutton Roof Crags, to the sea, beyond Carnforth's railway junction, it has a total length of about 8 miles. Still, it lends its name to several bridges and geographical features on the Lancashire–Westmorland border.

Dalton has no modern village. But AW gives it four pages in *Westmorland Heritage* and seems fascinated by its wealth of ancient monuments and archaeological remains.

The development of the villages of Burton and Holme is largely a result of their position in flat moss land between limestone hills to the

Burton street scene

east and west. This area became the natural route for north–south lines of communication between Lancaster and Kendal. Turnpike roads, the Lancaster Canal and the Lancaster to Carlisle Railway passed through these two villages, which found themselves the first point of entry to Westmorland for travellers from the south. This is so today, with the Burton-in-Kendal motorway services on the M6 being literally on the Cumbria county border. This service station was opened in 1970, along what would have been a new motorway when AW came to sketch the parish a few years later.

AW sketched Burton's Georgian street scenes for his book as well as a variety of houses and village views in Holme. He certainly preferred well-preserved Burton and laments the building of characterless new houses in Holme that turned it into a 'sprawling suburb', not helped by the motorway near by. Holme parish stretched eastwards to include a large part of Farleton Fell, also sketched by AW. This huge steep-sided limestone hill is usually the first exciting sign for travellers on the M6 that they are nearing the Lake District – that and the large brown 'Welcome to CUMBRIA: The Lake District' sign on the motorway at the point where the defunct Lancaster Canal crosses under the high-speed carriageway.

The Lancaster Canal, once the most important transport artery crossing the Lancashire–Westmorland boundary, was slowly leaking into extinction by the time AW moved to Kendal. Commercial traffic on the waterway ceased completely in 1947. AW never got to see the 'black and white' canal in its heyday, when coal came north from industrial Lancashire and limestone went south from rural Westmorland. He does, though, include several sketches of the disused canal and its various bridges as he charts his way through the parishes south of Kendal.

THE ROUTE

Wray Institute to Keer Holme (6½ miles)

From Wray Institute continue along the Main Street to the George and Dragon Inn and the B6480 Hornby–Wennington Road. Turn left and cross over to the opposite side, passing the Friends' Meeting House on the left. Turn right opposite the Methodist Church along the way signed 'Lane Head leading to Kiln Lane'. Walk through the housing development and as the houses end continue straight ahead along the bridleway following a wide hedged track.

At a crossroads of tracks turn left along another hedged track – Back Lane. Ignore the first field gate on the right but go through the second field gate (easy to miss) on the same side. It is a wooden gate in a hedged field corner, waymarked as a footpath. The field path heads diagonally across a large field in the direction of a barn, marked on the OS map as 'Peasber Barn'.

The fields here give an excellent view eastwards to the distinctive Yorkshire peak of Ingleborough. Although it remains distant on the horizon, its outline accompanies you for much of this stage of the walk. A fan of Ingleborough, AW calls it in *Walks in Limestone Country* 'a mountain of many talents', 'a magnet for the eyes', 'the undisputed overlord' and 'the most compelling presence'. Fine praise indeed.

Cross a stile to the left of the barn and continue in roughly the same direction through the next field. Cross the old Lune Valley railway line by the remains of a concrete kissing gate. Cross a stile on the

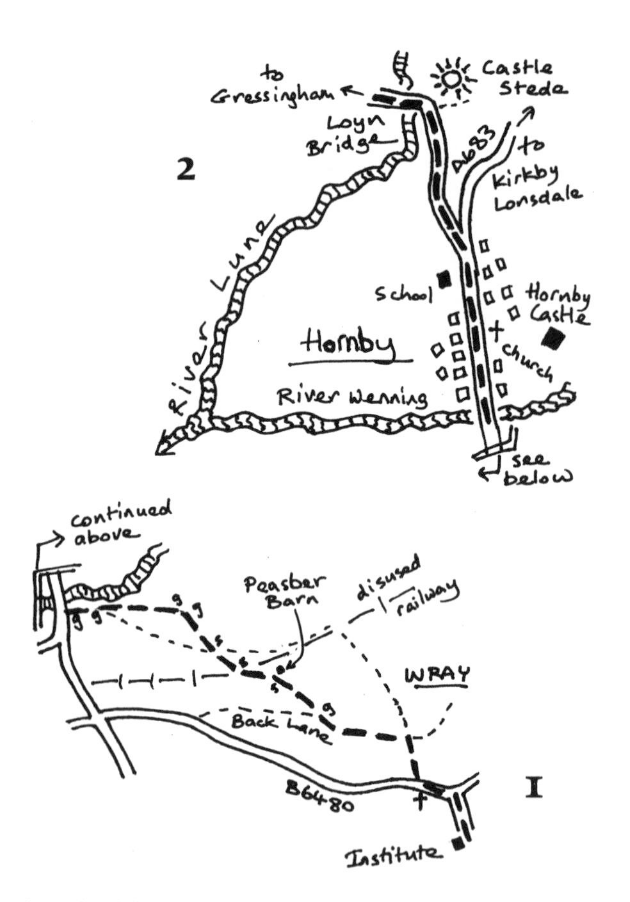

far side of the railway and head straight towards Hornby Castle through the next flat field. At the next boundary, where you reach a path junction, follow the path straight ahead through the field and come out at the access gate on the far side, where you join a track, running left to right.

The disused railway line, which had a station at Hornby, was part of Midland Railway's 'Little' North Western Railway line

Hornby Castle

from Morecambe and Lancaster to Leeds. It ran up the Lune Valley to Wennington Junction, where it linked with the Furness railway system going towards Carnforth. The Lune Valley line closed in 1966.

Turn left and go through another gate to join a concrete track. The River Wenning winds in from the right. The gated track leads between assorted farm buildings and passes through a large metal gate to reach the main A683 Lancaster–Kirkby Lonsdale road in Hornby village. Turn right and cross the river, continuing along the pavement of the main street to pass the church on the right.

Hornby is the site of two castles, both of which AW sketched for *A Lune Sketchbook.* His view of the grandiose castle overlooking the weir on the River Wenning was from the road bridge in the village. Apart from the base of the central tower, the original thirteenth-century castle on this site has largely been obliterated and replaced by the present nineteenth-century Gothic building. It was once owned by the Stanleys, the Earls of Derby, and Sir Edward Stanley fought in the Battle of Flodden in 1513. James I stayed a few nights at the castle in 1617 and in 1643, during the English Civil War, Hornby Castle was captured by Colonel Assheton and the Roundheads.

The wide River Wenning, rising in the Craven district of Yorkshire near Clapham, flows westwards towards Lancashire via the villages of High and Low Bentham and Wennington.

Supplemented by its Bowland tributaries, the rivers Roeburn and Hindburn, it meets the River Lune a mile west of the road bridge in Hornby village.

AW's *A Lune Sketchbook* also includes a view of Hornby's main street with not a single car on it! His sketch looks to the parish church of St Margaret with its early sixteenth-century octagonal tower, built by Sir Edward Stanley. It seems that AW took his photo for the sketch from the corner of the former Castle Hotel, as his sketch includes the hotel canopy.

Continue along the main street, passing the Royal Oak on the left. Just after you pass the school and swimming pool, turn left down the road signed to Gressingham. Take care, as there is no pavement along this road, which drops downhill for about ¼ mile to reach the River Lune at Loyn Bridge. Just before you reach the river, the old fortification of Castle Stede can be seen in a field on the right, next to a wartime pillbox. A footpath on the right-hand side of the road enables a closer look, as it skirts by the historic site.

Much more interesting and accessible than the fancy folly overlooking the River Wenning is Hornby's original defensive site at Castle Stede. Here is the best-preserved motte and bailey fortification in Lancashire. The Lune Valley is thought to have the biggest concentration of motte and bailey castles outside Wales. There are six of these Norman fortifications between Kirkby Lonsdale and Halton.

Castle Stede, dating from around 1100, made use of the natural defence provided by the steep east bank of the River Lune. The 'motte' is the big flat-topped defensive mound, on which a tower would have stood. The 'bailey' was the enclosure below it, where people would have lived together with stables and granaries, surrounded by a series of defensive ditches and fences.

On his sketch of this site, AW refers to it as 'Castlemede'. He took his photo from the road and now over thirty years later, the trees growing on top and around the defensive mound are

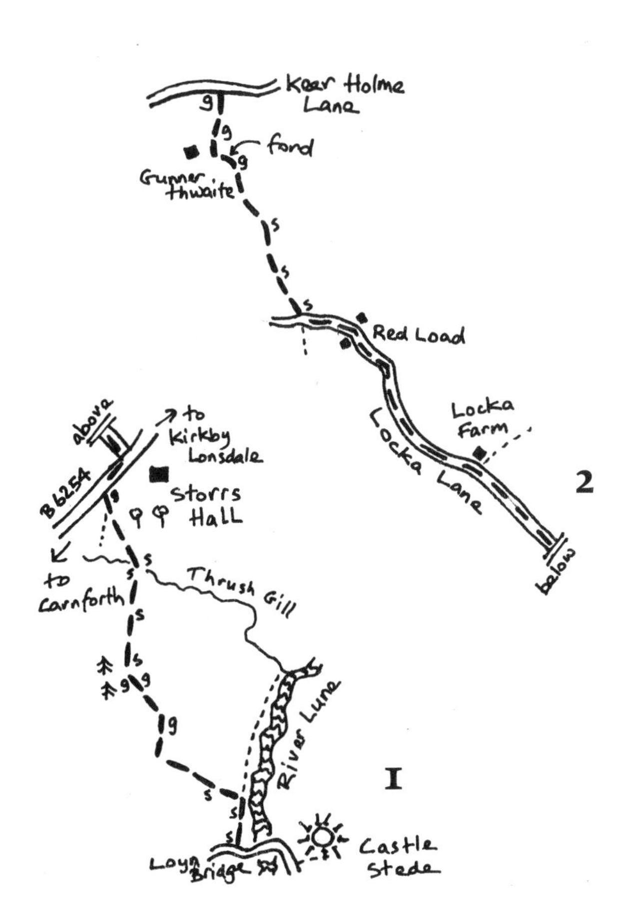

considerably bigger than they are in his sketch. Just downhill, he also sketched the graceful arches of the Loyn Bridge from the east bank of the River Lune. The bridge dates from 1684 and is a scheduled ancient monument, replacing an earlier structure on this important crossing of the river. 'Loyn' is the old word for 'Lune'.

At Loyn Bridge you leave the Forest of Bowland Area of Outstanding Natural Beauty. Now is the time to forget any lingering memories of the boggy morass of Upper Whitendale, especially as limestone country lies ahead.

Cross Loyn Bridge and join the footpath on the right at a stile. The path is signed as the 'Lune Valley Ramble – Arkholme 1½ miles'. Keep the river on the right and cross to the far side of the field. Enter a wooded section of the river bank and reach a stile in a fence by a waymarker post. Take the path pointing left uphill and leave the riverside. Aim for the gate at the top of the field. This is the first hill of the day.

Cross a stile by the gate and enter a field on the right. Follow the left hedge side with a view over to the walk's next objective, Storrs Hall. Turn right at the field corner and continue along the left hedge side of the same field to reach a gate on the left halfway along the field boundary. Go through this and aim diagonally right across the next field, aiming for gates in the top right corner. Go through a series of gates between two fields along the edge of Thrush Gill Wood. Cross another gate and stile and walk straight ahead through a big field, aiming directly for Storrs Hall. Cross more stiles and a little stream, Thrush Gill. Then bear left of the hall through parkland, aiming for a clump of trees and a stile at a woodland boundary. Cross this, and follow a fenced path leading through a green gate to reach the busy B6254 Carnforth–Kirkby Lonsdale road.

Storrs Hall was an ancient estate, associated with the Storrs and Askew families and purchased by a Kirkby Lonsdale solicitor, Francis Pearson, in 1848. Although the original manor house dated back to Tudor times, it is no surprise to discover that it was largely rebuilt in the fashionable Gothic style by the Victorian owner. Francis Pearson was the son of a prominent local surgeon and founded his own firm of lawyers, still operating today as Pearson & Pearson.

Turn right along the road for a short distance; then cross it with care, turning first left up a side road, Locka Lane. The route follows this narrow country lane for the next 1¼ miles as it winds its way towards the old Westmorland county boundary with a view directly north to Hutton Roof Crags. The lane turns sharp left at Red Load Farm, then sharp right and then left. Leave it at this bend via the footpath on the right, starting at a wall stile. There are good views west from here to Warton Crag and Morecambe Bay.

Go straight ahead and drop downhill to cross a stile in a fence. Continue straight ahead through the next flat pasture, heading for gates in the wall on the opposite side. Cross the wall stile to the right of the gates and continue straight ahead along the left wall side. As you reach woodland on the left, bear slightly right away from the wall, go over a little hill and drop down to a clump of trees in the bottom right corner of the field. The valley below is that of the infant River Keer, beyond the large farm complex of Gunnerthwaite. The names of the farms are now sounding like Lake District names.

Ford a stream and go through a gate in the field corner; then turn left and join the farm road heading towards Gunnerthwaite. Follow this only as far as the point where it crosses the stream again at a wall corner. Turn right here, following a field edge with the stream on the left, to reach a gate. Go through this and walk straight ahead towards the farm on the far side of the field. Pass through a gate to reach Keer Holme Lane.

Join the concessionary path on the opposite side of the lane that begins at a stile. This avoids going through the yard of Brown Edge Farm. Skirt around the left-hand side of the farm and then cross two more stiles to rejoin the definitive footpath behind the farm. Turn left and walk under pylons, with the stream-sized River Keer and a fence boundary on the left. Cross a stile in this fence and then a footbridge over the river.

Crossing the River Keer does not quite get you into Westmorland, although the river does follow the county

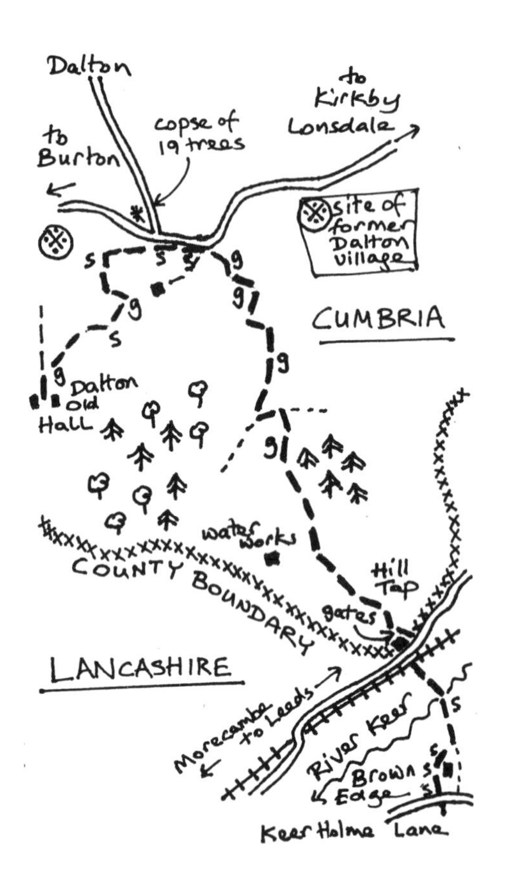

boundary between Lancashire and Cumbria less than a quarter mile upstream from here. This short-lived river rises in springs to the north of Docker Moor and follows a pleasant course before becoming little more than a drain under the M6 and A6. It is really Carnforth's river, as the railway town grew up at a crossing point of the Keer, just upstream from where it sluggishly creeps its salty way into Morecambe Bay. Keer Holme is marked on the OS maps and refers to the pastures hereabouts, reclaimed from the marshland of the River Keer.

'Holme' or 'holm', a common place name throughout the north of England where the Vikings settled, is a Scandinavian word for 'island'.

Go straight ahead through the next boggy field, aiming for white gates and a farm. Cross the Morecambe–Leeds railway line at the pedestrian crossing to reach a lane opposite Hill Top Farm. Turn right along the lane only as far as the signed public bridleway on the left just beyond the farm buildings. This begins at an uninviting pair of large metal gates. Welcome to Cumbria!

And goodbye Lancashire. The county boundary between Lancashire and Cumbria (formerly Westmorland) runs along the north side of the lane to the right of Hill Top Farm.

Keer Holme to Holme War Memorial (6 miles)

Our long journey through Westmorland starts at the gates by Hill Top Farm in a far-flung corner of the administrative parish of Burton-in-Kendal. Prior to 1974, this hill country north of Keer Holme was part of Dalton parish.

Go through the large metal gates and then through two field gates, following a bridleway waymarked as 'Lunesdale Walk'. The vaguest of tracks swings left around a hillside and climbs uphill to a gate and stile that will be visible at the top of the field. Cross this and continue directly uphill towards the ridge top. Keep below the squat waterworks tower on the hill to the left and skirt left around a boggy patch to reach two gateposts. Continue straight ahead uphill in the next field to join the woodland edge on the right. Walk along the side of the wood and join a grassy track leading downhill to a gate. Join a lower track and turn sharp left along this. The track soon turns sharp right to reveal a good view of Lakeland beyond Arnside Knott. Follow the gated track straight ahead for ½ mile until it reaches Dalton Lane, running between Burton and Kirkby Lonsdale.

As you approach the road, the large property you see over to the left of the track is Henridding, sketched by AW in *Westmorland Heritage*. The walk route shortly leads around the other side of this building. This is the first site of an AW sketch to be encountered since Loyn Bridge 5 miles to the south. Any withdrawal symptoms from AW will be soon be relieved, as he has sketched something for almost every couple of miles from here all the way to Buttermere.

Turn left only as far as the next access road on the left. Go straight across this to join a footpath beginning at a gate and wall stile adjacent to Dalton Lane. Keep to the wall side next to the road. The path leads through a little wood to cross another wall stile and enter a field.

At this stile, peep over the wall overlooking the road and view a circle of trees at a junction of lanes. AW sketched these nineteen trees and notes the circle as the possible burial place of nineteen men killed in a nearby English Civil War skirmish. The fields to the left of the road just downhill from here were the site of Dalton village, which was still in existence in the eighteenth century but cleared with the development of the Dalton Hall estate. AW marks the site of the old village in *Westmorland Heritage*, together with sketches of Dalton's Iron Age and medieval settlements.

Dalton copse of trees

Follow the left side of the field alongside the wood. When the trees end, cross a wall stile on the left to enter another field. Follow the left wall side and go through a gateway into the next field. Go diagonally left from here and pass through a gate in the wall. Henridding is to the left.

Turn right and follow the right wall side to cross a ladder stile. Go straight ahead, keeping to the right wall edge through an area of limestone boulders. Look out for an easy-to-miss stile in a fence on the right and cross this. Continue straight ahead, now with the wall on the left. The wall soon swings left but leave it here, bearing slightly right downhill and joining a grassy track that heads towards Dalton Old Hall below. The track follows the left wall side and joins the farm road at the bottom of the hill. Turn left along this and follow it between the farm buildings, keeping to the right of the Old Hall. Pass through gates and enter a field where a ford crosses a stream.

AW sketched the seventeenth-century farmhouse of Dalton Old Hall. To the rear of the farm are crumbling remains of the west wall of a pele tower that had previously existed here. The Dalton estate passed to the Hornby family in the eighteenth century. On the wooded hillside to the south of Dalton Old Hall are visible earthworks associated with an Iron Age settlement. AW mentions these and sketches the stone remains of walls that once marked the boundary of the site.

Cross the ford and follow the track that runs along the bottom of the hill. Leave the track on the right when you reach a footpath

Dalton Old Hall

waymarker post and gate. Follow the right edge of the next field. Over to the left, to the right of a large copse, the hillside earthworks of the Iron Age settlement can be seen. Cross a stile and continue along the field edge. When the wall ends on the right, bear slightly left across the field to go through a waymarked gate. Cross a bridge over a beck and then follow the right hedge side. Go through a gate on the right to follow a walled grass track around the front of Coat Green Farm. Another gate leads to the farm road. Follow this

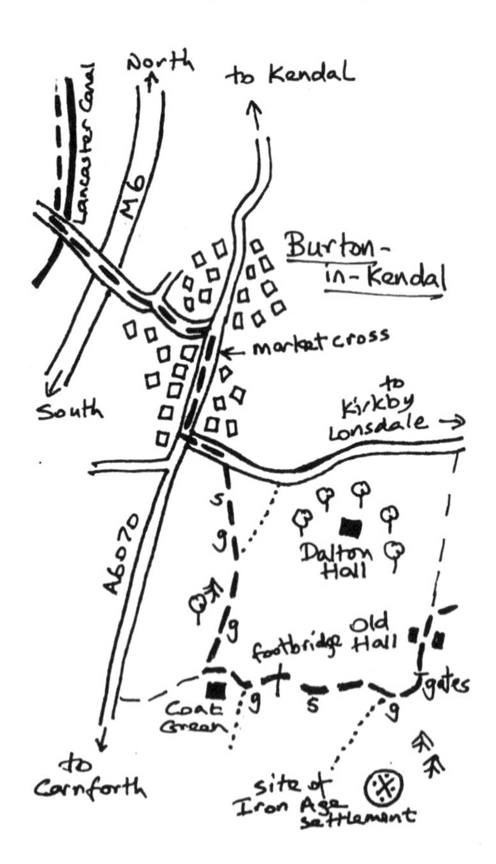

straight ahead only as far as the next signed footpath on the right leading along a hedged track.

Join this path, at the end of which a gate leads into parkland. Continue straight ahead, with the woodland on the left. At a junction of paths, bear left to go through a gate to the right of a small copse and then straight ahead, crossing a field with further stiles to pass under trees and reach Dalton Lane again. Turn left along Dalton Lane to reach the junction with the A6070 Carnforth–Kendal road. Turn right and follow the pavement of the main street to reach the old market cross in the centre of Burton.

Burton-in-Kendal had its heyday in the seventeenth and eighteenth centuries. It gained a royal charter in the 1660s and found itself sitting astride the old turnpike road halfway between Lancaster and Kendal. Burton established itself as Westmorland's main corn market. It was a prosperous Georgian market town and AW sketched the fine architecture of its houses in the 1970s. The market square remained the hub of town life, overlooked by the Royal Hotel, a halt for stagecoach travellers. Miscreants were often clasped in the leg irons attached to the market cross, which acted as the town stocks, for routine public humiliation.

The eighteenth-century turnpike road between Lancaster and Kendal benefited Burton but transport developments in the nineteenth century led to its decline. Despite Burton having a wharf on the Lancaster Canal and a train station on the Lancaster to Carlisle Railway, it could be largely bypassed, just as it is today by the A6 road and the M6 motorway. The arrival of the Lancaster Canal resulted in the county's main corn market, and just about everything else, moving north to the county's biggest town, Kendal. Subsequently a peaceful slumber has rested on Burton.

From cobbled yards and the sixteenth-century parish church of St James, to elegant Georgian town houses of the gentry like Burton House at the southern end of Main Street, AW's sketches of the village echo its proud past. Burton House was the residence of local magistrate, William Atkinson. In Victorian times, a private girls' boarding school was opened here.

Continue along the main street past the Royal Hotel. Between the village butcher's and post office on the right, turn left down Neddy Hill. Follow this lane as it swings right to a refurbished Westmorland County Council signpost to Burton and Holme station. At this junction turn left into Station Lane. Follow this lane as it crosses over the M6 and then goes under an aqueduct carrying the Lancaster Canal. Then join the canal on the left via steps. Turn left along the towpath, heading north.

The Lancaster Canal took over twenty-five years to complete. Having been given the green light in 1792, it was only finally opened all the way from Preston to Kendal in 1819. The main engineer was John Rennie. The Westmorland section was the last section to open, the aqueduct over Station Lane at Burton being completed around 1816. Station Lane led to the train station serving the villages of Burton and Holme on the Lancaster to Carlisle Railway, which is now the speedy West Coast Main Line. The station, the most southerly halt in Westmorland, was closed to passengers in 1950 and to goods traffic in 1961.

The walk now follows the canal towpath in the direction of Kendal for 1 mile. It winds between flat moss land to the west and the steep spur of Farleton Fell to the east.

Passing Holme Mills on the left, you enter Holme parish. Farleton Fell forms the high eastern boundary of this parish. AW sketched the workers' cottages built alongside the flax mill, thought to have been built on the site of a twelfth-century

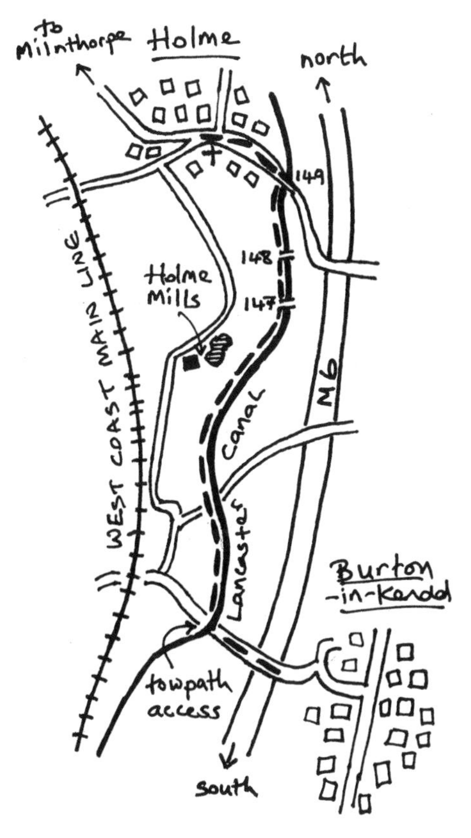

manorial corn mill. The arrival of the Lancaster Canal triggered the development of the factory complex here, which in turn led to the growth of Holme village. In the twentieth century the works diversified into matting and carpets. The firm of Goodacres specialized in the production of coconut floor matting, utilizing the simple, effective and possibly true slogan 'We Mat the World'. It was still employing a hundred people in the 1960s but closed soon after.

Leave the canal via the steps at bridge number 149. Turn left and follow the pavement into the village.

This stage of the walk ends in the centre of the village by the parish church and war memorial. Holy Trinity Church was built in 1839 to serve a growing population, as people – including Irish migrants – moved into the area to work in the mill. Around the same time a National School was built nearby. This is now the parish hall, adjacent to the war memorial.

One of the joys of *Westmorland Heritage* is that AW captured the essence of each parish and packed so much in. His entry for Holme parish is just three pages, but within these he managed to sketch and write about Holme Mills, Farleton Fell, the canal, the parish church, the war memorial, the main street and several pretty houses. He even manages to squeeze in several barbed comments about new housing and quarrying.

Holme war memorial and main street

Stage Five
HOLME WAR MEMORIAL TO KENDAL TOWN HALL
(13 miles)

'Roads and railways, like all the works of man,
have their day. The Kent is for ever.'
Three Westmorland Rivers

This stage of the walk takes the walker into the heart of Kendal through rolling limestone hills and elegant parkland. The route weaves its way through a succession of stately homes, medieval churches and fortified manor houses. Over a relatively short distance from Holme to the boundary of Kendal, you pass through no fewer than eight historic parishes of south Westmorland, all lovingly sketched by AW in *Westmorland Heritage.* The Lancaster Canal and the River Kent are twin channels that steer the walker towards the magnet of Kendal. In exploring the Lower Kent Valley you also travel in the company of AW's sketches in *Three Westmorland Rivers.* The halfway point of the entire route is passed in the vicinity of Sedgwick village.

Along the River Kent

The river geographically closest to AW in the second half of his life was the River Kent, running wide and fast through Kendal. It dominates the town and was crossed no fewer than six times in the town centre by four road bridges and two footbridges. In 1993, shortly after AW's death, the town got a fifth road crossing at Romney Road. Kendal has always been justly proud of the river that not only gave birth to the town but also provided its name.

AW's first sighting of the River Kent would have been when he crossed Levens Bridge on the A6, travelling north on the Ribble bus for his first Lakeland holiday in 1930. Here he would have seen the mature river sweep grandly around a bend through the Elizabethan deer park before passing under the road bridge and entering the marshland of its circuitous estuary. As the bus travelled the 4 miles north between Levens Bridge and Kendal, the River Kent would have remained largely hidden from the A6 road beyond fields and woods until it came into view under the stone-arched Nether Bridge in Kendal town centre.

On the second day of AW's first Lakeland holiday, he climbed up to the mountain ridge between Froswick and High Street and looked across to Kentmere Head. Here he saw the source of the river he had seen for the first time just two days earlier as he sat on a bus from Lancashire. Less than a year later, on the first day of his ambitious 1931 Whitsuntide tour of the Lakes, AW and a gang of Blackburn Town Hall colleagues found themselves on this same ridge, looking down on the infant River Kent, fast falling from high buttresses to the glacial valley below. At which point the heavens opened and they were severely drenched.

So the upper reaches of the Kent Valley provided the backdrop to some of AW's earliest Lakeland experiences; and throughout the 1930s, while he was still tied to his job and his life in Blackburn, this part of the Lakes was a firm favourite of AW's. Kentmere was convenient for him to get to and from in a day, taking advantage of cheap train excursions to stations on the Kendal to Windermere line. Then when he moved north to Kendal in 1941, a happy AW had the River Kent right on his doorstep.

Hunter Davies notes in his biography of Wainwright that in the early years of the 1940s the Wainwright family – AW, wife Ruth and son Peter – would go on local walks together. In a letter written to Lawrence Wolstenholme back in Blackburn, only two months into his new life in Kendal, AW positively gloats as he describes a snowy family expedition up the Kentmere Valley and over the Garburn Pass back to Windermere. When AW built his new house at the top end of Kendal Green in 1949, he enjoyed his own view of the Kent Valley out of his back window.

We have seen how, during his 'retirement' years in the 1970s with the *Pictorial Guides* complete, AW went on to develop other projects, including Lakeland ones. He had published five *Lakeland Sketchbooks* and his guide to *The Outlying Fells of Lakeland* even before he brought out the mammoth *Westmorland Heritage* in 1975. He followed these with the unique *Kendal in the Nineteenth Century,* followed by two *Furness Sketchbooks* and *Walks from Ratty.* It was after this that he hit on the original idea of producing a book of sketches charting a river from source to sea. The first river he chose for this was, of course, his old friend the River Kent, together with its main tributaries, the rivers Sprint and Mint. *Three Westmorland Rivers* was published in 1979 and it became the template for the series of river sketchbooks covering the Lune, Ribble, Eden and Wyre that followed.

Three Westmorland Rivers: The Kent, The Sprint and The Mint is a collection of seventy-five AW sketches, with more than half of these concentrating on the 20-mile long River Kent from the head of Kentmere to its estuary beyond Arnside. The smaller rivers Sprint and Mint also rise in the Far Eastern Fells, the Sprint flowing down lonely Longsleddale and the Mint flowing down the even lonelier traffic-free Bannisdale. AW dedicated the book to the ladies of Animal Rescue Cumbria. In his introduction to the book he also acknowledges the contributions and research undertaken for the book by a Mrs W. Inglesfield and local historian John Marsh.

This stage of the walk follows AW's footsteps through the Lower Kent Valley, taking in the sites of ten of his sketches, from the Watersmeet of the Bela and Kent upstream to Watercrook on the outskirts of Kendal. These include a considerable number of sketches in the environs of the Levens Hall estate. As well as river views, he sketched the grand mansions and historic buildings of the Lower Kent Valley – Dallam Tower, Levens Hall, Nether Levens, Sedgwick House and Sizergh Castle. He also did not forget that the river had powered industries here, as he reminds readers with his sketches of the water-powered Snuff Mill at Helsington and the Old Gunpowder Works at Sedgwick.

The subjects of these sketches were all on AW's home turf, many being places to which he had walked on summer evening

Watersmeet

jaunts from his Kendal home back in the 1940s. He had also got to know south Westmorland very well through his travels with Betty in the mid-1970s while taking photos for *Westmorland Heritage*. In fact, many of the sketches along the River Kent which appeared in *Three Westmorland Rivers* in 1979 were recycled sketches that had already appeared in *Westmorland Heritage* four years earlier.

This stage of our walk crosses the boundaries of no fewer than eight of the traditional county parishes featured in *Westmorland Heritage* before finally entering the town of Kendal from the south after crossing Natland Beck. The River Kent winds its way south through all but one of these parishes. The various other north–south highways of past and present – canal, railway, A6 road and M6 motorway – are also a recurring theme of these parishes. In order as you walk upstream, the parishes are: Holme, Beetham, Milnthorpe, Heversham, Levens, Sedgwick, Helsington and Natland. These eight parishes are traversed over a distance of little over 10 miles.

Each parish's entry in *Westmorland Heritage*, usually covering three or four pages, followed a similar format. AW presented a detailed map of each parish with general commentary, followed by a series of drawings covering significant architectural and landscape features – churches, war memorials, old bridges, village streets, farms, manor houses, pele towers, waterfalls and hill summits. In the eight parishes he sketched between Holme and Natland, AW drew every parish church – seven in total, as Sedgwick, the smallest parish in Westmorland, did not have one. (For the record, the largest parish in the old county of Westmorland was Shap Rural.)

On reading AW's comments in *Westmorland Heritage*, there is a strong sense that he had considerable affection for the parishes south of Kendal. His only gripes – and they are his usual gripes – are about increased traffic and the characterless sprawl of modern residential estates. The latter, AW thinks, has particularly blighted villages like Holme and Natland.

North of Natland parish, the walk reaches Kendal and the last 1½ miles go through the town that prior to the local government changes in 1974 was administered by AW's employer, Kendal Borough Council. AW came to know every cobble and yard of the town he lived in for fifty years. He walked through it every day. As Borough Treasurer he knew all its business and its people. And through his long associations with Abbot Hall Art Gallery and Kendal Museum he became immersed in its culture, history and antiquities.

AW was already sketching the historic buildings of his adopted town in the 1940s, years before the *Pictorial Guides* took shape. But when the obsession with drawing mountains engulfed him, AW had to wait until his retirement years in the 1970s to put his wealth of knowledge about Kendal into a meaningful publication.

As the biggest town in the county, Kendal featured heavily in *Westmorland Heritage*, where AW dedicates eighteen pages to it (though the vast rural parishes of the Langdales and Patterdale both get twenty pages). Within these eighteen pages were crammed all the sketches of the 'auld grey town' one would expect to find, including ones of the Town Hall where AW worked, the numerous churches, the bridges over the River Kent, traditional yards, curious street signs and the ruined hilltop Norman castle.

Three Westmorland Rivers marked the River Kent's passing through the town with sketches of its stone-arched bridges – Stramongate, Miller and Nether Bridges – the first two of which were reproduced from *Westmorland Heritage* – but it was not until he wrote *Kendal in the Nineteenth Century*, published in 1977, that he gave the town the proper Wainwright treatment.

If the River Kent made a lasting impression on AW, the same cannot be said of the ailing Lancaster Canal. This artery which had helped transform Kendal in the nineteenth century was dying just as AW was beginning his new life there. Only the coal still being brought from Lancashire up to Kendal Gas Works kept the canal going, but the final nail in its coffin came in 1944, when this coal began to be transported by road. At the time AW's first *Pictorial Guide* was published, the Lancaster Canal was officially closed and subsequently filled in.

This stage of the walk comes to a close at Kendal Town Hall. It is a fitting end, as his job in this building was the reason AW had the opportunity to move to Kendal in the first place. It is also fitting that this stage takes in Kendal Castle with its magnificent panorama looking north to Lakeland. In the 1940s, the ruin of Kendal's baronial stronghold was a very familiar sight to AW, as he and his family lived just below it. His first residence in the town was a council semi, 19 Castle Grove, on a newly built estate lying slightly detached from the town, east of Castle Hill.

To get to work AW could either go over Castle Hill or walk around the bottom of it. It is difficult to visualize AW walking around the bottom of a hill, so it is a fair bet that AW habitually followed the footpath over Castle Hill several times a day. He probably pinched himself to check he was not dreaming. From Kendal Castle he could look northwards to Kentmere and the High Street ridge. Yes, it was really true, he had actually fulfilled the dream he had nurtured since 1930 and was now living in Lakeland.

Holme War Memorial to Levens Bridge (6½ miles)

Facing the war memorial, turn left along Duke Street and then right into Moss Lane, crossing Holme Beck. Follow the lane under the West Coast Main Line railway, ignoring the first footpath on the right.

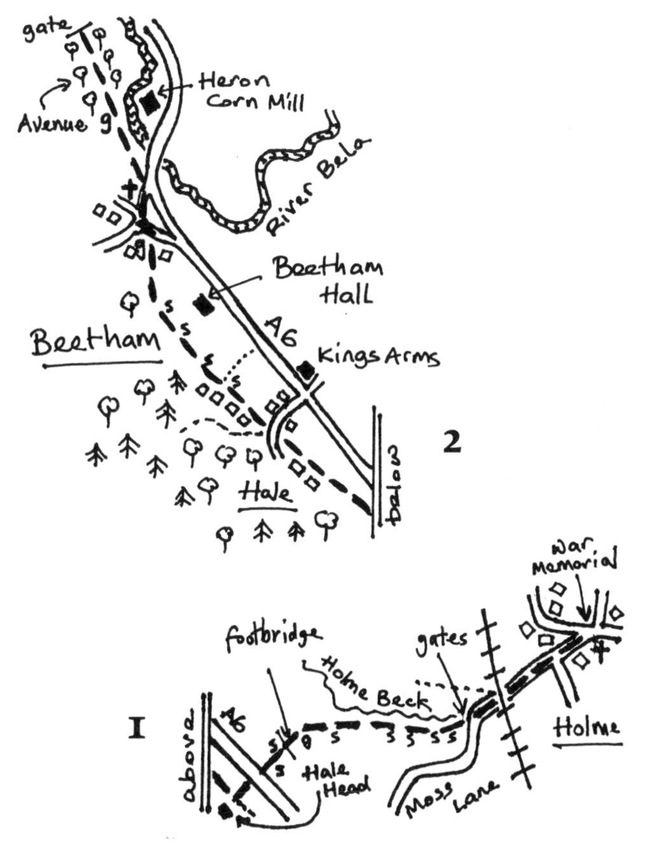

Walk a little further around a bend and join the next signed path on the same side. This starts at two gates. Follow the right field edge to another gate; then turn left and follow the right field edge to a squeeze stile with Holme Beck on the right. Follow a beck-side path through a series of stiles and cross the parish boundary between Holme and Beetham. Enter a big mossy field and walk along the right field edge to a stile at the far end. Continue straight ahead, bearing slightly left to a gateway in a hedge. Cross a track and continue straight ahead towards houses on the nearby A6 road. Cross a footbridge over a drain and follow the right field edge of the next two fields (which can be very boggy), crossing further stiles to reach the A6 Carnforth–Kendal road.

Boggy Holme Moss between the village of Holme and the A6 road is Westmorland at its flattest. Do not be despondent though, as limestone, woodland and even sea views are just around the corner. In crossing the A6 you enter the second Area of Outstanding Natural Beauty on this journey – Arnside and Silverdale. This AONB was designated in 1972 as a limestone landscape of national importance. Here rare plants and butterflies like the lady's slipper orchid and the high brown fritillary mingle with the lesser spotted Lancashire caravan owner.

Take care crossing the A6 road and join the path going up a driveway directly opposite, signed to Fell End. Turn right in front of Hale Head House and follow the narrow access road that leads past houses towards the incongruous 'suburbia' of Hale village, close to the King's Arms pub on the A6. When you reach a road, go straight across it, continuing along a farm track almost opposite signed as a footpath to Slackhead and Beetham. Ignore paths leading off to the right and left, and go straight ahead through a series of squeeze stiles to enter a large field with a woodland and wall on the left. A line of limestone rock outcrops runs along the top of this field, close to the wall. Bear slightly right and follow the edge of the field

Beetham Hall

straight ahead, keeping the rocks to the immediate left. The fortified farmstead of Beetham Hall can be seen straight ahead beyond the next wall boundary.

AW sketched Beetham Hall from these fields, along with the nearby ruined pele tower at Hazelslack. Pele towers were little defensive castles built to protect the locals, largely from Scottish raiders, and there are many sites of these hereabouts, just as there were in Lancashire's Lune Valley. Dallam Tower, Levens Hall, and, of course, the castles at Sizergh and Kendal, were all medieval fortifications built to defend the Lower Kent Valley. Beetham Hall and Hazelslack Tower, which is on the other side of the wooded ridge to the west, were constructed in the fourteenth century. Beetham Hall passed into the ownership of the Wilson family of nearby Dallam Tower in the eighteenth century.

Go through the squeeze stile in the left corner of the field to follow a path between woodland and wall. Cross another squeeze stile and take the path signed to Beetham, forking diagonally right across a large field and heading directly towards the village. A gate in the far right corner of the field leads into Beetham. Turn left by the phone box and pass the village stocks. Turn right at the next junction to reach the Wheatsheaf Inn and St Michael's Church. Keep the church on the left and continue along the lane to reach the village war memorial near the verge of the A6 road.

Recorded in the Domesday Book, Beetham developed thanks largely to its position on the banks of the River Bela, where a convenient section of fast-flowing waterfalls, a legacy of the Ice Age, led to the siting of a corn mill here. The eighteenth-century Heron Corn Mill presently occupies the same site; it is now a working museum. The original mill was here in the twelfth century and in 1220 it is recorded that monks from Yorkshire were granted the right to grind corn at Beetham. The picture-postcard parish church also has twelfth-century origins and the architecture of the village shows that it flourished in the seventeenth and eighteenth centuries, building its own grammar school (rebuilt in 1827 and now the home of the Heron Theatre) and the seventeenth-century Wheatsheaf Inn. AW sketched Beetham's church and war memorial.

Up until the 1820s, when the new turnpike road was built towards Ulverston and Kendal, the villages of Beetham, Milnthorpe and Heversham were not on the main south–north route, as this went up to Kendal via Burton, further to the east. The 1820s turnpike road – now the A6 road – crossed the River Bela at Beetham over a new bridge.

Turn left along the access road to Heron Corn Mill. The River Bela flows past on the right. Go through the gate in the left corner of the mill's car park, following the path signed to Dallam Park. This leads gradually uphill through an avenue of trees to a gate at the top. There is a good view down to Milnthorpe and the River Bela from here. Follow the waymarker posts straight ahead through the parkland. The path skirts around the left-hand side of the next rolling hill and descends to the river, with good views north across the Kent Estuary to the limestone of Whitbarrow Scar and the Lakeland fells beyond. Dallam Tower is over to the left. Cross the river via the footbridge straight ahead to reach the B5282 Arnside–Milnthorpe road.

Dallam Tower and its surrounding parkland are still part of Beetham. The northern boundary of the parish is the River Bela and the footbridge across the river leads to the parish of

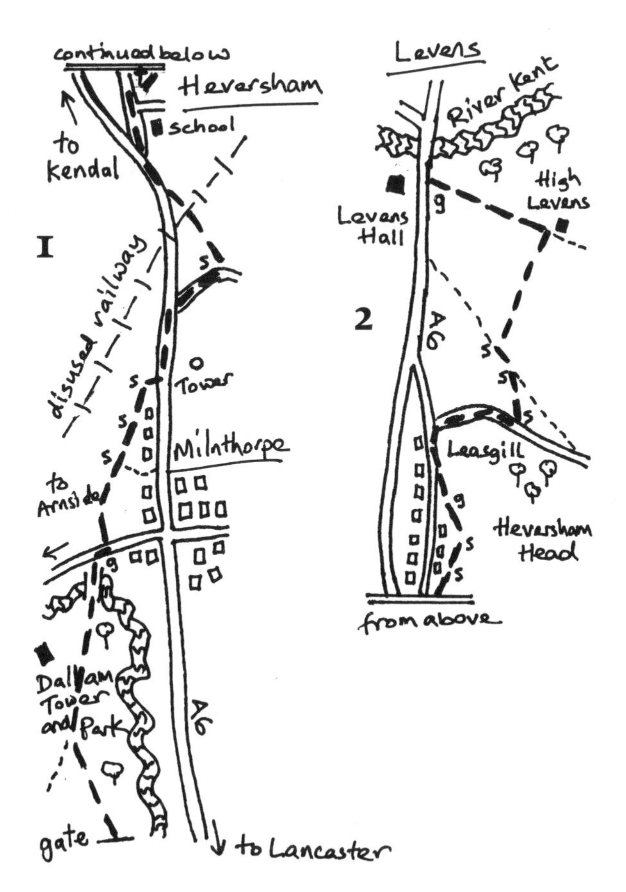

Milnthorpe. The building of the present Dallam Tower, on the site of an earlier fortified residence, was started in 1720 by local bigwig and Westmorland MP Daniel Wilson (1680–1754). The OS Explorer map shows an 'earthwork' on the wooded hill east of the mansion, locally known as 'the clump'. This is thought to be the remains of an Iron Age settlement. AW sketched the 'handsome and elegant mansion' and the drawing appears in both *Westmorland Heritage* and *Three Westmorland Rivers.* In the latter he also includes a drawing of the point just downstream of here where the River Bela meets the River Kent.

The River Bela was important in the development of Milnthorpe. Its waters powered numerous corn, cotton and paper mills along the length of the river and its little estuary into the Kent Channel helped Milnthorpe flourish as Westmorland's only port in the eighteenth and nineteenth centuries. Ships sailed up as far as Milnthorpe Sands near Sandside and cargo was offloaded into smaller vessels and carts. Among the sketches AW included in his entry for Milnthorpe in *Westmorland Heritage* are views of Bela Mill and the footbridge over the river, where you exit Dallam Park.

Turn right along the pavement but walk only as far as the bus stop on the right. Turn left and cross over here, following an access road signed as 'Public Way Church Street'. When the road bends continue straight ahead along an enclosed path signed as a bridleway. When this bends sharp right, go straight ahead across a stile and follow the left field edge to a squeeze stile in the top field corner. Continue straight ahead through the next field, aiming for the end of the row of houses on the right. There are good views in all directions on the top of this hill, including to the Kent Viaduct and nearby Heversham Church, the walk's next objective. Go through a squeeze stile in the wall at the top right of this field and turn sharp right, looking directly across to St Anthony's Tower on the hillside opposite. Steep steps and a gate lead down to the A6 road.

St Anthony's Tower

AW sketched St Anthony's Tower, which was used as an observation post on the lookout for German aircraft in the Second World War. It was built by local mill owner Henry Smithies as a memorial to the passing of the Great Reform Act of 1832.

Cross the A6 road with care and turn left to walk in the direction of Kendal. You will pass a milestone indicating that Kendal is 7 miles away by road. Follow the pavement for less than ¼ mile until you reach a road junction on the right. Turn right along narrow Kirkgate Lane, which is the parish boundary between Milnthorpe and Heversham. At the sharp right-hand bend leave the lane on the left, crossing a wall stile and following the field path signed to Heversham. Follow the right field edge uphill along the boundary of a large residence. Go through a kissing gate and turn left along a driveway, crossing over a disused railway. Then immediately after passing the garden gate of a house on the right cross a field diagonally through an open gateway to rejoin the A6 road.

The disused railway crossed to the south of Heversham was the Furness Railway's branch line, which linked the station at Arnside with what is now the West Coast Main Line near Hincaster. The line opened in 1876 but was closed for passengers in 1941 and removed in the 1960s. Heversham had its own train station, on the south side of the village, which opened in 1890.

Turn right along the A6 road but leave it shortly on the right, following the bypassed lane into Heversham village. Pass Dallam School on the right and you will soon reach the parish church of St Peter.

With access to the sea along the River Kent, Heversham had a surprising significance in the Dark Ages as a point of entry for Norse Vikings from Ireland and the Isle of Man, who subsequently settled in 'thwaites', the woodland clearings that formed many a Cumbrian place name. Even before the Vikings came to Westmorland there was a coastal monastery close to

Heversham Church

the site of the present Heversham parish church and the surviving shaft of an ancient cross remains on show in the church porch. AW sketched it and refers to it as '9th century Anglian'.

The present St Peter's Church has twelfth-century origins but was largely rebuilt and underwent a major Victorian restoration in 1869 by the Lancaster architects Paley and Austin. Probably without knowing it, AW sketched many of the churches and country houses either built or restored by Edward Paley (1823–95) and Hubert Austin (1845–1915) who, from the 1860s to the 1890s, worked up and down the northern counties of England. They also built churches in Blackburn and this walk has already encountered their craftsmanship in the churches at Wray, Beetham and the restored Hornby Castle.

The present Dallam School occupies buildings of the former Heversham Grammar School, established in 1613. AW sketched the original site of the school, together with a nearby cockpit, which was in a field above the church and below the hilltop of Heversham Head. One of Heversham School's most famous pupils is Ephraim Chambers (1680–1740), who had a very interesting life journey: he was born a Westmorland farmer's son and ended up a member of the Royal Society, being buried in the cloisters of Westminster Abbey. His achievement was writing a totally original book (just like AW!): the *Cyclopaedia, or an Universal Dictionary of Arts and Sciences*, the first of its kind in Georgian England.

Go through the lychgate of the church and join the path signed at the church entrance to Heversham Head. This leads around the right-hand side of the church to a gate in the wall at the rear of the churchyard. Continue straight ahead uphill through a field of limestone boulders. Go through a squeeze stile at a wall end and keep going uphill, with the wall to the left, to reach another gate and stile. Join the access track to a house and turn left along it. The track crosses a cattle grid and passes a primary school on the right, soon joining the main street in the hamlet of Leasgill.

Continue straight ahead only as far as the next lane on the right. Turn right and follow this lane steeply uphill. After nearly ¼ mile join a footpath on the left at a squeeze stile in a wall. The path goes straight ahead through an avenue of trees to another squeeze stile at the wall boundary. Turn left here briefly along an enclosed path but only as far as the next path on the right, signed to Hincaster and Levens Bridge. Join this via the squeeze stile and follow the right edge of a large field sloping downhill to Levens Hall. The path keeps woodland to the right and reveals great views to the north and west. The route is now in Levens parish.

Keep going straight ahead until you reach the old farmhouse of High Levens on the right. Turn left here along the farm track signed to the A6. This leads downhill and goes through a gateway to meet the main road opposite Levens Hall. Turn right to reach Levens Bridge over the River Kent. You can gain a good view of Levens Hall and its gardens by crossing the busy A6 with care and going through the car park entrance.

This is the halfway point of this stage and the deer park makes an ideal lunch stop. The brief dalliance with the A6 road at Levens Bridge is the only point where you encounter the Cumbria Coastal Way, a long-distance path that is here making its way from Arnside around to Grange-over-Sands. AW enjoyed sketching Levens Hall and deer park, and his drawings of it turn

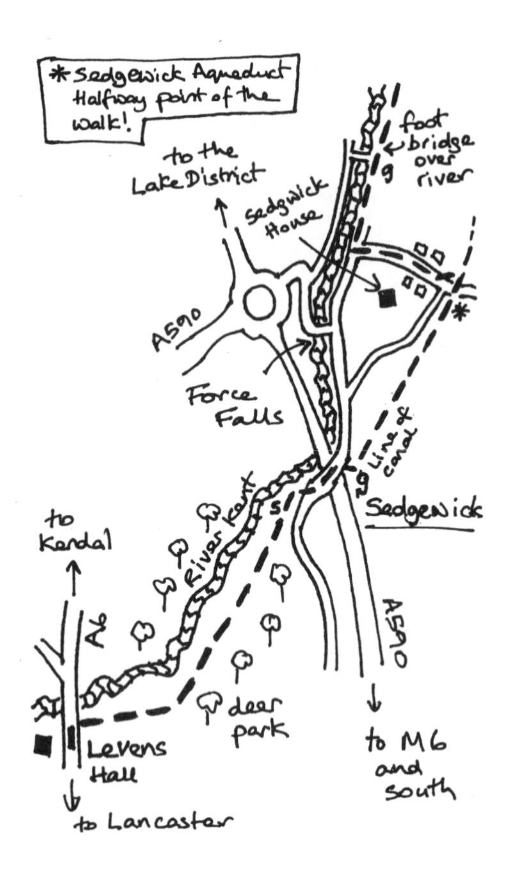

up in both *Westmorland Heritage* and *Three Westmorland Rivers*. The Bagot family have lived here for the last four hundred years.

Levens Bridge to Kendal Town Hall (6½ miles)

To continue the walk route do not cross the road bridge but enter Levens Park by the gate on the right and follow the right-hand side of the River Kent through the deer park. The footpath through Levens Park follows a track for almost a mile until you reach a wall stile by a

Levens Bridge

gate on the far side of the deer park. A limestone seat to the left gives a good view of the river here.

Levens Park gives you an opportunity to see the River Kent up close at last. Just upstream from here are Force Falls, where salmon leap and canoeists struggle. AW drew these fast-flowing falls, which run under the equally fast-flowing A590 link road between the M6 motorway and the A6 road to Kendal. This is the busy main road into the Lakes from the south. On leaving Levens Park you enter the parish of Sedgewick.

Cross the stile and turn left along the lane, crossing the bridge over the A590. A Lancaster Canal Trail wooden fingerpost indicates that Kendal is 4 miles away (via the disused canal). Turn right up steps at a kissing gate by another canal trail fingerpost. Go uphill through a field and follow a well-used path following the line of the disused canal, with Sedgwick House over to the left. Keep to the top end of the field and you will soon reach a canal bridge. Go through a kissing gate under the bridge and follow the old canal towpath straight ahead to the aqueduct, where there is an information board.

Sedgwick Aqueduct is a scheduled ancient monument, built at a skew to a design of the Lancaster Canal's chief engineer, the Scotsman John Rennie (1761–1821). The route of the canal between Crooklands and Kendal – it takes a diversion west through the Hincaster Tunnel – was influenced by the location of the Wakefield Gunpowder Works at Sedgwick.

The aqueduct can be taken as the halfway point of the whole walk. You have now walked approximately 63 miles from Blackburn train station.

After crossing the aqueduct over the main village street, leave the canal on the left down a steep set of steps. Turn right and walk straight ahead through the village, passing Sedgwick House on the left.

Sedgwick House

AW gives the little parish of Sedgwick two pages to itself in *Westmorland Heritage.* He sketched Sedgwick House, Force Falls and the gunpowder works but no parish church, as Sedgwick did not have one. It was the Lancaster Canal and the Wakefield family that put Sedgwick on the nineteenth-century map. Sedgwick House, in the Perpendicular style, was completed in 1869 by Paley and Austin. It was the home of William Wakefield, a member of the influential Kendal family who had established the first gunpowder works on the west side of the River Kent hereabouts in 1764. Mary Wakefield (1853–1910) organized local singing competitions at Sedgwick, pioneering an international movement of amateur music festivals. She is commemorated by a plaque in the foyer of Kendal Town Hall.

In the eighteenth and nineteenth centuries Westmorland was an important centre for gunpowder production, not just for use in mine and quarry blasting but also for military use. The Wakefields established works on both banks of the River Kent, the key ingredient being the plentiful supply of charcoal in the coppice woods. The odd accidental explosion led to the loss of workers' lives, and the possible use of the Quaker-funded gunpowder for military use and even in the slave trade led to John Wakefield of Kendal being excluded from the Society of Friends.

Follow the road straight ahead down to the River Kent. Facing the river bank, turn sharp right along a bridleway, following a lane that soon ends at gates. Continue straight ahead through the gates, following a lovely riverside path past a suspension bridge over the River Kent. You are now briefly in the parish of Helsington. Go through a gate and the path continues along a hedged track. When the track soon bears slightly right away from the river, leave it along a path forking left into woodland overlooking the river. This turning is easy to miss.

Further stiles lead along the edge of woodland to a gate on to the riverbank by 'Dorothy's Seat'. Continue straight ahead along the path that follows the top of the river bank. Pass under power lines and you enter the parish of Natland. As you approach Hawes Bridge the first glimpses of Kendal can be seen looking north. Cross a stile to join the narrow lane to the right of Hawes Bridge.

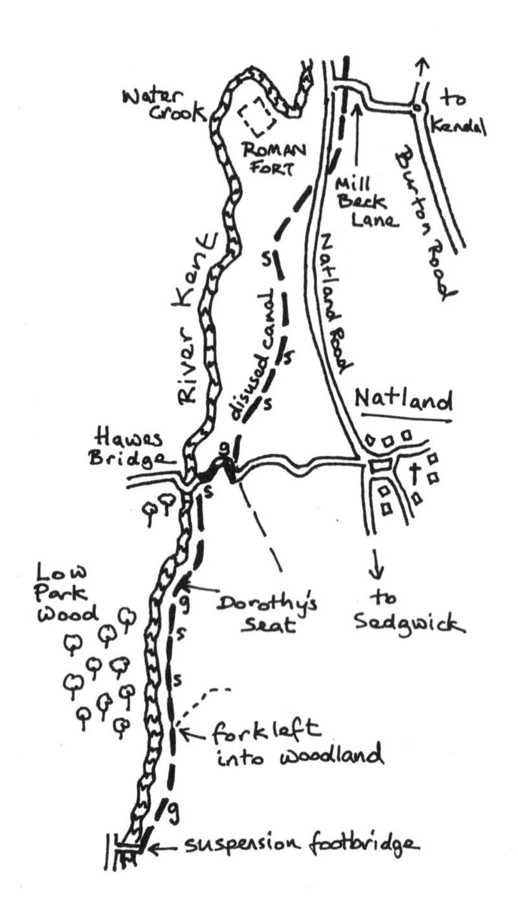

Hawes Bridge appears in both *Westmorland Heritage* and *Three Westmorland Rivers*. AW also sketched the Roman fort excavations at Watercrook, which lie in a bend of the River Kent, still within Natland parish, and climbed and sketched Natland's local viewpoint, the hill known as the Helm, which rises to the east of the village.

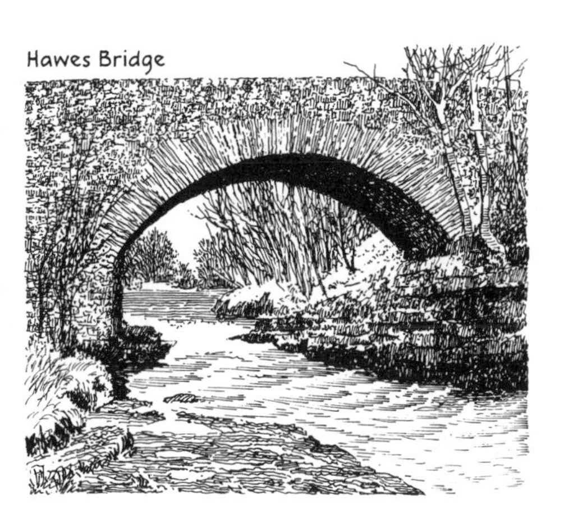

Do not cross Hawes Bridge but turn right, following the lane uphill. Carry on up the road until you reach a kissing gate on the left by a Lancaster Canal Trail fingerpost indicating that Kendal is 2¼ miles away. Join the line of the empty canal here and go straight ahead in the direction of Kendal, with a view down to the River Kent on the left. Crossing several stiles, follow the old line of the canal for about ¾ mile until you reach Natland Road.

Hidden in woodland to the right of Natland Road is Helme Lodge, built in 1824 for the chairman of the Lancaster Canal committee. He had his own private landing stage on the canal here so that he could jump aboard a fast packet boat going south.

Cross Natland Road and continue straight ahead along the line of the canal, which is signed as a footpath to Canal Head. This passes under one of the original canal bridges under Natland Mill Beck Lane and soon joins the A65 Burton Road. Cross the main road at the traffic island and continue straight ahead along the line of the canal, which is now a tarmac footpath and cycleway. The well-used route passes behind a leisure centre and Kirkbie Kendal School to reach Change Bridge (number 186).

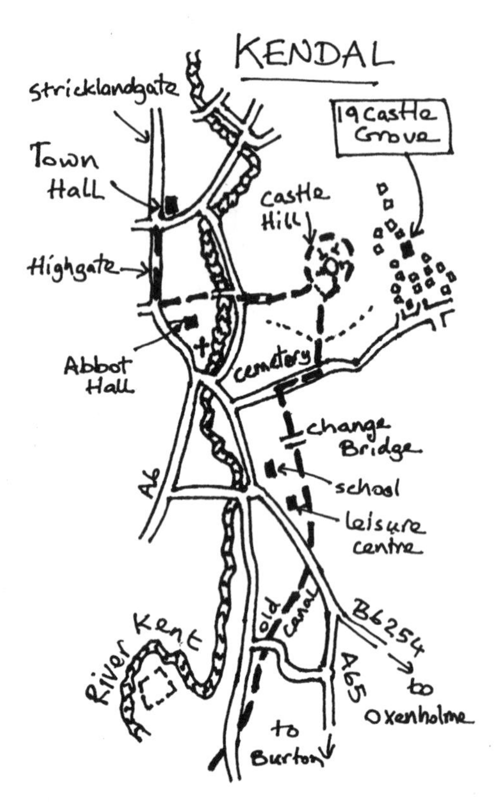

Change Bridge was the point where the canal towpath changed sides. Horses towing barges would have to cross over it and continue along the towpath on the opposite side. The changeover was necessary to avoid interference with barges loading and unloading at the bustling wharves at Little Lound that were to be found here in the nineteenth century. The canal-side house to the left of Change Bridge was built and lived in by the Kendal architect Miles Thompson (1800–72). He designed many Victorian buildings in Kendal, including the one that is now a Wetherspoons pub named after him.

The arrival of the canal in Kendal in 1819 solved the town's fuel crisis. It now had easy access to Lancashire coal and much of the resulting industrial activity was centred on the area of the Lound. Here was the town gasworks, a timber wharf and the Lound Iron Foundry, which manufactured iron girders.

AW harked back to the old days of Kendal's canal with two sketches in *Kendal in the Nineteenth Century*. His first sketch shows a working barge on the canal, overlooked by the parish church. His second sketch, the atmospheric 'Whitsunday on the canal', was created from an old photo and depicts a barge crammed full with day trippers (from the Fellside Sunday School) enjoying an annual outing to Levens.

Continue straight ahead along the line of the canal to meet Parkside Road. Cross over but leave the canal here, turning right and following the pavement alongside the town's main cemetery. When you reach Kendal Town Football Club on the right-hand side of the road, leave it on the left along a hedged path between cemetery plots. This path begins at steps and is signed to Kendal Castle. It leads beyond the cemetery to the open hillside of Castle Hill.

Kendal Castle

At the junction of paths beyond the wall gap, take the path signed for the castle that leads straight uphill. The short steep climb leads to the substantial ruin of Kendal Castle with brilliant views in all directions. Turn right and follow the circular path around the castle's walls. This follows the outer bank of a defensive ditch and leads around to the north side of the castle and its main gateway. There is an excellent view indicator on this side of the hill, showing a panorama of fells. Lakeland has finally arrived!

AW's drawing of Kendal Castle in *Westmorland Heritage* presents it as a romantic ruined folly complete with grazing sheep. AW's first house in Kendal, 19 Castle Grove, was on the opposite side of Castle Hill to the town, a council semi in the housing estate between the sports fields and the Oxenholme–Windermere railway line, which rattled behind AW's house.

Information boards inside the castle highlight its history. It was certainly here in the twelfth century as the defensive base administering the barony of Kendal, the first lord of which was one Ivo de Tallebois. He was granted the lands hereabouts by William Rufus, who had conquered Cumbria in 1092 and established the English–Scottish border at Carlisle. The castle is most well known for being associated with the sixteenth-century Parr family, as Katherine Parr (1512–48) became the sixth wife of Henry VIII and outlived him to be the guardian of the future Elizabeth I.

Eagle-eyed walkers can plot their journey over the next few days using the viewpoint indicator on the north side of the castle. Scout Scar can be seen rising directly west above Kendal: this is the first objective of stage six of the walk. The ridge rising above Troutbeck towards Froswick will be joined on stage seven.

Facing the viewpoint indicator at the castle entrance, turn left, continuing along the path encircling the castle. Take the right forking path that drops down to a bench and an information board. Continue downhill from here via cobbled steps to a kissing gate. Join the terrace of late Victorian villas (this is Parr Street) and walk along it to Aynam Road. Turn right and cross at the zebra crossing to reach the River Kent. Cross the footbridge over the river and enter the little park. Go straight ahead along the tarmac path, past the stone memorial to James Cropper, with the children's playground to the left.

Abbot Hall and its parkland were acquired by Kendal Borough Council in 1897, the grounds being opened as a public park. Holy Trinity Church and Abbot Hall were much sketched by AW, even before he started working on his *Pictorial Guides* in the 1950s. Built around 1759, Abbot Hall was originally the private residence of Colonel George Wilson, son of Daniel Wilson who built the Georgian Dallam Tower, passed earlier. James Cropper (1823–1900) was a paper manufacturer who was Kendal's Liberal MP in the 1880s.

Continue straight ahead, passing under a stone archway at the park entrance, until you reach Kendal's main shopping street at Highgate. Turn right along this until you reach Kendal Town Hall, overlooking the junction with Lowther Street. Cross this junction with care to arrive at the Town Hall entrance.

You are now at the epicentre of Wainwright's Kendal.

Kendal Town Hall

WAINWRIGHT'S KENDAL

'I walked to the office through green fields and amongst trees beside a river, and there were hills in the distance. Life was good.'
Ex-Fellwanderer

This 3-mile circular walk explores Kendal, AW's adopted home. The walk links places and people that played a significant role in the Wainwright story, and recreates his walk to work at the Town Hall from the house he had built on the edge of Kendal Green. It looks into the rich history of Kendal, which fascinated AW so much that he devoted a whole book to it, *Kendal in the Nineteenth Century*. There is also the chance to re-enact a scene from Wainwright's Kendal life by standing at a bus stop on Windermere Road.

A Man of Some Importance

When AW arrived to take up his new job on Monday 1 December 1941, Kendal was in sombre mood. Like Blackburn, the town was on a war footing and there were evening blackouts and grim weekly newspaper reports of deaths of local people in action. Women were signing up for war work, and there were fundraising efforts to 'Aid Russia' and Home Guard dances in church halls. Like the rest of the country, Kendal adopted the patriotic policies of 'Make Do and Mend' and 'Dig For Victory'. The big difference between Blackburn and Kendal was that the latter took in evacuees and was not considered under any great threat from German bombs. That said, only seven months before AW took up his post, a stray bomb left over from a Luftwaffe raid on Belfast wiped out a farm and eleven people in the countryside north of Kendal.

When AW arrived in Kendal at the end of November he stayed at digs known as Stanegarth on Burneside Road but quickly moved his wife, Ruth, and son, Peter, into his new council semi at 19 Castle Grove. In the week he arrived, the film showing at St George's

Cinema on Stramongate was *Pimpernel Smith*, starring the dashing Leslie Howard, advertised with the strap line 'the mysterious rescuer, who baffles the Nazis'. In the spirit of the film's hero, AW, in his mid-thirties, was to do his bit. He was almost called up, but being third in line below the Kendal Borough Treasurer, William Ernest Carter, he spent the rest of the war keeping Kendal's finances in good order and boosting morale by organizing the town's 'Holidays at Home' programme in the summer months from 1942 to 1945. He was responsible for producing souvenir brochures for the August events and illustrated them with his own scenes of Kendal, such as views of Holy Trinity Church and Abbot Hall.

Life was good for AW. He had swapped *the Blackburn Times* with its reports of cotton riots and industrial decline for the provincial farmers' weekly, the *Westmorland Gazette*, with its rural round-up of village whist drives, hunt balls and bad weather conditions on Shap summit. He had swapped views of the West Pennine Moors for views of proper mountains. He had left a Borough Treasurer's office of over fifty staff for a Borough Treasurer's office of just fourteen people, where the workload was much lighter. In 1948, AW was appointed Borough Treasurer at Kendal Town Hall and started to move in the professional circles of Westmorland's administrative capital. It was a job he could confidently expect to keep until his retirement. In Kendal, the air was fresh, the fields were green, the factories were small and the people were happy. In 1949, he would have his own detached house built on a green field site on the edge of Kendal Fell. He achieved all this through hard work; it was a just reward for all those years spent hidden away in the 1920s, studying to become a municipal accountant.

In the 1940s, from his house at 19 Castle Grove, AW could enjoy a half-hour stroll to work, past the ruins on Castle Hill and across the River Kent into town to arrive at the Town Hall, overlooking Kendal's main shopping street. In the 1950s and 1960s, he would have a similar half-hour walk to work from his new house, 38 Kendal Green. Whatever route AW walked to work, there were always views of green limestone hills.

AW's new detached house at the northern end of Kendal Green had a prospect from the back garden looking to the Kentmere fells, and was built at the end of a quiet cul-de-sac of just five houses, the two oldest of which were only built in the 1930s. From the front door of his house AW walked at least four times a day (as he came home for lunch) along the oval-shaped Kendal Green, a planned open space upon which trees were planted. Around the green, the Kendal Fell Trustees had released plots of land for the building of fine Victorian villas. Prior to development this whole area was known as Low Tenter Fell, and was one of several scattered sites where Kendal's coarse woollen cloth was stretched out and attached by hooks to rows of tenter frames.

A delightfully detailed account of the history of this part of Kendal, where AW lived for over forty years and wrote his *Pictorial Guides*, can be found in John and Jean Coopey's *Kendal Green: A Georgian Wasteland Transformed*. This book highlights the affluence associated with Kendal Green, its original trustees being formed from the town's influential Quaker families, such as the Wakefields, Wilsons and Braithwaites. The green's residents were predominantly middle-class professionals: manufacturers, bankers, architects, shop managers and wine merchants.

The plot of land on which AW built his house was purchased from Samuel Gawith, who lived in the nearby villa of Holmfield and was involved in the family firm of Gawith, Hoggarth & Co., Kendal's well-known tobacco and snuff manufacturers. For most of the period AW resided at Number 38 Kendal Green, his neighbours are recorded as Leslie Hill at Number 39 and the exquisitely named Alice Golightly at Number 37. AW kept himself to himself; the socializing with neighbours was largely left to his wife, Ruth, who eased the monotony of being home alone by spending afternoons walking her dogs with female friends who lived nearby.

Beyond the green lay Windermere Road, the old turnpike road linking the centre of Kendal with Ambleside and Keswick. This was the busy road into the Lakes from the south, which became another fashionable residential area, lined with a ribbon development of semi-detached houses uphill from St Thomas's Church. From the 1940s to the late 1960s, AW witnessed an explosion in the volume of motor traffic coming to the Lakes and the clogging up of Kendal in the process. In the early 1970s, he got some good news: the Kendal bypass opened and took the Windermere-bound traffic out of the town centre and over the top of Kendal Fell.

AW walked up and down the bottom end of Windermere Road every day of his working life. The corner shop, where he stocked up on tobacco, is still there. Higher up on the right, Number 78 Windermere Road was the home and studio of the photographer Ken Shepherd, who worked magic on the negatives of AW's dull camera snapshots. On Windermere Road, AW waited virtually every weekend in the 1950s and 1960s for the Keswick-bound bus, as he embarked upon his thirteen-year project to survey the Lakeland fells. He would often wait (and occasionally walk) with another Windermere Road resident, the bank manager of Kendal's Lloyd's Bank, Weaver Owen. They were just two of countless professional men who took advantage of living and working in Kendal to escape to the hills on their days off.

AW was certainly not the first, or the last, of the 'offcomers' who had moved to Kendal to climb mountains. One such was the journalist A. Harry Griffin (1911–2004), destined to become a Lakeland legend himself. From his family home at Cunswick End, just beyond the edge of Kendal, Griffin had a gentle commute to the Stricklandgate office of the *Lancashire Evening Post*, where he was Northern Editor. In January 1951, almost two years before AW started work on his first *Pictorial Guide*, Griffin posted off his first short 'Country Diary' to the *Manchester Guardian* from Kendal's main post office. He was still writing this column, his observations on Lake District life, right up until his death over half a century later.

AW and Harry Griffin had a lot in common. Griffin was a fellow pipe smoker and Lancastrian, born in Barrow-in-Furness. Like AW, Griffin moved to Kendal in the 1940s to be nearer the fells, although, unlike AW's, Griffin's mountain expeditions were usually on the end of a rope. An experienced rock climber, Griffin had no interest in bringing up his young family in the city, even if it meant turning down jobs with big newspapers. Both AW's and Griffin's writings were essentially love letters to the fells and they shared similar views on environmental issues affecting the Lake District, particularly when it came to the problem of increasing tourist traffic.

The work of Harry Griffin and AW was finally brought together posthumously in a 2008 publication, *The High Places*. This was a collection of Griffin's *Lancashire Evening Post* weekly features, 'Leaves from a Lakeland Notebook', combined with illustrations by AW from his Lakeland sketchbooks. AW had dedicated Book Five of his *Scottish Mountain Drawings* to Harry Griffin and they had, on a few occasions, walked together in the fells. There is even a story that AW avoided Griffin on the fells because he talked too much. Griffin was certainly AW's link to a more adventurous Lakeland, as he had encountered and written about characters like the cave hermit of Borrowdale, Millican Dalton, and the speed merchant Donald Campbell.

At Kendal Town Hall AW had a responsible position that took up a lot of his time. But he coped more than adequately with his duties, including the long dull committee meetings. The fact that AW handled his job confidently, as well as the relative security of his employment, meant he could concentrate his thoughts on the project that obsessed him, the writing of the *Pictorial Guides*.

In its external appearance at least, Kendal Town Hall retains the air of late Victorian grandeur that greeted AW when he came to work here. After 1945 the great symbols of nineteenth-century local government lingered on – the aldermen, the Mayor's Parlour, the boxes of bunting for civic parades, the chain of office and the carefully preserved Charter of Incorporation. AW always attended civic occasions, as he was required to do, along with Town Clerk Harry Jones, and he was Borough Treasurer when Kendal formally appointed its first lady mayor in 1955 and when the Queen visited the Town Hall in 1956.

Internally, Kendal Town Hall is now a shadow of its former self. Seven years after AW retired from local government in 1967 Kendal Borough Council ceased to exist. Kendal's importance as a local authority had started to wane once the larger Westmorland County Council had been created in 1889. This new tier of local government had the grand County Hall built at the northern end of Stricklandgate in the 1930s and became a big employer in the town.

AW's long-time deputy, Percy Duff (1922–2011) filled AW's shoes as Borough Treasurer from 1967 to 1974, after which he became number two at the new authority that replaced it, the much larger South Lakeland District Council. Born and bred in Kendal, Duff was a motorbike enthusiast and local historian, who became AW's closest male friend in Kendal. Like Harry Griffin, Percy Duff was much more gregarious and adventurous than the taciturn AW. He had a greater knowledge of Kendal's history than AW and, with his wife, Margaret, produced a number of books of old photographs of the town. The Duffs' extensive collection of photos helped AW when he came to write *Kendal in the Nineteenth Century*.

From the Town Hall, it was a short walk for AW, then largely unrecognized by his legion of readers, along Kendal's ancient north–south highway past Burton's the Tailors to 22 Stricklandgate, the address of the *Westmorland Gazette*. This weekly newspaper had been the voice of the county since 1818, when it was the mouthpiece of its Tory landowners, the Lowthers, who set up the paper with the support of William Wordsworth. The poet's disgraced friend Thomas de Quincey became its second editor, but lasted only fourteen months in the job. Born in Manchester, de Quincey was an early example of another Lancastrian moving to the Lakes.

By the time Harry Firth, Printing Manager at the *Westmorland Gazette*, got to see AW's handwritten manuscript of *Pictorial Guide* Book One, *The Eastern Fells*, in 1955, AW had already shown his precious baby to two people he knew already from the Town Hall. The first was Henry Marshall at Kendal Library (one of many libraries funded by Andrew Carnegie, and known as Carnegie Libraries); the second was Sandy Hewitson, a printer of council leaflets. The printers Bateman and Hewitson Ltd had traditionally operated from premises in Grosvenor House, Stramongate, but had been taken over by the *Westmorland Gazette* by the time AW came to call. Their previous publishing ventures extended no further than little books like *Shrubs: Their Pruning and Arrangement*.

In the mid-1950s an axis of creativity evolved along Stricklandgate. At one end, hidden by billowing puffs of pipe smoke, sits the author AW at his Town Hall desk; at the other end, beavering away in Kendal Library, is Henry Marshall, who acted as AW's first publisher for the *Pictorial Guides* during the years 1955–63. Halfway between the two was the *Westmorland Gazette*, whose printing arm in May 1955 rolled out the first 2,000 copies of AW's Book One, *The Eastern Fells* and which later published his books too. Add into this mix a glowing first review of the book by Harry Griffin of the *Lancashire Evening Post* in the paper's Stricklandgate office and it is clear that this short stretch of one of Kendal's oldest thoroughfares gave birth to the Wainwright phenomenon.

While the Town Hall and Library remain intact, the premises of the *Westmorland Gazette* have altered since AW's day. The *Westmorland Gazette* sign hanging over 22 Stricklandgate is still there, as is the adjacent walkway leading into what was Gazette Yard. But the old offices have been rebuilt as part of the 2007 retail development involving Booths supermarket. AW still lords it over his old publisher, as the *Westmorland Gazette*'s address is now 1 Wainwright's Yard.

Kendal in the post-war years must have appeared to AW as a town brimming with larger-than-life personalities. It had an influx of 'offcomers' like himself – artists, writers, adventurers and municipal accountants – who had moved to the town for inspiration and excitement in the hills, or to live out their days pottering through Kendal's historic yards wearing spotted neckerchiefs and eccentric hats. AW was not particularly bohemian, but through his work he found himself on the periphery not just of Harry Griffin's world of adventure but also Mary Burkett's world of art.

The spirited Miss Burkett, born in 1928, was brought up in County Durham and moved to the Lake District in 1955 to lecture in art at Ambleside. She came to work at Abbot Hall Art Gallery in Kendal when it opened in 1962 and became its Director in 1966. She held this position for the next twenty years and, through her outstanding efforts and devoted support of the arts in Cumbria (in the late 1960s she found herself championing the forgotten work of Ambleside's German refugee Kurt Schwitters and supporting the troubled ex-footballer-turned-West-Cumbrian-artist Percy Kelly), she turned Abbot Hall into one of northern England's most prestigious cultural centres.

Through her dealings with the Borough Council, Miss Burkett befriended AW and three exhibitions of his work were put on at Abbot Hall, the last of which, in 1987, was billed as 'An 80th Birthday Tribute'. One of the exhibitions displayed original drawings from AW's *Kendal in the Nineteenth Century* to raise money for the charity Animal Rescue Cumbria. AW did not turn up to the launches, as he was not a man for cheese and wine soirées. Mary Burkett shared the credits with AW in *Wainwright in Lakeland,* produced in 1983 by Abbot Hall. This book was a collection of sketches and comments from AW's publications to date, issued as a limited edition of 1,000 signed and numbered books to raise funds for the gallery and mark the twenty-first anniversary of the opening of the Abbot Hall Art Gallery. With a foreword by A. Harry Griffin, two years later it was reissued by the *Westmorland Gazette.*

When AW's first wife walked out on him at the end of 1967, there were naturally rumours flying around Kendal about the Borough Treasurer's 'other woman'. During the subsequent divorce proceedings, suspicion fell on Mary Burkett. Fuel to the fire was no doubt stoked by Miss Burkett giving AW a lift in her car to the Peak District in 1966, where she was on business and he was researching his *Pennine Way Companion.* They stayed overnight in adjacent rooms in a Buxton hotel before driving back the next day.

Miss Burkett was also a staunch ally of Kendal Museum on Station Road, where AW helped out, as both honorary clerk and curator, for over forty years. AW was given responsibilities for managing the popular town museum as early as the 1940s. The museum became his hobby: he didn't just look after the financial side of things but got stuck into labelling, indexing and cataloguing the exhibits, which included birds' eggs, the hunting trophies of old colonels and a large polar bear. During his tenure an extension was built on the former wool warehouse in which the various collections were housed.

While he worked at the Town Hall, AW conducted much of his unofficial business relating to his *Pictorial Guides* there, holding meetings with Harry Firth, Printing Manager of the *Westmorland Gazette*, for instance. After his retirement in January 1967, AW continued working at the museum in a voluntary capacity for two days a week and the museum became his new office, where he could use the phone and meet people. He was still to be found there in the 1980s. Now he too has joined the stuffed animal menagerie as a neatly labelled exhibit: a small collection of his writings together with personal effects like his pipe and glasses can be found in the ground-floor Wainwright Gallery. The Wainwright Society, formed in 2002, now uses the museum as its base.

Through his connections with Abbot Hall, Kendal Museum, Kendal Library and Deputy Treasurer Percy Duff, AW expanded his knowledge of local history and put this to good use in 1977, when he produced *Kendal in the Nineteenth Century*. With access to Victorian photographs AW was able to reproduce old town scenes in a series of sketches, which appear in the book with old maps and a potted history of Kendal. The book is dedicated to 'The First Men in Kendal with Cameras'.

AW's collaborator on this big book was again the local historian John Marsh, a police sergeant in the Cumbria Constabulary, who had previously provided material for AW's *Westmorland Heritage* and *Three Westmorland Rivers*. They were also to work together in 1980, when AW illustrated *An Antiquarian Map of Cumbria*, based on the researches of John Marsh. This was published by the Cumberland and Westmorland Antiquarian Society and sold at the time for £3.

A look at Wainwright's Kendal is hardly complete without considering Betty, who became the major force in AW's life from the late 1960s onwards. Betty Hayes (1922–2008) was educated at Casterton School and worked as a teacher and hospital registrar before her marriage to and subsequent separation from an Irish doctor brought her by chance to Kendal with her two young daughters in tow. Her married name was Betty McNally and she first met AW on official business at his Town Hall office in 1957. A second meeting in the same place in September 1965 marked the start of several years of trials and tribulations before AW divorced Ruth and he and Betty were finally united in marriage. Their low-key nuptials took place on 10 March 1970 at the register office at County Hall, just down the hill from Kendal Green.

In the late 1960s, in the days between their illicit meetings in Keswick cafés, AW would wander past Betty's rather grand residence, Fowl Ing House, hidden in the trees at the end of Fowl Ing Lane, just off Appleby Road. This Georgian mansion was built in 1812 by local Quaker, John Gough (1757–1825), a blind mathematician and botanist, who was friends with the scientist John Dalton. Betty McNally moved into the house in 1952, together with her parents and two children, Jane and Anne. AW recuperated at Fowl Ing after a bout of pneumonia in the early months of 1970, just before he and Betty were married. AW sketched the house and the joy for Wainwright fans is that they can now stay at Fowl Ing, as it is now a guest house, renamed Wainwright House.

After their marriage, 38 Kendal Green became their marital home, although Betty insisted on making a few changes. For the remaining twenty years of their life together, Betty, who had trained as a nurse, not only drove the car that enabled AW to carry on and write all his books about the north of England in the 1970s and 1980s, but also worked tirelessly with him, often by organizing exhibitions of his original drawings or raising money for Animal Rescue Cumbria.

While AW's first thirty-four years in Blackburn produced one manuscript that he hid in a drawer, his fifty years in Kendal saw the publication of nearly sixty books, including *A Pennine Journey*, the unpublished book he had written in 1938. Being at the foot of the fells, Kendal was a springboard for AW. As well as giving him the opportunity to brush up against creative and adventurous people, it had a tradition of mountain adventure. Two decades before AW and Harry Griffin settled in the town, a Kendal-born mountaineer, Dr Howard Somervell (1890–1975), was part of the 1920s British expeditions that attempted to conquer Everest. Somervell was born into the family of wealthy boot manufacturers who created K Shoes and, naturally, he attempted to conquer the world's highest peak in a pair of Kendal-made boots. On a more practical level, Kendal's position as a transport hub enabled AW to catch a bus on Sundays to even the remotest corners of Lakeland at a time when he had no other means of travel. After he married Betty, AW's life in Kendal was further transformed.

THE ROUTE

Start the walk outside Kendal Town Hall.

Unlike Blackburn's purpose-built Italianate Town Hall, in 1859 Kendal's municipal offices took root in an existing Georgian building, the White Hall Assembly Rooms, designed by the Kendal architects Francis and George Webster. This still forms part of the present Town Hall, the older part of which overlooks Lowther Street. As Kendal flourished in the late nineteenth century, the Town Hall was extended northwards in the direction of Stricklandgate, the foundation stone of the new building and its clock tower being laid in 1893.

The original building on this site had been a cloth exchange hall and the Kendal coat of arms, engraved over the entrance of the Victorian Town Hall, has a representation of bale hooks and a

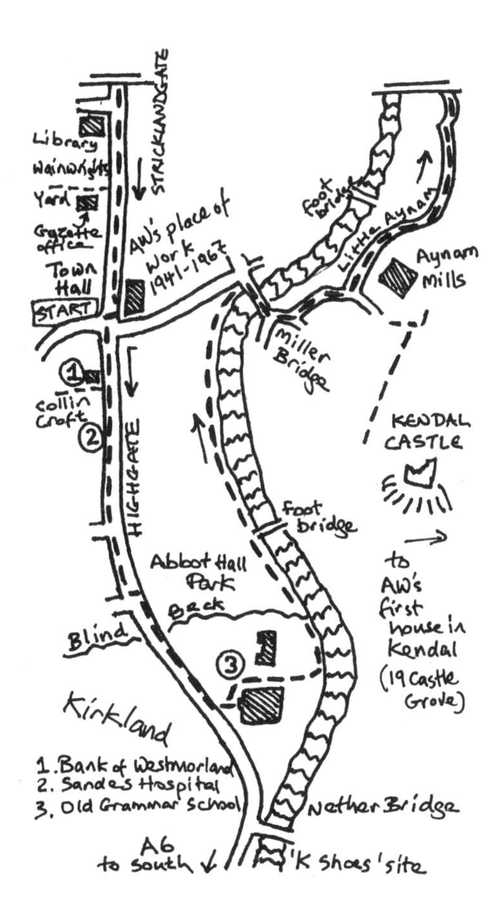

Latin motto that translates as 'Wool is our bread'. This highlights the importance of the wool trade to the development of the town from the Middle Ages to the early nineteenth century, after which the textile trade became heavily mechanized and moved to Lancashire and Yorkshire, influencing the creation of huge industrial towns like Blackburn.

Cross over to the corner of Allhallows Lane, turn left and walk down the right-hand side of Highgate. You soon reach HSBC bank and the entrance to Collin Croft yard on the right.

In the eighteenth and nineteenth centuries Kendal's manufacturers were given a boost by first the canal and later the railway. Highgate, the north–south road through the town, developed as the main shopping street; this remains largely intact. The intricate arrangement of alleys leading to yards can still be seen on both sides of the street, a layout that developed to allow the town's growing population to take full advantage of both the nearby fellside and the River Kent. AW sketched many of Kendal's historic yards for *Kendal in the Nineteenth Century* and *Westmorland Heritage*.

Kendal Civic Society has done an excellent job of marking the town's historic sites with green information plaques. These are easily spotted by the casual walker, so there is no need to reproduce them here.

Collin Croft, adjacent to the Bank of Westmorland, was designed by George Webster (1797–1864) and is a restored example of a typical town yard. In the nineteenth century it would have been unsanitary and overcrowded, a ramshackle collection of cottages and workshops.

Kendal Collin Croft

Continue along Highgate passing the Shakespeare Inn, the entrance to the Sandes Hospital and the junction with Captain

French Lane, all on the right. Cross over to reach the junction with Dowker's Lane on the left at the entrance to Abbot Hall Park.

It was wool money that built most of Kendal's oldest buildings, like the 1659 Sandes Hospital, a school and almshouses built by cloth merchant Thomas Sandes (1608–81). The almshouses were rebuilt in the 1850s by Miles Thompson, an architect in the Websters' firm. A memorial to the Websters, who left a rich legacy of churches, halls and banks in and around Kendal, can be seen behind the gates at the entrance to the more recently named Webster's Yard. Oddfellows Hall, on the left-hand side of this part of Highgate, is another George Webster-designed building, dating from 1833.

Many of Kendal's historic properties were demolished in the post-war years and buildings that AW would have known at the entrance to Abbot Hall Park on Dowker's Lane were swept aside in the 1970s.

Continue along the left-hand side of Highgate to cross Blind Beck, visible beyond railings on either side of the street.

Blind Beck is a mere trickle over limestone boulders but formed an important historic boundary in old Kendal. South of the beck, towards Nether Bridge, was the old township of Kirkland, 'church land', with Holy Trinity Church at its heart. North of the beck, back towards the Town Hall, was the newer borough of Kendal, with its market granted by a royal charter in 1575. Kirkland remained a separate community with its own court and regulations and was not fully absorbed into Kendal Borough until 1908.

Continue along Kirkland to reach the ornate gates of Holy Trinity Church on the left. The church is definitely worth a visit and reveals much about the history of AW's adopted town.

Holy Trinity Church

Built on the back of Kendal's prosperous wool trade on the site of an older place of worship, the oldest parts of Kendal's original parish church date from the thirteenth century. It is one of the widest churches in the country, with five aisles. The town's most important families of the Elizabethan and Tudor ages, like the Bellinghams and Parrs, had their own chapels inside the church. Kendal's first Norman baron, Ivo de Tailbois, gave the 'Kirkland' at Kendal to the Benedictine Abbey of St Mary's in York and the abbot built his own residence, the original Abbot's Hall, adjacent to the church. In the churchyard is the grave of John Gough, the Quaker mathematician who built Fowl Ing, where Betty McNally lived until she married AW.

Continue the walk by turning left at the church gates and following Church Walk between the churchyard and Kendal's Old Grammar School. This leads to a tarmac path overlooking the River Kent.

To the right, the River Kent flows under the stone-arched Nether Bridge, a much-widened seventeenth-century structure that marked the ancient crossing point into the town from the south. Just beyond the bridge on the east bank of the river was the site of the Netherfield Boot Factory, which made Kendal

Kendal Old Grammar School

famous in the nineteenth and twentieth centuries as the home of K Shoes. When AW lived in Kendal the town was still well known for its boots and shoes, and the Netherfield shoe firm started by the Somervell Brothers here in the 1840s remained one of the town's biggest employers.

Turn left along the riverside path to view Abbot Hall on the left. The path crosses over Blind Beck again, which enters the River Kent close to its weir.

As noted earlier, some of AW's earliest sketches in Kendal were of Abbot Hall and Holy Trinity Church. The present art gallery was opened in 1962 in what was then a derelict building, the former Georgian residence of Colonel George Wilson. Kendal Borough had bought the property in 1897 and turned the little parkland into a public open space. The stables behind Abbot Hall were opened as the Museum of Lakeland Life in 1971.

As part of the August 'Holidays at Home' programme for which he was responsible during the Second World War, AW organized activities and events in Abbot Hall Park. A 1940s photo in the collection of Percy and Margaret Duff captures a fresh-faced AW, in his suit and tie, presenting prizes to children at the annual Abbot Hall sports event. AW sits smiling alongside Kendal's Chief Constable.

Continue along the riverside path, often known as the Colonel's Walk, to pass on the right the concrete footbridge over the River Kent.

The present footbridge over the river here replaced the older Jenning's Yard Bridge, removed when the river was widened as part of a town-centre flood alleviation scheme in the 1970s. AW may well have used the old footbridge on his route to work in the 1940s, as he had to cross the river at least twice on a daily basis. This was when he lived at Castle Grove, about half a mile due east from the footbridge, on the other side of Castle Hill.

Continue straight ahead along the riverside path to the next river crossing at Miller Bridge.

Just before you reach the bridge, look on the left for a stone plaque in the wall which records Kendal's historic flood levels. The year 1898 saw the biggest flood recorded in the town while the highest flood of the twentieth century occurred in 1954.

Miller Bridge was another link between AW's place of work, the Town Hall at the top of Lowther Street, and his first house in Kendal on the east side of the river. The present bridge opened in 1818 and was part of a scheme that built a new complex of warehouses and wharves, designed by Francis Webster, at the head of the newly arrived Lancaster Canal on the east side of the river. Miller Bridge replaced an earlier structure that had led to the Castle Corn Mill.

Miller Bridge

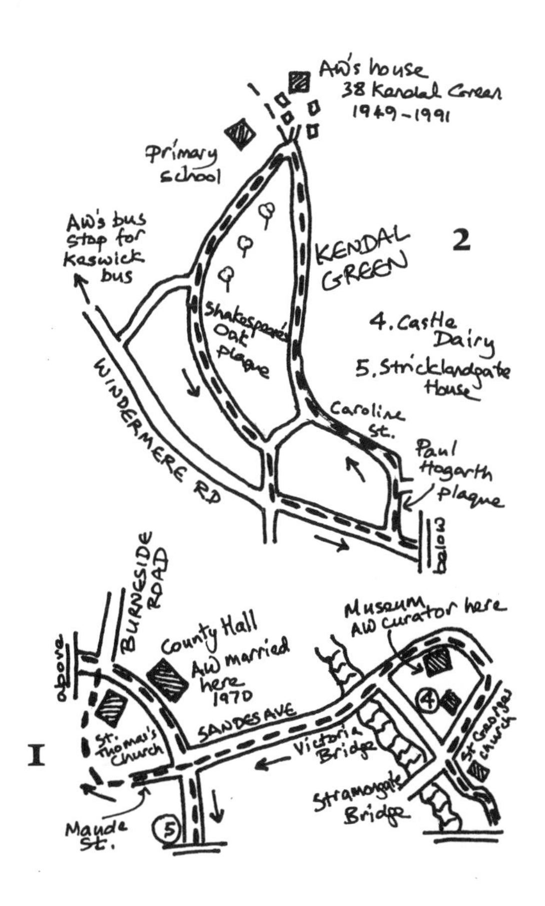

Cross over Miller Bridge to the east bank of the river. Turn left into Bridge Street and left again along Bridge Lane to face the Aynam Mills complex. Continue straight ahead along Little Aynam, which leads to the Georgian terrace of Thorney Hills. Walk along the terrace, signed as a private road, and then join the road that runs along the left-hand side of St George's Parish Church. This leads back to the river and Stramongate Bridge.

Aynam Mills were built for the wool industry but AW would have known them as the premises of J.T. Illingworth & Sons, one of Kendal's tobacco and snuff manufacturers. The elegance of the villas at Thorney Hills, formerly known as Kent Terrace, is somewhat faded, but in the nineteenth century this was the fashionable part of town, the home of gentlemen and wealthy industrialists. The architect George Webster, a dominant figure in Kendal's Victorian townscape, lived at what is now Number 4. He was also responsible for designing two parish churches in Kendal that were built to serve the population of the town when it was expanding north and eastwards in the mid-nineteenth century. One of these was St George's, completed in 1841.

Stramongate Bridge marks another ancient crossing point of the River Kent, a bridge recorded here in the fourteenth century, replacing a ford. The present four-arched bridge dates from 1794 and was built on either side of a much narrower sixteenth-century packhorse bridge. The bridge, leading to Stramongate and Finkle Street, carried the main road entering the town from the north and Scotland.

Castle Dairy

Do not cross the bridge but turn right into Wildman Street and pass the Castle Dairy on the left-hand side.

AW sketched the Castle Dairy, reputed to be Kendal's oldest occupied house. Parts of it date from the fourteenth century, when it was a single-storey hall, owned by the barons of Kendal, who lived at the nearby castle. The structure was greatly enlarged as a gentleman's residence in Elizabethan times. The building retains original internal features and can be visited by the public, as in 2011 it opened as a restaurant and art gallery run by Kendal College.

Continue to the next junction and turn left down Station Road, with the County Hotel on the corner. Beyond this is the entrance to Kendal Museum.

Looking across the busy junction at the County Hotel, the road going under the railway bridge is the route north out of the town that soon splits into Shap Road (the A6) and Appleby Road. There were probably countless occasions in the mid-1960s when a lovelorn AW, a respectable married man, wandered the half mile up Appleby Road and turned right to join the track that ran alongside Fowl Ing, in the hope of glimpsing Betty, the woman of his dreams.

The building that became Kendal Museum after the First World War was an old woollen warehouse operated by Whitwell, Hargreaves & Co., which had been linked with a private siding and goods yard on the railway next to Kendal train station. During his half century in Kendal, AW not only saw the closure of the town's canal but lived through the gradual demise of the railway. In the 1940s, the Kendal to Windermere Railway was still an integral part of the London Midland and Scottish Railway, the biggest operator in the country. By the mid-1970s, there was no goods traffic on this line and it had been downgraded to a single track.

The museum has a long and illustrious past in the town. Founded in 1796 by William Todhunter, a Hawkshead bookseller and natural history enthusiast, in Victorian times it moved premises around the town as its collections grew with the involvement of the Kendal Literary and Scientific Society, whose founder members included Wordsworth, Southey and John Dalton. The surfeit of hunting trophies brought back by Victorian colonels were largely *in situ* by the time AW came to help out here, although he did witness the arrival of the Earl of Lonsdale's stuffed polar bear in 1947.

The museum was run by Kendal Town Council when AW worked there and the council still owns the building. A visit to the museum where AW worked for most of his Kendal years is a must, not least because it remains the only place in town where there is a permanent exhibition of AW memorabilia.

Continue past the museum, turning left into Sandes Avenue and soon crossing the River Kent again at Victoria Bridge. Walk straight ahead to reach the crossroads at the junction with Stricklandgate.

Victoria Bridge was the fourth road crossing over the river to appear in Kendal. It was opened in 1887 for Queen Victoria's Golden Jubilee, along with the new thoroughfare of Sandes Avenue, built as a link to the railway station.

At the junction, cross Stricklandgate and continue straight ahead along Maude Street. There are views straight ahead to the fine houses

Borough Museum

perched on the side of Kendal Fell. At the end of the street, go through the gates and enter the little public park known as Noble's Rest.

Traditionally a recreational area known as Maude's Meadow, this park was renamed when it was donated to the town in 1929 by Mary Ellen Noble, in memory of her surgeon husband. A stone memorial in the centre of the park records this. AW may well have walked across this open space to add a bit of variety to his walk to and from work.

Bear right along the tarmac path to reach gates at a sensory garden. Go through these and continue along the path on the right-hand side of a meadow to reach another gate next to St Thomas's Church.

You are now firmly in AW's home territory. On the far side of the junction is Burneside Road, where AW stayed when he first arrived to take up his new job in Kendal at the end of November 1941. On the same side can be seen the name of Titus Wilson, printers since 1860, emblazoned over premises adjoining an old carpet factory. When AW came to Kendal this big printing firm operated at 24–28 Highgate, and in the 1940s it printed six

The Parish Churches of St George and St Thomas

Christmas cards of Kendal scenes he had drawn; it was thus his first publisher. Perhaps this encouraged AW to take his idea of a big Lakeland project more seriously. The other big building that would have been familiar to AW here is the Stricklandgate Methodist Church. At the end of December 2011, there was a memorial service here for Percy Duff, the man who helped Betty take AW's ashes up Haystacks.

Cross the junction to the Methodist church and turn left up Windermere Road. Take the second turning on the right and walk up Caroline Street. Continue uphill as it swings left to reach the large open space of Kendal Green.

At Number 28 Caroline Street, a Kendal Civic Society plaque marks the terraced cottage where the artist Paul Hogarth (1917–2001) was born. Although he had left his native town in the 1920s long before AW arrived, he still embodies the Kendalian spirit of adventure, having fought in the Spanish Civil War and been the first British artist to set foot in Communist China. He became a renowned book illustrator as well as a member of the Royal Academy. His work has been exhibited at Abbot Hall.

In Victorian times, Kendal's workhouse was to be found on the site now occupied by new houses on the left-hand side of Caroline Street. AW would have frequently passed the old workhouse buildings here, which during his time in Kendal were mostly used as a hospital for the elderly. The houses around Kendal Green itself were laid out largely between the 1860s and the 1880s on land opened up for developers by the Kendal Fell Trustees. Newer twentieth-century houses, including AW's, occupy the northern end of the green.

Walk along the right-hand side of the green. At the top end, the lane bends sharp left but a private road leads straight ahead. This can be followed only as far as the footpath signpost on the left, signed for 'Carus Green ¾ mile', as the road leads into a private cul-de-sac.

AW's former house, 38 Kendal Green, can be glimpsed from the start of the footpath. It is the slightly sunken white detached house seen face on at the top end of the cul-de-sac. The newly appointed Kendal Borough Treasurer had this house built in 1949 and moved into it with his family in 1950. AW's second wife, Betty, moved into the house in 1970 and shared it with him until his death in 1991. Please respect the privacy of the present owners of AW's house and their neighbours by not lingering around their homes.

By following the footpath to the left of the houses for a few yards beyond a gate, the open view from the back of AW's house is revealed, looking beyond houses to the Kentmere fells. The adjoining St Thomas's School opened in the 1960s.

Return to the road around Kendal Green and complete a loop by turning right and walking down the right-hand side of the green.

At Underley Road on the right just after the school, AW may well have cut through to Windermere Road where he could catch the Keswick-bound bus at 8.30 a.m. on Sundays. There is presently a stop for buses in both directions, close to where the two roads meet. On his return from the fells he would have got off the bus, which departed Keswick at 6.30 p.m. on Sundays, at the top of Underley Road and walked downhill to his house. A bit further along the right-hand side of the green is a plaque in the wall commemorating the planting of an oak in 1864 to celebrate Shakespeare's 300th birthday, when Kendal Green was officially named.

At the very far end of the green turn right down Green Road, which leads back to Windermere Road.

AW's corner shop is here, and a bit further up on the opposite side of the road is a bus stop that AW may well have used. At this point you can re-enact AW's typical weekend activity of waiting for the Keswick bus.

Turn left and walk downhill back to the traffic lights. Cross to St Thomas's Church and walk straight ahead along Stricklandgate, passing the Cumbria County Council offices on the left.

The quickest way for AW to get to work at the Town Hall from his house was simply to drop downhill to Windermere Road, probably via Caroline Street, and continue along the straight, slightly rising shopping thoroughfare of Stricklandgate. It was about a mile and could be walked in a fairly leisurely twenty-five minutes. This circular walk ends by taking AW's regular route to work along Stricklandgate, which has so many buildings and yards familiar to AW.

Stricklandgate, the road to the 'pasture land of young cattle', begins at St Thomas's Church, the third parish church in Kendal passed on this walk. The church dates from 1837 and was built to serve the northern end of the town. On the left-hand side of the road is County Hall, Cumbria County Council's offices, purpose built in 1938 and occupied by Westmorland County Council prior to 1974. AW married Betty in County Hall's register office in March 1970.

Continue straight ahead, passing the crossroads with Sandes Avenue, to join the pedestrian shopping street. You soon reach Kendal Library on the right at the junction with Library Road.

The fine Georgian town house of Stricklandgate House, passed on the left, was built in 1776 for Joseph Maude, an influential merchant who established the Kendal Savings Bank in 1815. In the 1890s the house was occupied by the town museum and later became the private residence of Dr Samuel Noble, whose widow still lived here in 1945. After the war it became council offices and the South Westmorland Rural District Council, a relatively short-lived authority, was based here from 1948 to 1974.

The present Kendal Library was opened in 1909; it is relevant to the AW story as it was the workplace of AW's first publisher, Borough Librarian Henry Marshall. Almost opposite it is the post office, opened in 1930, where the journalist Harry Griffin would post off his fortnightly 'Country Diary' to the *Manchester Guardian.*

Continue along Stricklandgate, passing the Market Place on the left, to reach Wainwright's Yard on the right.

AW's walk to work along the main street would have taken him past the old Market Place with its narrow ginnels and market stalls, a much smaller version of the Blackburn market he had grown up with. This circular walk around Kendal draws to a close with the town's slightly bizarre tribute to the Wainwright name – a shopping development! Wainwright's Yard is not even a gateway to a world of tobacconists and old map sellers, the kind of shops that might have interested AW. Wainwright's Yard, officially opened in 2007, is still worth a look at, as it has a well-designed display of AW's sketches, taken from his *Pictorial Guides.* A Kendal Civic Society green plaque has been placed on the wall of the new *Westmorland Gazette* offices and includes a sketch of AW. This newspaper's name will always be synonymous with that of Wainwright.

Continue along the main street and you soon reach the Town Hall on the left.

The final stretch of street AW plodded along to his office is where Stricklandgate merged with Highgate. The Lloyds Bank branch on adjoining Finkle Street was once managed by Weaver Owen, AW's very occasional companion on the fells in the early Kendal days. The *Westmorland Gazette*'s famous old address, 22 Stricklandgate, is now occupied by Toni and Guy, hair salon. The retail landscape has changed so much since AW walked through Kendal that even some of the famous high street names that spanned AW's life, and with which he grew up, have gone, like the Woolworths' store on Highgate, opposite the Town Hall. The thought of AW popping over the road for some pick and mix is a pleasant image on which to end this walk.

Stage Six
KENDAL TOWN HALL TO TROUTBECK BRIDGE
(15 miles)

'Dare we hope there will be another Orrest Head over the threshold of the next heaven?'
The Outlying Fells of Lakeland

This stage of the walk is the momentous day when you enter the Lake District National Park and climb one of AW's Lakeland fells for the first time on the journey. It is the day when the soft limestone dales of south Westmorland give way to the craggy foothills of mountains. Morecambe Bay still glistens in the south, but there are tantalizing views of the Langdale Pikes, Bowfell and High Street ahead. It is another day spent amid the rich treasures of *Westmorland Heritage* as the walk heads directly west out of Kendal and climbs the escarpment of Scout Scar, recorded by AW in *The Outlying Fells of Lakeland*. The route then heads north-west towards Windermere in search of other Outlying Fells, culminating in the climb up Orrest Head, a little crag almost as closely associated with AW as Haystacks.

The Dream Begins

Consider AW as a gangly twenty-three-year-old youth, enthusiastic and excited at the prospect of visiting proper mountains for the first time in his life. Then consider a stocky AW with his mutton-chop whiskers, newly retired, slow moving but still raring to go, slightly reluctant to shut the door completely on his *Pictorial Guides* to Lakeland. These two versions of the same man collide in this stage of the walk: the AW on his first visit to the Lakes in 1930 and the AW who wandered extensively through the Outlying Fells in 1973.

The early months of 1930 saw several firsts. A Mickey Mouse comic strip appeared for the first time and Birds Eye frozen foods went on sale. Then on 24 May 1930 the Yorkshire born aviator

Amy Johnson (1903–41) landed in Darwin, Australia, having flown solo, a distance of 11,000 miles, from London in a Gipsy Moth. The first woman to do so, she was showered with awards and even had a song written about her. It rather overshadowed a momentous event for AW two weeks later. There was no celebratory chorus of 'Alfred, Wonderful Alfred' ringing around Blackburn Town Hall when he climbed his first Lakeland hill on Saturday, 7 June 1930.

William Wordsworth (1770–1850) had feared the 'rash assault' of the proletariat coming to spoil his beloved Lakes and in 1844 he even wrote a *Sonnet on the Projected Kendal and Windermere Railway,* which specifically mentions Orrest Head. The railway line opened in 1847 and cheap excursions meant holidaymakers from industrial Lancashire indeed arrived in their droves. Orrest Head, less than 800 feet high, was a viewpoint not to be missed, according to all the late Victorian and Edwardian guidebooks that catered for the thousands of day-trippers who arrived every year by train to Windermere, the gateway to the Lakes.

In Baddeley's *Guide to the English Lake District,* one of the most popular guidebooks, Orrest Head is top of the list of walks from Windermere village and the view is described as 'perhaps, the finest in Great Britain'. Arriving from Lancashire on his own 'rash assault', courtesy of the Ribble bus, having studied his map and his Baddeley AW headed straight for the top of Orrest Head, just like everyone else.

AW was in the company of his Yorkshire cousin Eric Beardsall, another local government employee. Orrest Head is a little rock outcrop above Elleray Wood, a public open space accessed by a footpath through the woodland at the back of the Windermere Hotel. On this open hillside, the scales fell from AW's eyes and his life found new meaning. In his own words from Ex-*Fellwanderer,* it was as though 'a curtain had dramatically been torn aside'. The psychological effect the panoramic view of mountains from Orrest Head had on this 23-year-old from industrial Blackburn is perhaps the key to understanding the man. AW sums up the

View from Orrest Head

rest of his life in a few short sentences in Ex-*Fellwanderer*: 'I felt I was some other person; this was not me. I wasn't accustomed or entitled to such a privilege. I was an alien here. I didn't belong. If only I could, sometime! If only I could! Those few hours on Orrest Head cast a spell that changed my life.'

AW was not the first person to have a revelatory moment on the fells, nor the last. People who live in towns or cities today have their own 'Wainwright moments' when they first encounter the countryside and suddenly their own lives are put into perspective.

In his conclusion to his first *Pictorial Guide* in 1954 (*The Eastern Fells*, published in 1955) AW admits that his first climb up Orrest Head was 'the first time I had looked upon beauty, or imagined it, even'. He was an urban dweller who suddenly discovered heaven on earth, the awesome natural beauty in the shape of mountains. AW's life so far had been one of urban constraint. His employer dictated his daily routine, chaining him to the office five and a half days a week. In the little free time he had, lack of money limited his social mobility. He was more or less tied to Blackburn. Here he was physically constricted by a man-made landscape built of brick and iron and blanketed in the fog of noxious fumes belched out by factory chimneys. He could not wander at free will through a town owned by private rent-collecting landowners where public open spaces were restricted to the council-owned Corporation Park and Queen's Park with their ornamental lakes and ducks. The local jaunts on to the moors with Lawrence Wolstenholme provided some respite but even there he was limited to walled lanes and official footpaths. The moors were largely privately owned, either by grouse-shooting landowners who saw ramblers as a menace or by water authorities who saw ramblers as a source of pollution to the water supply. He could not roam wherever he liked. In 1930 when AW stood on top of Orrest Head for the first time the sweeping panorama of mountains before him knocked the views he had experienced from Darwen Tower into a cocked hat.

Mountford John Byrde Baddeley (1843–1906) had already sketched the fells in view from the top of Orrest Head. His Lakeland guidebook includes several prints showing panoramas of fells, engraved by John Bartholomew & Co., the Edinburgh mapmakers. One of these prints depicts forty-eight peaks, all numbered and named, that can be seen from Orrest Head, and this drawing must have been familiar to AW as well as an influence on his work.

Baddeley was the Victorian equivalent of Wainwright. His first Lake District guide was published in 1880 and catered for the new visitors arriving by train at Windermere. After his death, his impact on the popularization of this area was considered worthy of a memorial, the Baddeley Clock Tower, which still stands by the main road down to the lake, halfway between Windermere and Bowness.

AW's life-changing experience at Orrest Head, followed by his night in a Windermere B&B, was the start of a week AW and his cousin spent walking in Lakeland. AW was transformed by this holiday in June 1930 and almost a year later, in May 1931, he returned for another week of climbing mountains. Taking on the role of expedition leader, he persuaded three other colleagues from

Blackburn Town Hall to join him for a six-day Whitsuntide walking tour of Lakeland. AW had planned for the first day a gruelling 16-mile hike north to Patterdale. So it was that after alighting by bus at Windermere train station on a Saturday lunchtime, AW led his party of novices – Jim Sharples, Eric Maudsley and Harry Driver – up to Orrest Head as the first port of call on his hand-written itinerary.

Orrest Head is so ingrained in the cult of Wainwright that his panoramic view of the fells from this viewpoint found itself engraved on the summit plinth. In June 2010, members of the Wainwright Society celebrated the eightieth anniversary of AW's first visit to the Lakes by re-enacting his 1930 journey from Blackburn to Orrest Head. This involved dressing up in period clothes, catching an old Leyland bus (or two) from Blackburn to Windermere, and retracing AW's footsteps from the train station and the short walk up to Orrest Head, where they were joined by local schoolchildren.

If Orrest Head is right up there with Haystacks in the pantheon of revered Lakeland places associated with AW, then it may come as a surprise to discover that it never made it into the *Pictorial Guides*. Orrest Head is not one of the 214 fells recorded in the seven volumes of AW's guides to the fells. It was simply not high enough. In the 1950s AW was obsessed with recording the high fells, not the little hills on the fringes. If it had been a few hundred feet higher, Orrest Head could have sneaked its way into *The Far Eastern Fells*, as did Sallows and Sour Howes, its loftier but fairly nondescript neighbours to the north.

Orrest Head did eventually get the *Pictorial Guide* treatment, however, when it appeared in *The Outlying Fells*. Its four-page entry, sandwiched between Reston Scar and School Knott, includes an acknowledgement that this was AW's 'first ascent in Lakeland'. His sketched view from the summit also turns up in *Westmorland Heritage*, in the parish entry for Windermere.

'Wainwright' peak baggers might like to note that this stage of the walk takes in three of *The Outlying Fells*. Just to the south of Orrest Head it visits School Knott the haunt of Windermere dog walkers. But first, after the steep climb out of Kendal, it follows the limestone ridge of Scout Scar, the haunt of Kendal dog walkers. AW was very familiar with the popular viewpoints of Scout Scar and Cunswick Scar, which rise above the western edge of the town to reveal a dramatic panorama of mountains beyond the Lyth Valley. The ridge was only a few miles walk from his house via the footpaths across the golf course on Kendal Fell. AW's sketches of the Scout Scar escarpment and the 'Mushroom' shelter sitting upon it turn up in both *The Outlying Fells* and *Westmorland Heritage*.

AW notes in his introduction to *The Outlying Fells* that the book was requested by readers. He dedicates it to 'The Old-Timers On The Fells' and there are jokey references running through the book to old age, physical ailments and the imminence of death. AW was sixty-six when he wrote it but did not resemble the cartoon figure on the front and back covers of the book, of a skinny bald old man running out of puff. AW was big and heavy, with a full head of white hair, and still capable of getting up mountains despite all his years of pipe smoking.

This book, written in 1973, was a return after nearly eight years to the successful format of the *Pictorial Guides*. AW put a lot of effort into *The Outlying Fells* and the book has a sense of enjoyment that suggests AW was back doing what he liked best. He was to spend the rest of the 1970s and 1980s producing straightforward sketchbooks and large-format books illustrated with photographs, so whether he realized it or not, *The Outlying Fells* is something of a swansong, in that it was the last time he wrote a book in this format. Following on from *Pennine Way Companion* and *A Coast to Coast Walk*, there was even a 'Personal Log' section at the back of the book for readers to record details of their own journeys.

In the period of over forty years that had elapsed between AW's first walk up Orrest Head in 1930 and his rediscovering it for *The Outlying Fells* in the early 1970s, AW's life had been transformed, but perhaps not as dramatically as the world outside. In 1930 Adolf Hitler was still to rise to power in Germany on the back of the Great Depression, while Mahatma Gandhi was being arrested for fermenting unrest in British India. But four decades on from Amy Johnson's solo adventure in a Gyspy Moth, not only had man landed on the moon but scientists were splicing genes. In 1973, the international community was on the brink of crisis as war broke out in the Middle East and oil rocketed in price to trigger a new global depression.

Technological advancements had seen off Kendal's post-war Borough Treasurer. AW retired from his council post in 1967, slightly unnerved at the rise of machines, in the form of computers and calculators, in local government offices across the land. As he states in Ex-*Fellwanderer*, 'Mechanics were taking the place of clerks.' He left office in a huff – and a puff of Three Nuns tobacco – and was content to sit at his desk at home in Kendal Green and remain within the comforting old world of pen and ink.

This stage of the walk passes through five county parishes that AW sketched in *Westmorland Heritage*. Beyond the Kendal bypass, the route enters the parish of Underbarrow and Bradleyfield (one parish) and follows a north-westerly line across the boundaries of Helsington, Crook, Nether Staveley and Windermere. The towns of Kendal and Windermere are largely separated by the extensive rural parishes of Underbarrow and Crook, with their scattered hamlets and pretty becks flowing south through the Lyth Valley.

AW had a liking for this countryside of winding hedged lanes, rolling hills and whitewashed cottages, as he thought it the landscape most typical of Westmorland. Added to its attractiveness was the fact that it was unspoilt countryside free of fast roads, most of the traffic between Kendal and Windermere being carried by the speedy A591 road further to the east. AW's sketches of this area for *Westmorland Heritage* show his usual rich mix of subjects: prominent viewpoints, parish churches and old farmsteads, together with the new country houses of industrialists on the shores of Windermere.

Kendal Town Hall to Crook Old Church (7½ miles)

Cross the junction outside the Town Hall and walk up All Hallows Lane past the Miles Thompson pub. Continue steeply uphill as the road bends left into the beast of a hill that is Beast Banks.

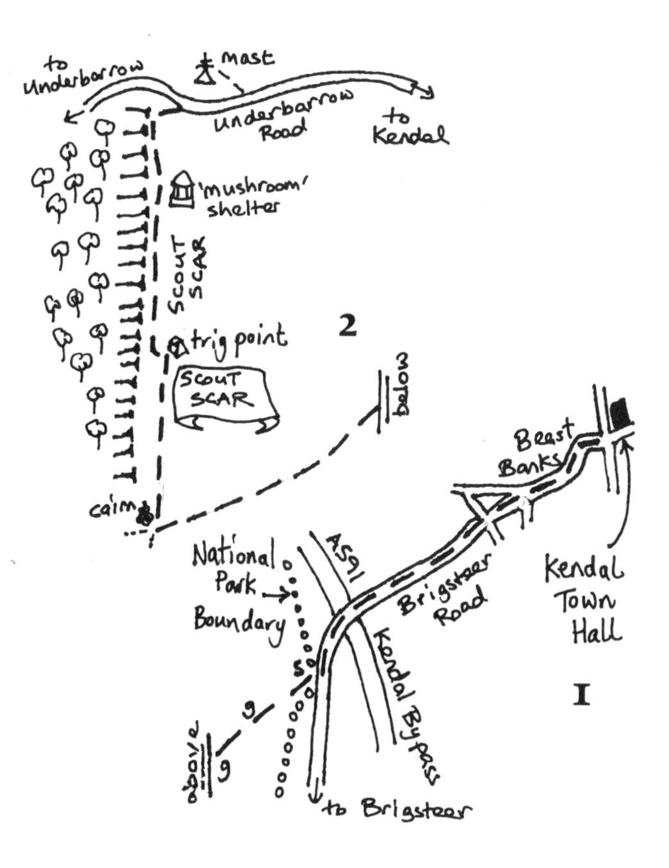

All Hallows Lane once led to All Hallows Chapel, on the right-hand side of the lane opposite the Black Swan Inn. Beast Banks takes its name possibly from the ancient cattle fair held hereabouts, or from a bull-baiting site, and led uphill to Kendal Fell, which in the eighteenth and nineteenth centuries was a patchwork of limestone quarries, kilns and terraces of tenter frames on which cloth was stretched. Beast Banks was also the site of a Presbyterian chapel, and the entrance to the old burial ground can be seen higher up on the left-hand side of the road, where an inscribed gateway reads 'Scotch Burial Ground 1760–1855'.

The Miles Thompson pub is named after the Kendal architect who became a partner in the firm of George Webster. Miles Thompson designed this pub; it was formerly Shearman House, Kendal's public washhouse and baths, built in 1863. Thompson also built houses further up Beast Banks on the same side. Beyond the Black Swan, Number 21 has a gable end, on the top of which sits a little statuette of Miles Thompson himself.

Keep walking uphill until you reach a junction where a road signed for Brigsteer forks left.

AW was not the only writer living in Kendal in the 1970s. At Number 32 Greenside, a terraced cottage at the top of Beast Banks, ex-mobile librarian John Cunliffe was creating Postman Pat, the incredibly successful children's TV character. The terrace of Greenside can be seen on the right-hand side of the road where the road to Brigsteer forks left. A red pillarbox stands outside Number 10 Greenside, the old Beast Banks sub-post office that provided the inspiration for the character. In 2004, Kendal Civic Society placed a plaque on the wall of the sub-post office which, unlike its fictional 'Greendale' equivalent, closed in 2003.

Join the Brigsteer road and follow the right-hand side of it along the edge of a green. At the next road junction, cross over and continue straight ahead along the pavement of Brigsteer Road. The road soon climbs steeply again to cross over the A591 Kendal bypass. Follow the wide grassy verge of the road, which enters a straight flat section. Look out on the right for an old milestone (dated 1900) in the wall and join the footpath on the same side by crossing a wall stile.

Every Kendal resident must have been relieved when the town's bypass opened in 1971, taking most of the tourist traffic away from the congested town centre. At the wall stile you enter the Lake District National Park for the first time, and pass from Kendal into the parish of Underbarrow and Bradleyfield. Beyond the next few fields the footpath leaves the National Park very briefly when it enters the parish of Helsington, but the ridge top of Scout Scar brings you back into the National Park, where the route stays for the rest of the walk.

A grassy path leads across the former Kendal racecourse to a metal kissing gate in a wall at the boundary of open access country. Continue straight ahead to another metal kissing gate in the next boundary wall. Follow the main track gradually uphill, heading for the limestone ridge in the distance. The view opens up south and west to the villages of the Lyth Valley. Keep to the main track, which winds steadily uphill, aiming to the right of woodland, to reach the ridge top to the left of a large cairn.

Turn right at a crossroads of tracks and follow the ridge of the broad limestone plateau, heading directly north. You will soon reach the trig point (751 feet) on Scout Scar, in front of a wall. Turn left here and follow the right wall side down to its end, to join the path following the escarpment edge above a sheer drop down to the Lyth Valley. Turn right and follow the path along the grassy limestone edge that leads to the popular 'Mushroom' shelter.

Scout Scar is the first 'Wainwright' you encounter on the walk – if you include *The Outlying Fells* in your list of Lakeland

Scout Scar and Mushroom Shelter, Underbarrow

fells surveyed by AW; some don't, of course. Scout Scar, 764 feet high, is the first entry in *The Outlying Fells* and AW describes the walk up to the summit shelter from Kendal town centre as 'a pleasure every step of the way'. The highest point is where the 'Mushroom' summit shelter was constructed in 1912 as a memorial to the coronation of George V. The unique 360-degree view indicator inside the roof of the shelter will help you plot the route ahead. AW's walk along Scout Scar in *The Outlying Fells* also includes the slightly lower summit of Cunswick Scar, further to the north. Our walk follows AW's route towards this, although it does not visit it.

Continue north on the path along the limestone edge, which soon swings right at a bench, with a good view north to Cunswick Scar and Cunswick Fell. The path drops down the hillside to reach Underbarrow Road through a kissing gate.

Go directly across the road and join the path opposite leading up to the Scout Scar car park entrance in an old quarry. Turn right, following the path through trees around two sides of the car park. The main path then swings left and passes the fence of the Scar Quarry

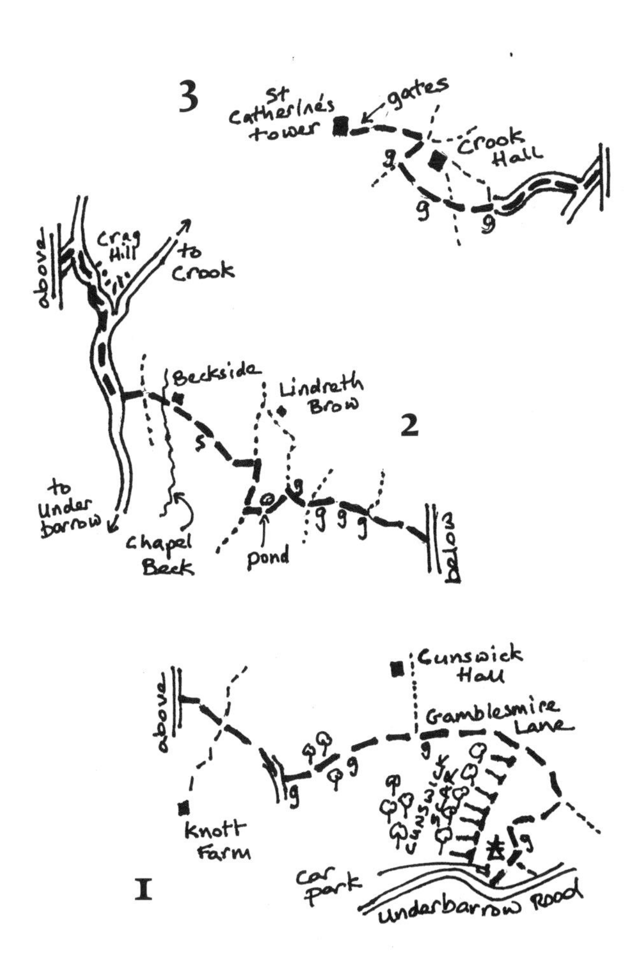

transmitter on the left. Join the access track and turn left along it through woodland to reach a kissing gate. Go through this and follow the left wall side to the wall corner. Turn right here, following the path for 'Cunswick Fell 1¼ miles'. Follow the left wall side along a grassy path looking down to Kendal. This soon leads to a crossroads of four paths by a gateway in the wall on the left.

Cunswick Hall gateway and farm

Turn left here through the open gateway following the track known as Gamblesmire Lane. This drops downhill and skirts woodland, continuing through a gate and following a right field edge to meet a path junction by an open gateway just south of Cunswick Hall.

AW sketched Cunswick Hall in *Westmorland Heritage* and notes it as the oldest residence in the parish of Underbarrow and Bradleyfield. There was a pele tower here and the hall became the ancestral home of one of the county's prominent families, the Leyburnes. Unfortunately it all went horribly wrong for them as a result of their misplaced allegiance to the Stuart cause in the Jacobite Rising of 1715. Their estate at Cunswick was forfeited and passed to the hands of the county's biggest landowners, the Lowthers.

Continue straight ahead, with the wall now on your left. Go through a gate and enter woodland. The stony track gradually drops downhill and leaves the woodland, continuing as a narrow hedged path, which passes through a gate and joins a farm lane. Turn right along this, crossing first a beck and then a cattle grid. Follow a hedged lane uphill to a crossroads of tracks. Go straight ahead here, following a hedged track uphill. This becomes a lovely coppiced bridleway enclosed by an archway of trees.

When you reach the track at the bottom of the hill go left through the gate along a bridleway. Bear slightly right and keep the hedge boundary on the immediate right. The bridleway passes through another gate just before it crosses a little beck over a bridge. Continue straight ahead uphill along the right wall side to reach the top field corner by two gates. Ignore the gate leading into the field on the right and go through the gate directly ahead.

In the next field ignore the obvious track swinging right alongside the wall. Instead continue straight ahead, uphill. On the brow of the hill there is a good view down to the pretty valley formed by Chapel Beck. Bear slightly right downhill to a wooden gate, the left of two gates at the hedge boundary. The gate marks a junction of bridleways. Bear left in the next field, continuing downhill and skirting around the left-hand side of a dried-up pond. On the far side of this is a faint track alongside a ruined wall and solitary gatepost. Swing sharp right here and follow a right field edge. This heads in the direction of a large white house, Lindreth Brow, nestling under Bell Hill. At the far right-hand corner of the field is a kissing gate but do not go through this.

Instead turn sharp left, now following the right-hand side of the same field. At the wall corner on the right follow the obvious grassy track climbing slightly uphill in the next field. The chimneys of the nearby farm, Beckside, come into view straight ahead. Go through a gate and join a farm track. Turn left along this farm track and follow it to Beckside, reached through a gate. Keep to the track as it runs around the side of the houses and becomes the access road, crossing Chapel Beck. Continue straight ahead to join the Crook–Underbarrow road.

Chapel Beck rises in hillside springs north of Crook and flows south through Underbarrow, fed by numerous other streams to form the River Pool. Here it joins the River Gilpin, its close neighbour to the west, which rises in springs on hillsides above Bowness. Together, the rivers Gilpin and Pool drain the flat mosses of the Lyth Valley, an area of impassable peat bogs until nineteenth-century drainage improvements, and they meet the River Kent near its Morecambe Bay estuary.

Turn right along the road and follow it uphill. At a sharp right-hand bend leave it by going straight ahead along a narrow lane, which climbs over the side of Crag Hill. This minor road is the boundary between the parishes of Underbarrow and Crook, and beyond Crag Hill you enter Crook parish. After approximately ¼ mile leave the lane via the first side lane on the left, beginning at a gate signed for Crook Hall Farm. Turn right at the next side lane, following the signs for Crook Hall. This lane winds uphill and swings right at a cattle grid. Leave the track to Crook Hall Farm on this bend by going straight ahead through a gate signed as a bridleway to 'Birk Moss ¾ mile'. Follow a grassy track through the field, aiming for the church tower that can be seen straight ahead a few fields away. Crook Hall can be glimpsed over to the right.

AW mentions Crook Hall in *Westmorland Heritage* when referring to its resident Royalist sympathizer, known as 'Robin the Devil'. This was actually Robert Philipson, who rode into Kendal to do battle with Roundheads. The Philipson family lived at Crook Hall, formerly Thwatterden Hall, in Tudor and Stuart times.

Pass a small pond on the right and go through a gate into the next field, now following the right wall side to reach a path junction. This indicates a bridleway left to High House. Ignore this by turning right along a path following a right wall side towards two gates to the left of the farm. Do not go through the gates but turn sharp left in the same field and follow the faint path leading to a gate in the wall in front of the old church tower. Go through this and enter the enclosed old churchyard of St Catherine's.

Crook Old Church to Troutbeck Bridge (7½ miles)

Only the restored bell tower, built around 1620, remains of the original St Catherine's Church, which served Crook Hall and the surrounding parish for nearly 400 years. When the church was demolished before it fell down, the tower was kept as a local landmark while a brand-new St Catherine's Church was built a quarter of a mile away on the B5284 Crook–Windermere road.

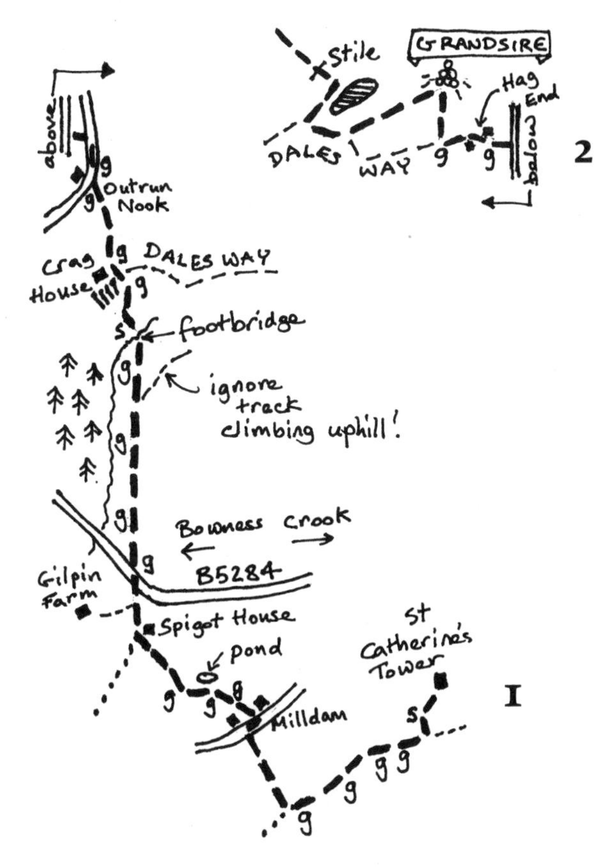

A peep over the north side of the wall enclosing the old church site reveals the new church, built in the 1880s, and offers a view of the twin peaks of Grandsire and School Knott. They remain on the horizon for the next few miles and are the next objective of the walk. For *Westmorland Heritage*, AW sketched both the old bell tower and the new Victorian St Catherine's Church, the latter of which he was not over-excited by.

Return to the path outside the churchyard and turn right to a wall corner. Continue directly ahead to meet a wall on the left. Keep between the wall and gorse bushes and cross a squeeze stile into the next field. Head downhill along the left wall side to join a farm track. Turn right along this track and go through another gate, continuing along the right edge of the next field. When the hedge boundary swings right, bear slightly left and continue through a gate into the next field. Walk straight ahead along the right wall side of the next field; the path continues straight ahead as an enclosed track. Go through another gate and turn sharp right, following a narrow farm road downhill. This soon meets a lane opposite Brow Head Farm.

Turn right downhill along the lane only as far as Milldam House, the next cottage on the left. Turn left along the track next to the

The new church and the old church, Crook

house: this leads between the beck and the garden before crossing the beck. Leave the track on the left and go through a gate on the left, signed as a byway. Skirt around the left-hand side of a tarn and then follow a track with a wall to the right. Ignoring a footpath on the right, go through a kissing gate and continue along a walled track leading to Spigot House. Continue straight ahead around the left-hand side of the house, following the driveway to the junction with the B5284 road.

Cross this road with care and join the path directly opposite, following a gated track uphill. When the track bends right and starts to climb steeply uphill, leave it by going straight ahead through bracken and gorse to a gate and wall stile in the next field boundary. With a beck down to the left follow the waymarked path straight ahead. This winds its way through gorse clumps and drops down to a footbridge over the beck. Turn right on the far side of the footbridge and follow the left wall side to cross another gate and wall stile. Follow the left wall side alongside the little beck.

The beck here is actually the infant River Gilpin, flowing south to Morecambe Bay. Upstream of the footbridge you have just crossed, the beck briefly marks the parish boundary between Crook and the neighbouring parish of Nether Staveley. With a landscape of bracken, heather and bare rocks now facing you, there is a sense that you have reached true Lakeland, with the softer limestone landscape that encircles Kendal now at an end.

On reaching the bracken at the bottom of the fell, bear right and then swing left uphill, climbing towards the farm, Crag House, glimpsed to the right of a large rock. The path runs around the side of the rock to reach a gate below the farm. Go through this and pass a gate on the right signed as the Dales Way. You join the Dales Way at this point and follow it for the next ½ mile.

The Dales Way is an 80-mile long-distance footpath from Ilkley to Windermere, which has proved popular since its inception. The way was devised by the West Riding Group of the Ramblers Association in 1968, and the original guidebook to the walk was written by Colin Speakman. At Crag Farm the Dales Way is almost near its end: it has only to skirt around School Knott and Brant Fell to reach its official end by Bowness Pier.

Follow the Dales Way by going straight ahead along a gravel path. Keep to the right wall side and skirt around the base of another crag to go through a gate in the next wall boundary. School Knott and Grandsire are straight ahead. Drop downhill, keeping the wall on the near right. Near the bottom of the field the path swings away from the wall and comes out at a kissing gate opposite the farm of Outrun Nook. Turn right along the road here and continue along the road for a short distance until you reach the access track to Hag End Farm on the left.

Turn left and follow the track to the farm. Go through the gate into the yard and bear right to pass between the tea room and the farmhouse. A gate leads around the back of the tea room and the path goes straight ahead, with a wall on the right, to pass through a kissing gate at the boundary of open access land.

Here, on the lower slopes of Grandsire, you are back in Crook parish, having briefly passed through the adjoining parish of Nether Staveley. Grandsire, 818 feet high, appears in *The Outlying Fells* as the supporting artiste of its near neighbour School Knott. Not deemed by AW worthy of its own chapter, Grandsire was climbed by AW and for that reason it is visited on this walk. He climbed it from Windermere, having first climbed over School Knott and seems to find Grandsire the more interesting of the two, recording it as 'a nice place for a siesta'.

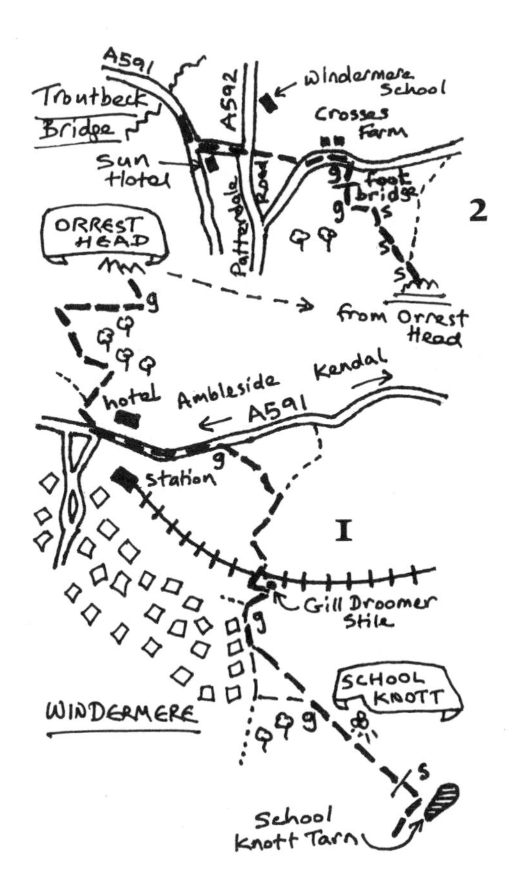

To reach the top of Grandsire, turn right after the kissing gate and walk uphill, close to the wall boundary on the right. There is no obvious path but this stretch of grassy fell is an open access area. The top of the hill is marked by a cairn on a rock outcrop and looking west, you can clearly see the well-used path going up School Knott from its tarn. To reach the tarn, follow the faint ridge path from Grandsire, aiming left of School Knott, to an open gateway in a wall. Go through this and continue straight ahead through rough pasture. Bear slightly left

downhill to rejoin the Dales Way footpath on the other side of a ruined wall in the left corner of the field. Follow the Dales Way down to a gate, which marks a parish boundary, where you leave Crook and enter Windermere. The Dales Way now turns left but leave it by turning sharp right and walking to the tarn. Turn left at the tarn and cross a stile in the wall to follow the obvious path to the top of School Knott.

School Knott, 760 feet high, provides a good view of Windermere, both town and lake, with the Langdale Pikes beyond. In *The Outlying Fells* AW climbs it from the train station, noting that the traditional approaches to the hill have been altered since the building of the post-war Droomer housing estate. AW points out that from the summit four sections of the lake are in view – at least, for those old timers who can still see!

Follow the path down the other side of School Knott and pass through a gate in the wall. The path forks into two by the bench and both forks lead to a tarmac path on the other side of the meadow; it is easiest to take the right fork and drop downhill through the open meadow. Bear right at the bottom of the meadow to join the tarmac path and turn right along this to pass through a gate. The track leads to an estate road (Mill Beck Close): cross this and continue opposite along a path running between a beck and houses. This leads to an old bridge over the beck to the left. Do not cross this but continue straight ahead up the driveway to a house, Gill Droomer Stile, with a pretty garden. Cross the beck on the left in front of the house and turn right around the fence boundary to reach a stile and railway crossing.

Cross the Kendal–Windermere railway line with care and climb steps to enter parkland. Walk straight ahead along a grassy path that soon bears left, leading to a gate in a wall. Join the bridleway track in the next field and turn right. Follow the track through the next two fields: it soon swings left and follows a left wall side to reach a kissing gate on the A591 Kendal–Windermere road. Turn left and follow the pavement downhill into Windermere.

Summit outcrop, School Knott

Summit outcrop, Grandsire

Grandsire and Schoolknott Tarn

Just before you reach the access road to the train station on the left, you pass a row of stone cottages known as the Terrace on the same side. These five houses had gardens running down to the railway line and were built in 1855 for the executives of the Kendal and Windermere Railway Company. On the other side of the main road is the Windermere Hotel, built in 1854 as a joint venture between the railway company and the hotel's first owner, Richard Rigg. When AW arrived here in 1930 the establishment was still known as Rigg's Hotel.

Even before the working classes arrived in the village on cheap day excursions, the train link with Lancashire led to many wealthy Manchester industrialists building houses in the wooded hills around the lake that gave the station its name. The introduction of an express train meant that prosperous businessmen could travel between Manchester and Windermere in just over two hours. When the train line from Kendal first arrived here in 1847 it terminated in fields in the tiny hamlet of Birthwaite. Ten years of urban development around the station followed and in 1858 the new village of Windermere was officially recognized by the Post Office.

Windermere village was already a tourist mecca by the time AW got off the bus by the train station in 1930. Despite the traffic, the area around the road junction between the A591 and Victoria Street winding downhill towards Bowness and the lake is much the same as AW encountered it. The old station buildings remain; they are now Booths supermarket. The Victorian edifices of the present NatWest Bank and Rigg's Windermere Hotel still overlook the junction, although the ornamental fountain that once stood here has now gone.

To continue the walk to Troutbeck Bridge, take care and cross the busy A591 by the road junction. Take the Orrest Head path, clearly signed by a noticeboard and beginning at the furthest left of the three driveways here. Go straight ahead up a tarmac drive, ignoring the footpath sign on the left. Keep to the driveway – waymarked for

Orrest Head – view from the north

'Orrest Head Viewpoint' – as it zigzags uphill through woodland. A good view of Windermere village and lake is soon revealed. After passing Elleray Cottage on the right, the driveway becomes a track and soon swings sharp right to follow the woodland edge between a wall and fence. This leads to a kissing gate between the memorial stones to Arthur Henry Heywood. From here you soon reach the top of Orrest Head.

As a fitting memorial to the landowner Arthur Henry Heywood, his family gave Orrest Head to Windermere Urban District Council in 1902 so that the public could enjoy the viewpoint. Old photos confirm there was a view indicator erected on a stone plinth here when AW first arrived. This would have helped him identify all the summits that can be seen from here. The present plinth with a viewfinder showing a panorama of the fells was erected in 2002 to commemorate the centenary of Orrest Head being open to the public. The viewfinder had gone missing but was replaced in 2012, in a joint venture with Windermere Town Council and the Wainwright Society, who were celebrating their tenth anniversary. There were probably one or two cast-iron seats on top of Orrest Head when AW first came here but, at the time of writing, there are a total of seven seats in various styles!

The view across the lake to the fells has not changed since 1930. This is due to the fact that the Lake District was designated a national park in 1951, which has protected this area from inappropriate development ever since. The unchanged view from Orrest Head is justification alone for the often-criticized tough approach taken by the planning authority for this national park.

Take one of the well-used paths leading down the back of Orrest Head looking across fields towards the white-painted Causeway Farm. The paths drop steeply to a wall corner and a path junction. Go through the kissing gate on the left, following the path signposted 'Crosses Farm ½ mile'. Head uphill directly towards the lake and on the brow of the hill drop to a ladder stile and gate in the next wall boundary. The grassy path continues downhill to a kissing gate in a wall at another path junction. Go through the gate and continue along the path, now signed as 'Crosses Farm 400 yards'. Follow the right wall side downhill and at a waymarker post, drop down a steep bank and go through a gate in this wall. The path enters the National Trust estate of St Catherine's, once the property of the Earl of Bradford. Continue straight ahead through Low Hag Wood, still following the signed footpath for Crosses Farm. The path crosses a footbridge and continues straight ahead to reach a gate on to a lane.

Turn left along the lane, passing the Victorian slate buildings of Crosses Farm on the right. A short distance beyond the farm, a track forks right off the lane at a wall corner. Join this stony track between walls, which drops downhill between the private grounds of Windermere School to reach the A592 Patterdale road. Cross this main road with care and continue downhill along the narrow lane directly opposite. This drops steeply to the roadside village of Troutbeck Bridge next to the Sun Hotel on the A591 Windermere–Ambleside road.

Stage Seven
TROUTBECK BRIDGE TO PATTERDALE POST OFFICE
(13 miles)

'The Ordnance Survey map and Baddeley I knew by heart: something else was needed.I started to draw pictures . . . It was fun at first, then a fascinating pastime, building a mountain on a blank sheet of paper.'
Fellwanderer

Now the walk leaves the lesser fells behind and for the first time climbs one of the high ridges gloriously revealed at Orrest Head. This is the first true mountain day, as the route climbs to the summit of High Street, across which the Romans built a road. It also visits the tops of other 'Wainwright' peaks and takes you from Lakeland's longest lake, Windermere, to the second longest, Ullswater. This stage is a journey through Book Two of AW's *Pictorial Guides, The Far Eastern Fells,* as well as a continuing exploration of the parishes described in *Westmorland Heritage.* The last 4 miles, from the Knott to Patterdale village, also follow a section of AW's *A Coast to Coast Walk.*

A Man Obsessed by Mountains

AW's early experiences of the Lakes did not find an immediate outlet in prose, poetry, illustrations or even a diary. The images of mountains, lakes and tarns remained fresh in his mind's eye but in the 1930s when he returned from trips to the Lakes he largely sketched not the mountains but doodles of his office colleagues in Blackburn Town Hall. However, by the end of that decade AW was drawing landscapes and writing prose, in particular the unpublished manuscript he wrote of his 1938 Pennine journey. Along the route of this solitary walk from Settle to Hadrian's Wall and back, AW made detailed sketches on postcards of places passed along the way and sent them home to Lawrence Wolstenholme.

In the 1940s AW was sketching Kendal, while in his lengthy letters to Lawrence Wolstenholme he waxed lyrical about his idyllic new life amid the fells. Hunter Davies's *The Wainwright Letters* includes much of this correspondence, revealing that even during the war, AW had dreams of undertaking a big writing project. The 1940s for AW were a very busy period, in which he had to establish himself in a new job, settle his family into a new town and, at the end of the decade, take up the role of Borough Treasurer and plan the building of a new house and garden. At the same time he squeezed in weekend expeditions walking the fells, often in the company of his son Peter.

The new decade of the 1950s was the dawn of a new optimism for Britain, the start of an economic upturn and a consumer boom after years of wartime gloom. It also signalled a new dawn at Kendal Green, where the settled Borough Treasurer was unsettled by the thought of spending the next twenty years rattling around his new bungalow with a wife he didn't love. Some men would have got stuck into the garden, as indeed AW did. But an alpine rockery was not enough to satisfy a man with a natural flair for drawing and writing who had spent the past twenty years indulging in his passion for OS maps and exploring on foot the mountains of the Lake District. He was not going to let all that knowledge and interest go to waste by spending the rest of his life trimming the garden hedge.

Sunday, 9 November 1952 probably saw AW in his capacity as a chief town official attending the Remembrance Day Service at Kendal's Cenotaph. Apart from this event, it was a typically quiet autumn day. The town's cinemas were shut on Sundays; the weekend's latest issue of the *Westmorland Gazette* was full of no news, the most interesting headline being 'The Bisto Car is Coming Your Way Shortly'. On that particular Sunday it was unlikely AW stood by his window expectantly awaiting the Bisto Kids to pop in on Ruth with their free giveaway of one-pound grocery vouchers. In any case, he had something a bit different planned for his evening.

That night, while Al Martino became the first ever UK number one in the first ever UK pop chart, AW sat down in his house with pen, ink and a blank sheet of paper and completed the first page of his first *Pictorial Guide*, covering the Eastern Fells. Telling the story himself in *Fellwanderer*, he notes that the first page he wrote that night described the ascent of Dove Crag from Ambleside. Appropriately the lyrics of Al Martino's number one single, 'Here in my Heart' expressed AW's emotional predicament:

> Here in my heart I'm alone, I'm so lonely,
> Here in my heart I just yearn for you only.

Of course, AW's yearning was not for his wife Ruth but for Dove Crag and the other 213 Lakeland mountains with which he was going to become intimate over the next thirteen years of his life.

Between November 1952 and the autumn of 1965, AW was a man possessed by mountains. He had set himself the mammoth task of completing seven volumes of a comprehensive guide to the Lakeland fells and absolutely nothing was going to get in his way. Not council business outside the normal office hours. Not his wife Ruth, who walked her dogs, put AW's meals on the table and kept well out of his way. Not son Peter, who left home and moved to a new job in Windermere in 1953. Not family relations from Blackburn and Penistone, who occasionally dropped in and whom AW left for Ruth to entertain. Not Kendal acquaintances driving past the Windermere Road bus stop on Sunday mornings and attempting to offer the Borough Treasurer a casual lift. Not the weather. Not even the brief but unforgettable appearance in AW's office of a vivacious woman in 1957 –Betty McNally, AW's future wife.

AW started work on Book One in an age of wartime rationing but by the time he finished Book Seven, Britons were enjoying foreign holidays, buying TV sets and driving their own cars; those thirteen years had taken Britain from post-war austerity to never having had it so good, to James Bond and Mary Quant mini-skirts

Hunter Davies's biography of Wainwright evokes the pioneering spirit of the mid-1950s, when AW delivered his hand-written, personal love letter to the fells not to a big London publisher but to the entrepreneurial Kendal Borough Librarian Henry Marshall. Marshall's own residence at Low Bridge in Kentmere village acted as AW's first publishing house, where he stored the *Pictorial Guides*, boxed them up and sent them out, dealt with orders, and received all correspondence – for the fan letters soon trickled in – on behalf of the publicity-shy author. Henry Marshall is very much the unsung hero of the Wainwright success story, his close links with local booksellers proving invaluable in promoting AW's new book. Sadly the partnership ended badly when AW turned to the *Westmorland Gazette* to be his publisher, as well as printer, from 1963 onwards. Marshall was bitterly upset and, tragically, died only a year later. AW writes in *Fellwanderer*, 'Henry, too, has passed on, and lies in the little churchyard of Kentmere, amongst the hills.'

This stage of the walk takes the walker along the valleys and ridges of AW's second *Pictorial Guide, The Far Eastern Fells*, written in 1955 and 1956. He was cracking on with this book while at the same time trying to drum up sales for the 2,000 copies of Book One, *The Eastern Fells*, published in May 1955. After a slow start, by early 1956 AW had sold enough copies of *The Eastern Fells* to pay his printer's bill and another 1,000 copies were issued in Easter of that year. The AW bandwagon had started to roll, and with the first book clearly popular, even as early as 1956 there was little doubt that AW would have a market for his *Pictorial Guides*. All he had to do now was write the rest of them.

In researching *The Far Eastern Fells*, AW covered ground that was familiar to him, as in 1930 he had spent day two of his first ever week's holiday in the Lakes walking up the Troutbeck Valley and climbing Scot Rake, to reach the high mountain ridge overlooking Kentmere. He climbed Thornthwaite Crag and High Street and then continued along the route of the Roman road marked on the OS map, following it northwards for several miles over a number of grassy summits before dropping down to Ullswater. It is likely he visited Rampsgill Head, High Raise, Wether Hill, Loadpot Hill and possibly Arthur's Pike, before dropping down to the lake shore and a night in a Pooley Bridge hotel run by a man from Bolton.

AW was back in these fells less than a year later on his 1931 Whitsuntide tour. His intended itinerary for day one was a 16-mile hike from Windermere to Patterdale, taking in the summits of Yoke, Ill Bell, Froswick, Thornthwaite Crag, High Street, the Knott and Angletarn Pikes, but his walking party never got to Patterdale on the first day. Torrential rain meant they had to abandon their expedition on the Ill Bell ridge and return to the Troutbeck Valley. Hopefully on this route you will have better luck.

As AW embarked on his *Pictorial Guides* project in the early 1950s, his research was facilitated by the Ordnance Survey issuing a series of maps at the scale of 2½ inches to 1 mile; the detail of these was invaluable. Added to this he had a set of old 6 inch to 1 mile maps that revealed a wealth of detailed information, particularly about Lakeland's industrial past. AW's maps and camera were his essential tools.

Book Two, published in 1957 and dedicated to 'The Men Who Built The Stone Walls', is a guide to 36 fells, all over 1,100 feet, lying east of Ullswater and the Kirkstone Pass. This stage of our walk climbs to the summit of High Street, the highest of the Far Eastern Fells. It also visits two linked 'Wainwrights', Thornthwaite Crag and the Knott, both given their own chapters in *The Far Eastern Fells.*

As it is the highest of *The Far Eastern Fells,* AW gives a lot of attention to High Street. He seems particularly keen for the walker to head towards the vertical cliffs on the eastern edge of the summit so as not to miss the prospect down to Blea Water and Mardale. His favourite ascent of the mountain was from this valley, via the ridge of Rough Crag and Long Stile. He considered this climb a classic and it resurfaced as one of the eighteen walks in the 1980s Michael Joseph publication *Fellwalking with Wainwright.* High Street also reappeared in another Michael Joseph book, one of the last AW wrote, and published in 1991, the year he died: in *Wainwright's Favourite Lakeland Mountains,* AW included a chapter on High Street, as one of his twenty best summits.

The Far Eastern Fells is ingrained with familiar themes that recur in every volume of the *Pictorial Guides.* AW's love of wildlife and natural beauty contrasts with his detestation of man's impact on both. He deplores large man-made intrusions on the Lake District, particularly in the form of newly planted conifer forests and reservoir constructions, and is concerned that more ugly developments may come. He is generally annoyed and irritated by the increasing number of motorists in the Lakes and scoffs at their attempts to climb mountains. AW also has a persistent fascination with summit cairns, constantly pointing them out to readers and being slightly miffed when he discovers new cairns have suddenly appeared.

In Book Two, AW expresses his opinions. He deplores the grouse butts on Loadpot Hill and Sour Howes; he laughs at the 'sandals and slippers' brigade who park their cars and walk up Hallin Fell, which he calls 'the motorists' fell'; below Wether Hill he shows 'little interest' in cultivated farmland. Throughout the book he often treads a fine line regarding access, consciously trying not to upset landowners in sensitive areas like the Nab and the Martindale Deer Forest. Despite all the sweeping changes AW lived in during the twentieth century, open access to mountain and moorlands was not one of them. Officially sanctioned freedom to roam came too late for AW and his generation, so on unwelcoming hills like the Nab he was always a trespasser.

AW's overriding concern in *The Far Eastern Fells* is clearly man's interference in Mardale. In his lifetime AW had seen the village of Mardale Green and the Dun Bull Inn disappear under the waters of Manchester Corporation's Haweswater Reservoir. The valley had been flooded in the 1930s and at the time of writing *The Far Eastern Fells*, Manchester was also in the process of diverting water from the beck in the neighbouring unspoilt valley of Swindale into the new reservoir. AW had a fear of the engineers who had come to wreak havoc in his beloved Westmorland. In his comments relating to Selside Pike, he says, 'Please, Manchester, leave it [Swindale] as you nearly found it!' In the chapter on High Raise, AW laments the loss of the old inn at Mardale Green and does not like the new Haweswater Hotel, catering for motorists rather than walkers. Finally, in the conclusion, AW notes the 'aggressively ugly' tidemark of the new reservoir.

In 'Some Personal Notes in Conclusion' with which AW ended each *Pictorial Guide* readers gain a few insights into AW's personal life, and in *The Far Eastern Fells*, the reader learns that AW walked on his own and did not drive a car. It is also clear that he loves the fells east of the Kirkstone Pass for their complete solitude and the absence of traffic. The strange paradox in this conclusion is that AW, who preferred to have the hills to himself, positively encourages walkers (not motorists) to come and discover this little known area of 'neglected' fells.

This stage also takes us through the pages of *Westmorland Heritage*, leaving Windermere parish when the walk crosses the Trout Beck and continuing through the large rural parishes of Troutbeck and Patterdale, both of which cover extensive areas from mountain top to valley floor. Troutbeck parish went from the lake shore of Windermere to the summits of Stony Cove Pike and Thornthwaite Crag, enclosing Troutbeck Park in the valley below.

AW devotes twenty pages to Patterdale in *Westmorland Heritage*, which is not surprising, as its parish boundaries extend from the summit of Helvellyn in the west to the summit of High Street in the east, with the numerous valleys at the head of Ullswater in between. AW considered Patterdale the most perfectly fashioned parish in the whole county. This stage also briefly passes through another parish, Martindale, in the vicinity of Angle Tarn, before it re-enters Patterdale and descends to the bright lights of the village along AW's Coast to Coast route.

Troutbeck Valley

Troutbeck Bridge to High Street Summit (7½ miles)

From the Sun Hotel follow the pavement on the right towards the nearby pedestrian crossing and garage. Turn right at the crossing, joining the path signed to Patterdale Road, which runs uphill between cottages.

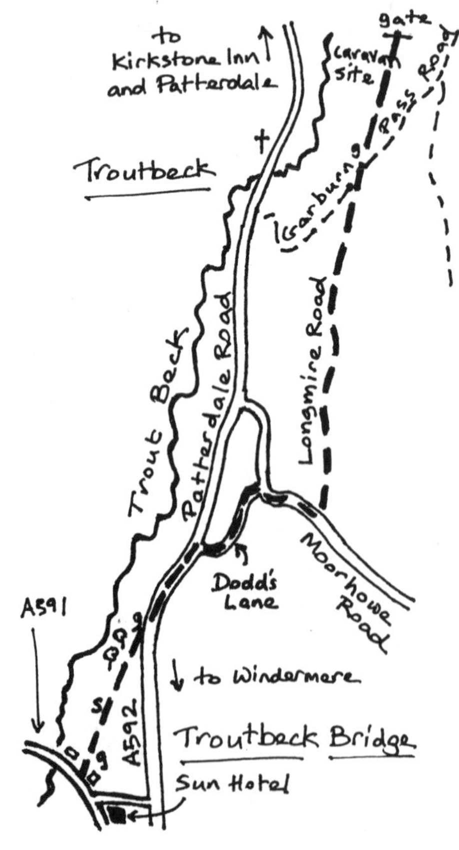

Some eight years before AW was born, the Sun Inn was where the one-time champion wrestler of England died. Thomas Longmire (1823–99) was a popular Victorian character around these parts; he won 174 wrestling bouts in the 1850s, became a Bowness publican and had eleven sons. He retired to the Sun Inn and is buried in the graveyard of Troutbeck's parish church.

The roadside settlement of Troutbeck Bridge largely lies within the parish of Windermere. The Trout Beck, crossed by the A591 road, forms the boundary with the adjoining parish of Troutbeck, which the route does not enter until a few miles up the valley at Troutbeck Park. AW sketched the cluster of old cottages at the start of the footpath heading north to Patterdale Road in *Westmorland Heritage.*

The path swings left and more cottages are revealed. It goes straight ahead and enters a large field at a kissing gate. It is a steady climb straight up through the field to a wall stile at the next boundary. Continue in the same uphill direction through the next field to the top left

corner, where steps in the wall and a gate lead to the A592, Patterdale Road. The valley of the Trout Beck, heading for Windermere, can be glimpsed down the steep wooded bank on the left.

Continue straight ahead along the pavement on the left-hand side of the road. Follow it for about ¼ mile until the first lane turning on the right by a postbox. Cross the main road with care and follow this lane, Dodd's Lane, uphill. It winds past cottages to meet a higher road. Turn right along this, Moorhowe Road, and follow it, still going uphill for about ¼ mile until you reach the second farm access road on the left, signed as a bridleway.

This is Longmire Road. Follow it straight ahead for almost a mile until it reaches a gate near a crossroads of tracks. Continue straight ahead, ignoring the track forking right, which leads over the Garburn Pass to Kentmere. Keep to the walled track that follows the contour line at the foot of the fell with the flat pastures of the Trout Beck over to the left. It keeps above Limefitt Park caravan site and passes through several gates to reach the farm of Long Green Head. Keep to the gated track above Long Green Head, which crosses several becks cascading down from the steep-sided western flank of Yoke. The track skirts woodland and reaches a gate in the wall with a footbridge over Hagg Gill down to the left.

At this gate you cross from Windermere into Troutbeck parish, leaving behind the flat meadows of the Troutbeck Valley. The farm at Troutbeck Park sits just above the point where the two feeder valleys come down from the mountains and meet as one. Separating the valleys of the Trout Beck and Hagg Gill is the long distinctive spur known as the Tongue. On the Tongue's western flank the Trout Beck heads upstream to its head at Threshwaite Mouth, but our route follows the eastern flank, along Hagg Gill. You are now surrounded by the hills in *The Far Eastern Fells* and AW included the Tongue, or Troutbeck Tongue as he calls it, in his list of fells. At 1,191 feet high, it is the lowest peak of the thirty-six fells recorded in Book Two.

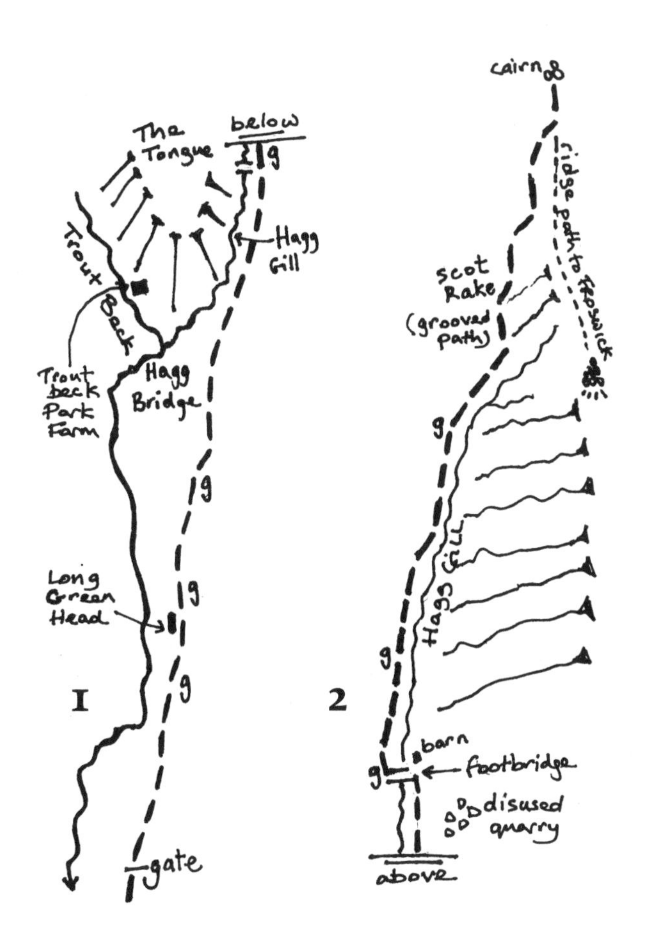

The Troutbeck Valley can lay claim to be the first real Lakeland valley that AW walked in, since day two of his June 1930 holiday took him this way as he climbed Scot Rake above Hagg Gill to reach the mountain ridge between Froswick and High Street. He sketched the valley's upper reaches many times and in *Westmorland Heritage* he comments that the large caravan and campsite in the valley had become an eyesore.

Beyond the gate, the track runs between Hagg Gill and the disused Park Quarry, soon bearing left to cross a footbridge over the stream by a barn. Climb up to the gate in the wall corner. Turn right along a track, now with the stream down on the right. Follow the track up the valley, keeping the wall on the right. After about ½ mile the wall turns sharp right; soon after this take the path bearing right and heading back towards the beck. Keep it on the near right and continue upstream. The path becomes steeper and climbs to a gate in a wall. Continue uphill, with a wall on the left and stream on the right. When the wall turns left, leave it and continue steeply up a grooved path, difficult to spot at first, which climbs the hillside through a series of terraced sections. This is Scot Rake. It climbs uphill almost for a mile, aiming for the ridge top north of the distinctive peak of Froswick.

Scot Rake is generally regarded as being part of the Roman road that climbed over High Street and linked the forts at Ambleside and Brougham, near Penrith. AW also accepted this view and seeing the 'Roman Road' marked on the OS map was the main reason why he chose this walk for his first mountain adventure. On the top of High Street the route of the Roman highway is clearly known, but there is some speculation about the route to the south – that it did not come up Scot Rake from Hagg Gill but took a more direct approach south, keeping to the high mountain ridge and crossing the peaks of Froswick, Ill Bell and Yoke. No Roman highway between High Street and Galava, the fort at the head of Windermere, has ever been identified with any certainty.

With a summit height of 2,359 feet, Froswick can lay claim to be the first proper mountain AW climbed on his 1930 June holiday, although he may not have actually visited the summit. Despite the mountain's terrifying aspect, in *Ex-Fellwanderer* AW indicates that he and cousin Eric climbed to the ridge below the highest point of Froswick and then continued north to Thornthwaite Crag and High Street. Froswick is, of course, recorded in *The Far Eastern Fells.* In order of height, AW records it as the twelfth highest fell out of a total of thirty-six peaks.

On reaching the ridge top you meet the path between Froswick and High Street. The summit of Froswick, a ½ mile away, can be visited by turning right here, but to continue the walk route turn left and almost immediately you will reach a fork in the path at a cairn. Take the left fork and the path climbs gradually to meet the wall leading to the tall stone beacon on the summit of Thornthwaite Crag.

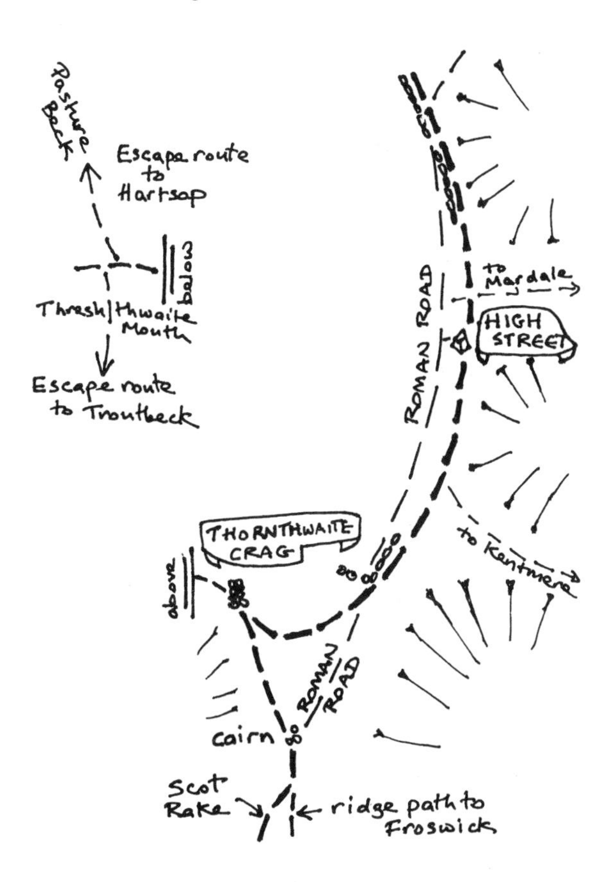

Along the ridge from Froswick runs the high parish boundary between Troutbeck, to the west, and Kentmere, to the east. Beyond the stone wall at Thornthwaite Beacon you enter Patterdale parish. Thornthwaite Crag, 2,569 feet high, is the fourth highest of the Far Eastern Fells and was well liked by AW for its commanding position and its view south to Windermere.

If weather conditions are bad and you do not wish to proceed over High Street, then follow AW's advice – given in The Far Eastern Fells – by following the boundary wall north-westwards from the beacon to descend steeply to Threshthwaite Mouth. From here you can follow a valley route along Pasture Beck northwards to Hartsop and eventually Patterdale.

In good weather, the route from Thornthwaite Crag to the broad escarpment of nearby High Street is easy to follow. Take the distinct path heading west from the beacon directly towards High Street. It soon meets a wall boundary. The Roman road follows the left-hand side of the wall but keep to the grassy path on the right wall side that leads to the 'trig point' on the summit on High Street less than a mile away.

The Roman road across High Street lies west of the summit 'trig point', and between them is the north–south stone wall that forms the boundary between the parishes of Patterdale, to the west, and Shap Rural, to the east. In *Westmorland Heritage*, AW includes sketches of High Street in his entry for Shap Rural. The summit is also a geographical watershed: to the south, streams flow to Windermere, the River Kent and, ultimately, Morecambe Bay, while streams flowing north head for Ullswater, the River Eden and, eventually, the Solway Firth. The mountain also forms the boundary between post-1974 district councils. In crossing High Street, you have left the administrative area of South Lakeland and are now in the district of Eden.

High Street Summit to Patterdale Post Office (5½ miles)

High Street, 2,718 feet high, is the highest of the Far Eastern Fells. The broad grassy plateau surrounding its summit meant it was ideal as a meeting place for shepherds from the numerous valleys below. For centuries, on 12 July, an annual fair was held on the top of the mountain, allowing stray sheep to be returned to their owners and attracting the locals with sports and events including wrestling and pony-trotting races. AW was aware of this story, perhaps intrigued that the OS map still recorded the summit of High Street as 'Racecourse Hill'.

The Roman road that gave High Street its name continued north, eventually reaching the fort at Brocavum, on the site later occupied by Brougham Castle. It was here that it joined the main military road to Carlisle and Hadrian's Wall. Sections of this other Roman highway, heading north from Bowland and the Lune Valley, have already been encountered in stages two and three of this walk.

Hayeswater from the Roman Road

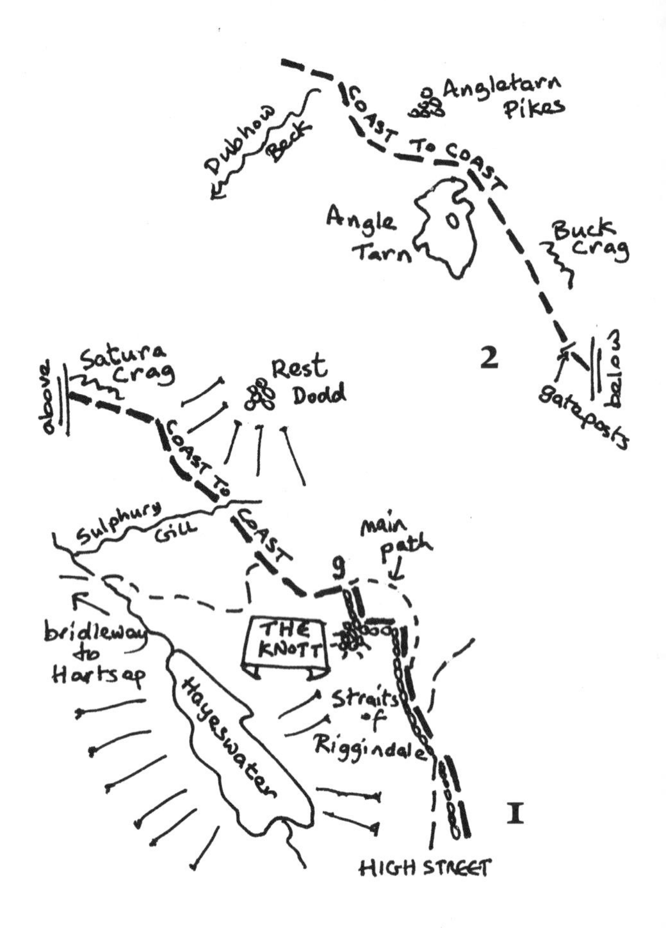

Continue straight ahead from the summit trig point, keeping the wall on the near left. You will soon reach a gateway in the wall at the Straits of Riggindale, the point where the ridge is at its narrowest. You briefly rejoin the Roman road here as it comes through the gateway on the left.

Continue straight ahead along the right wall side. Beyond the deep cleft of Riggindale a path forks right, but ignore this by continuing

High Street

straight ahead along the right wall side. You now leave behind the Roman road which heads directly towards Rampsgill Head. The path climbs again, heading for the rounded hill known as the Knott. The main path skirts around the side of this hill, but to visit the summit leave the main path by keeping to the wall side. The wall soon turns sharp left: turn with it to reach the summit cairn, which is on the other side of the wall.

The Knott, 2,423 feet high, is the tenth highest of the Far Eastern Fells and the third 'Wainwright' summit visited on this stage. When writing Book Two in the mid-1950s AW ascended it from Low Hartsop on the Kirkstone Road. It was also on the itinerary of day one of his 1931 Whitsuntide tour. The excellent view west from the Knott largely reveals the mountain peaks covered in AW's first *Pictorial Guide, The Eastern Fells*, dominated by the Helvellyn range. Pause for a moment on top of the Knott and reflect on the fact that in the 1950s AW was continuously walking up and down these fells on either side of the Kirkstone Pass, taking photos and making notes for the books that would change his life.

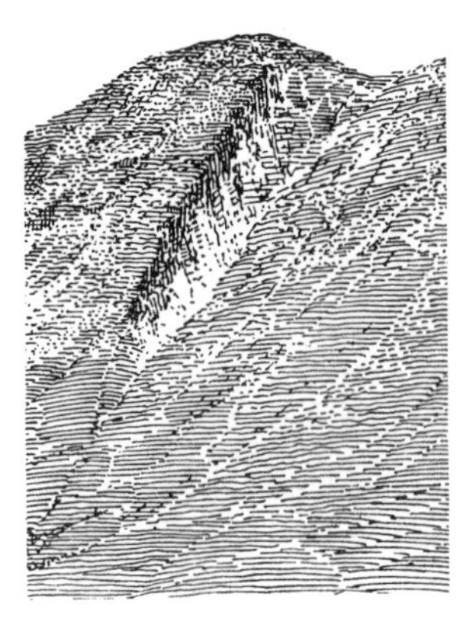

The Knott

Beyond the Straits of Riggindale, you enter the parish of Martindale and the path weaves between the adjoining parishes of Martindale and Patterdale for the next mile or so. The path that forked right off the ridge, heading east over Kidsty Pike towards Haweswater, is actually the route of the Coast to Coast Walk, the long-distance path that AW devised in the early 1970s. Our walk now follows this for the next 4 miles into Patterdale. In *A Coast to Coast Walk*, this section of the walk, which AW follows west to east, is part of stage four, Patterdale to Shap. On the flanks of High Street AW informs walkers they are on their last mountain and must soon bid a sad farewell to Lakeland.

From the summit of the Knott, simply continue along the right wall side, which drops downhill to rejoin the main path at a gate in a wall. Go through the gate and keep to the path, which soon turns right and heads through a boggy area, crossing the interestingly named Sulphury Gill and keeping the conical hill of Rest Dodd over to the right. The path follows an old fence line and turns left after a wall gap, heading for crags. The path crosses Satura Crag on the right, from where there is a good view down Bannerdale looking north. The path continues straight ahead to pass through two wooden gateposts at a wall junction. Keep going straight ahead to reach the tarn below the twin peaks of Angletarn Pikes.

AW liked the upland area around Angle Tarn, as it was an area of surprising views and unexpected twists and turns. He considered that the tarn 'ranks amongst the best of Lakeland tarns'. Rest Dodd and Angletarn Pikes classify as 'Wainwrights', but their summits

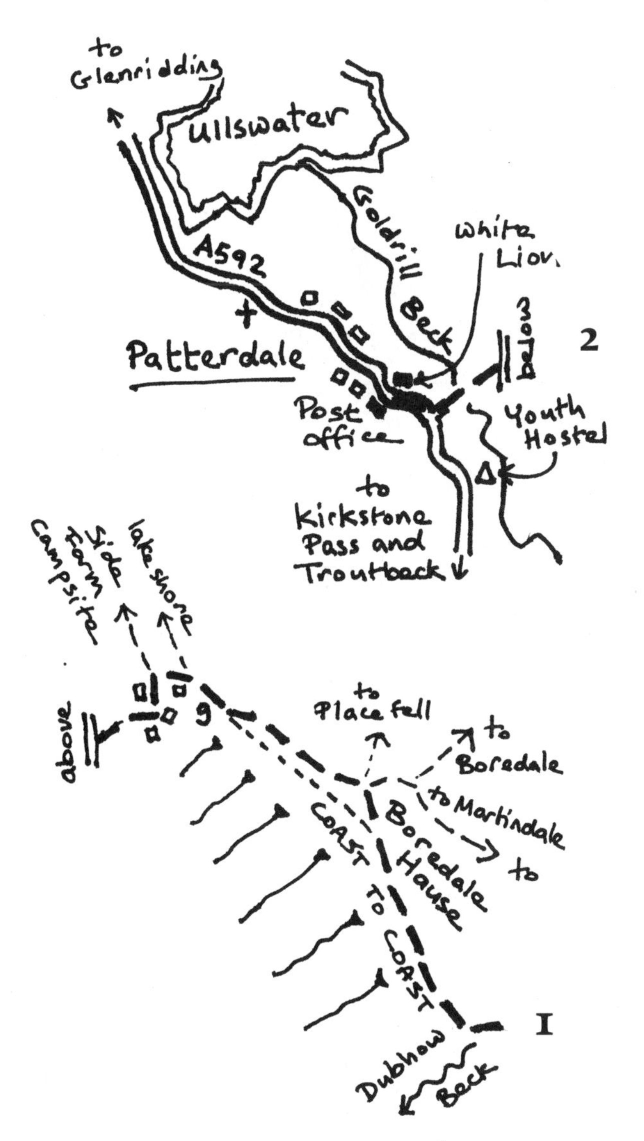
to Glenridding
Ullswater
Goldrill Beck
White Lion
A592
Patterdale
Post office
2
below 3
Youth Hostel
to Kirkstone Pass and Troutbeck
Side Farm Campsite
lake shore
above
9
to Place fell
to Boredale
to Martindale
to
Boredale Hause
COAST TO COAST
1
Dubhow Beck

Buck Crag and Heck Crag from Satura Crag

are not visited on this route. In the chapters on both these hills in *The Far Eastern Fells*, Satura Crag gets a mention as a good spot for an excellent view north down the secluded valley of Bannerdale. The shapely spur rising above the right flank of Bannerdale is another 'Wainwright', the Nab. This fell was off limits to walkers in the 1950s when AW wrote his guidebook, being part of the strictly private Martindale Deer Forest.

Follow the main path skirting around the right-hand side of the tarn and then left around the lower slopes of Angletarn Pikes. It then swings right, downhill, to reach a junction of numerous paths on the lofty pass between the hills known as Boardale Hause.

The common Lakeland term 'hause' derives from the Old Norse word for 'neck', referring to a neck of land forming a pass between mountains. From Boardale Hause the views across the valley take in most of the traditional parish of Patterdale, which stretches from Red Screes, near the top of the Kirkstone Pass, to the Helvellyn range, down to Ullswater and up to the summit of Place Fell. This

Patterdale

is the dramatic landscape of north Westmorland, so very different in nature to the gently rolling limestone hills in the south of the county. Boardale Hause, where numerous paths coming up from valleys and down from the fells meet, is also the start of a path leading up Place Fell, another of the Far Eastern Fells, and a hill highly regarded by AW for its spectacular view across Ullswater.

Continue along the path, heading downhill towards Patterdale, and when it splits into two take either path running down the bracken-clad fellside. The parallel paths run downhill towards trees and houses. Go through a gate straight ahead and leave the fell behind.

Turn left, and then right, along the driveway between the houses and follow it straight ahead. It crosses the Goldrill Beck, an inlet to Ullswater over to the right, and meets the A592 Kirkstone Pass road close to Patterdale Youth Hostel. Turn right along this road and follow it into the village. At the White Lion Inn on the right cross over to reach Patterdale Post Office. Take a well-earned rest in Patterdale, as the Eastern Fells are next.

Stage Eight
PATTERDALE POST OFFICE TO GRASMERE CHURCH
(8½ miles)

'I finished the Pennine Way with relief, the Coast to Coast Walk with regret. That's the difference.'
A Coast to Coast Walk

This stage celebrates the brilliance of AW's own long-distance walk, the Coast to Coast, by following a section of it from Patterdale to Grasmere. Weather permitting, the preferred but more arduous route is over a pair of grassy Eastern Fells, Birks and St Sunday Crag, although as with AW's Coast to Coast Walk, there is the option of the easier valley route along Grisedale. St Sunday Crag is the highest point on the entire walk, standing at 2,756 feet above sea level. Beyond the natural lunch stop of Grisedale Tarn, the path crosses into Grasmere parish, and it is soon downhill all the way to the much-visited resting place of a Lakeland icon even greater than Wainwright.

Coast to Coast

AW lived in an age when the British countryside movement made great strides in developing access opportunities for the urban man. There was the Kinder Trespass in 1932, the creation of National Parks and AONBs in 1949, and the formation of the Countryside Commission in 1968. The official opening of Tom Stephenson's long green trail, the Pennine Way, in 1965 also kick-started a fashion for long-distance walking at a time when outdoor leisure and tourism were rapidly growing. The 1970s saw a proliferation of 'unofficial' recreational routes as well as the first phase of government-backed trails like the Pennine Way, the Cleveland Way (1969), the Pembrokeshire Coast Path (1970), Offa's Dyke Path (1971) and the Ridgeway (1972). It was against this background that AW decided to write a guidebook to a long-distance walk.

First, though, came the *Pennine Way Companion*, published in 1968, AW's guidebook to what was then the only officially designated long-distance path in England. It took him over two years to produce this book, having employed four northern correspondents to do much of the donkey work before he set about tackling the boggy wet Pennines himself in 1966 and 1967.

His 'Personal Notes in Conclusion' at the back of the guidebook speak volumes. He did not enjoy the experience of the Pennine Way. In addition to the logistical headache of transport to and from the route (he happily accepted lifts in cars, including Mary Burkett's), he had no luck with the weather and found much of the route not to his liking. There were no mountain landscapes here, just dreary moors, farmyards and pastures of cattle. Then, slap bang in the middle of writing the book, his wife walked out, he retired, and he found himself alone at Kendal Green, incapable of making his own tea. The first sentence in his conclusion to his Pennine Way guide reads, 'Well, I'm glad it's finished, I must say,' but writing it at least provided a distraction from his deteriorating home environment.

Pennine Way Companion was not the official Her Majesty's Stationery Office publication on the route (that had been written by Tom Stephenson); nor was it the first – Christopher John Wright's more conventional *A Guide to the Pennine Way* came out in the same year. Even so, it was an unusual book for AW, arranged as a back-to-front annotated strip map, and it became the recognized route guide to the Pennine Way for a generation of long-distance walkers in the 1970s and 1980s. The book also showed that a long-distance walk could fit into the pictorial guide format (AW measured the Pennine Way at 270 miles) and its success possibly spurred AW on to thinking he could devise a better long-distance walk himself.

A Coast to Coast Walk was his original idea, a 190-mile route across northern England from sea to sea, passing through three national parks. When he devised and wrote it, during 1971 and 1972, AW was in a much better frame of mind than he had been

Ullswater
from the
north-east ridge

when writing *Pennine Way Companion*. First, he had the free time that came with his retirement. More importantly, he was married to the love of his life, Betty, who not only accompanied him on the walk and helped him plan it but also had a car in which to transport him across Lakeland and North Yorkshire. In the book he describes her as his 'good-looking, competent chauffeur'. Unlike AW's Pennine Way guide, in both the introduction and conclusion to *A Coast to Coast Walk* there is little mention of him being driven to despair by incessant rain.

AW ultimately preferred the experience of the Coast to Coast Walk to that of the Pennine Way because it was a route of his own making. He enjoyed the hours spent poring over the 1-inch Ordnance Survey maps to devise his walk, which he confidently proclaimed was scenically superior to the Pennine Way. With the exception of the unavoidable crossing of several miles of cow pasture between Richmond and Ingleby Cross, AW's Coast to Coast stuck to the uplands of Lakeland, the Dales and the North York Moors. AW also revelled in creating a route that was unofficial. He had a slight dig at the Countryside Commission and its officially designated trails, and scoffed at the waymarked Pennine Way, which attracted people in droves and was already suffering from path erosion and litter.

In 1972, the year AW completed the Coast to Coast, the Long Distance Walkers Association was formed. It was a boom time for long-distance walking and when AW's guidebook was published in 1973 he raised the bar. His philosophy of creating your own personal unofficial route, using existing public rights of way, with a meaningful (not arbitrary) start and finish point, had huge appeal, even though he was by no means the first person to adopt this approach.

The irony was that the huge popularity of AW's long-distance route, boosted in 1990 by a four-part BBC TV series, *Wainwright's Coast to Coast Walk*, meant that walkers began to abandon the official Pennine Way, not to devise their own journeys across northern England but to follow exactly and without deviation the paths used by AW in *A Coast to Coast Walk*. His informal personal journey from St Bees to Robin Hood's Bay turned into a semi-official waymarked route, attracting thousands of walkers every year.

In the mid-1980s AW collaborated with photographer Derry Brabbs, producing two illustrated books (for Michael Joseph publishers) covering both the Pennine Way and the Coast to Coast. AW's original *pictorial guides* to both long-distance walks were subsequently revised and reissued by publishers. For the record, while working at the Manchester office of the Countryside Commission in the early 1990s, I was involved in clarifying the exact legal line of the Pennine Way for amendments in Michael Joseph's first revision of *Pennine Way Companion*. It was the briefest of dalliances with the world of Wainwright.

Into the twenty-first century and while the Youth Hostel Association used the decline in numbers of people walking the Pennine Way as a reason to close hostels along the route, AW's Coast to Coast, over thirty years after it was devised, was named the second-best walk in the world in a 2004 *Country Walking* magazine survey (the number one spot was given to a New Zealand trail). Interest in the Coast to Coast continues unabated, so much so that in 2009, the BBC's television revival of Wainwright produced a whole six episodes of *Wainwright Walks: Coast to Coast*, in which broadcaster Julia Bradbury retraced AW's route from the Irish Sea to the North Sea.

Stage Eight of this walk covers part of section three of AW's Coast to Coast route, Rosthwaite to Patterdale. This very long stretch, recorded by AW as being 17¾ miles, goes from Borrowdale to Grasmere via Greenup Edge and Helm Crag, then from Grasmere to Patterdale via high and low alternative paths. AW suggests taking two days to complete the walk from Rosthwaite to Patterdale, with an overnight stop at the conveniently placed Grasmere village. Our walk follows the Coast to Coast from Patterdale to Grasmere using AW's alternative St Sunday Crag route. AW of course walked his long-distance trail going west to east, from the Cumbrian coast to the Yorkshire coast, because of the prevailing westerly weather; it was more favourable to head eastwards with any rain and wind more likely to be behind the walker.

AW's route between Grasmere and Patterdale allowed walkers to arrive at Grisedale Tarn and consider their options. For the strenuous walker in need of a challenge there was the Helvellyn ridge and the descent along Striding Edge; for the walker wanting to take it easy already (blistered feet perhaps?) there was the valley route through Grisedale. AW also provided a middle way. This was his route along the high ridge on the south side of Grisedale Beck, going over the summit of St Sunday Crag, which he described as 'a mountain for connoisseurs'.

The first 60 miles or so of AW's Coast to Coast go through his beloved Lakeland. This made it a fairly easy section of the guidebook to write and AW reproduced many of the sketches and sketch maps which he had used in his *Pictorial Guides*. St Sunday Crag and, of course, Helvellyn had featured in the first volume, *The Eastern Fells,* and the drawings of the summit of St Sunday Crag and its view to Ullswater turn up in both *The Eastern Fells* and *A Coast to Coast Walk*. Similarly, sketches of Grasmere village and Patterdale turn up in both publications.

This walk follows faithfully the route of AW's Coast to Coast between Patterdale and Grasmere while also celebrating the mountain landscapes AW explored methodically in 1953 and 1954 as he put together *The Eastern Fells*. It climbs two 'Wainwrights' recorded in *The Eastern Fells*: St Sunday Crag, 2,756 feet high, and its subsidiary, Birks, 2,040 feet high. AW certainly liked the imposing St Sunday Crag, as it had a proper mountain profile, but did not waste many pages describing Birks.

The entry for St Sunday Crag in *The Eastern Fells,* which apparently takes its name from St Dominic, includes one of the most beguiling AW sketches to be found in the seven volumes of the *Pictorial Guides*. It appears on page eight of the St Sunday Crag chapter and is a view of Ullswater from the north-east ridge. It includes the solitary figure of a woman, sitting on a rock admiring the view and seen only from the back. As Hunter Davies notes in his biography, this mysterious figure is generally accepted to be, at least according to AW's old Town Hall colleagues, Betty Ditchfield (not to be confused with AW's wife Betty), the secretary who was the object of AW's desires in the 1930s, but to whom he proposed and was rejected.

The Eastern Fells were well known to AW long before he sat down to write about them in the 1950s. They were his 'old favourites', starting with the principal mountain, Helvellyn, which he had climbed with his cousin Eric on Monday, 9 June 1930, the third day of his first Lakeland holiday. This was also his first day in Patterdale village, having arrived there on the bus along the shore of Ullswater from Pooley Bridge. Despite mist and rain, AW led Eric along the flanks of Birkhouse Moor overlooking Grisedale and ascended Helvellyn via Striding Edge. They then descended to Thirlspot and walked into Keswick where, soaking wet and dishevelled, they were revived by a guest house landlady in Stanger Street. AW was certainly not put off by this experience (Eric probably was), as he returned to the Lakes in 1931 and marched unsuspecting work colleagues over Striding Edge and Helvellyn again.

Indeed AW spent the 1930s and 1940s climbing the Eastern Fells, so when he sat down in November 1952 to pen a sketch of Dove Crag – the first page of Book One – he was rekindling fond memories of past walks. *The Eastern Fells* provided him with an easy-to-define area of concentrated high peaks lying between Thirlmere and the Keswick road to the west, and Ullswater and the Kirkstone Pass to the east. To the south, the Fairfield group of fells tapered to an apex at Ambleside, and to the north, the grassy Dodds petered out into the marshy ground of Threlkeld Common. AW's 2½ inch maps were the key to his ambitious project. so it is fitting that he dedicated Book One to 'The Men of the Ordnance Survey'.

AW could still be found in the valleys of the Eastern Fells towards the end of his life, as in 1989 he was filming in Grisedale for the BBC's Coast to Coast series. AW recounted to Eric Robson how he had spent a night in the old stone barn near Elmhow

Farm, by the flat pastures of Grisedale Beck, on Coronation Day, Tuesday, 2 June 1953. In fear of being caught by the farmer, he chain-smoked all night and left at dawn, walking to Grasmere, where he caught the Kendal bus and was back in his office at the Town Hall at 9 a.m. On his return to the office, news had filtered through that Hillary and Tenzing had conquered Everest (almost ten times higher than Helvellyn).

Patterdale and Grasmere are the two Westmorland parishes through which this stage passes. The parish boundary between them is crossed at the watershed on the high upland pass of Grisedale Hause. AW sketched both parishes at length, not least in *Westmorland Heritage*. He sketched Patterdale's main street, including the White Lion, and St Patrick's parish church; and his Grasmere village sketches include the two churches and the Swan Hotel on the A591 road. Between the two, it is clear AW preferred Patterdale, not just for its situation at the head of unspoilt Ullswater but because Grasmere was more 'touristy', attracting carloads of day trippers and the ice-cream brigade that AW disliked so much.

Grasmere was also the home of William Wordsworth (1770–1850), who not only put his fears of the 'rash assault' of mill-town dwellers invading the Lakes into verse but also complained bitterly to the *Westmorland Gazette* about the detrimental impact of the Windermere railway. In post-war Britain, AW was a less vociferous echo of Wordsworth, his books containing various little jibes aimed at townies who treated the Lake District like Morecambe, as well as complaints about increasing litter and parked cars spoiling the view.

It is hard to comprehend that the lives of Wordsworth and Wainwright were only separated by fifty-seven years. In truth, AW's Lake District was separated from Wordsworth's by that tumultuous epoch known as the Industrial Revolution. While Wordsworth witnessed the arrival of the railway, which allowed a wave of industrialists and manufacturers to build Gothic piles and summer retreats in an arcadia far removed from grim northern mill towns, Wainwright witnessed the arrival of the car and the creation of national parks, in a post-industrial society where increased leisure time created mass tourism in the Lakes. The irony was that in moaning about the vulgar intrusions man had made into the countryside in their own lifetimes, Wordsworth and AW both played a part in attracting visitors to the Lakes.

What Wordsworth and Wainwright had in common – on a few occasions, AW jokingly compared himself to Wordsworth – was a passion for Lakeland and a desire to express this creatively. The main difference was that AW saw the Lake District through the eyes of a man who had never experienced natural beauty. Wordsworth's childhood, in which he was surrounded by countryside, was alien to AW, just as his own childhood, in which he was surrounded by mills and urban poverty, would have been alien to Wordsworth. AW was the 'weaver poet', inspired by natural beauty as an antidote to the industrial mill town, while Wordsworth was the Romantic poet. They both interpreted the beauty of the Lake District but through different lenses. Wordsworth's scale was grand and epic, AW's was municipal and meticulous – after all, he was an accountant.

The two men shared the same biographer, the peerless Hunter Davies, and in 2008, they were two of the three Lakeland icons (the other being Beatrix Potter) to have their images emblazoned on the sides of some new Stagecoach buses operating in the Lake District.

Like AW, Wordsworth wrote a guidebook to the Lakes and had a Kendal publisher. *A Guide through the District of the Lakes* was published by Hudson and Nicholson of Highgate, Kendal, in 1835. While AW could claim to have written his first *Pictorial Guide* principally for his own enjoyment, Wordsworth's book was aimed specifically at the increasing number of tourists visiting the district. Of course, Wordsworth did not invent tourism in Lakeland, any more than AW invented footpath erosion on the fells. Both men popularized the Lakes but people were going to come anyway. If the Lake District's fragile landscapes have been damaged by over two hundred years of visitor pressure, then perhaps blame should be laid at the real culprits – the stagecoach, railway, motor bus and car.

That said, the impact of Wainwright is clear to see if you wander into Patterdale post office. In a one-shop village, the post office clearly benefits from having the Coast to Coast route outside its front door. A whole cottage industry of Coast to Coast souvenirs has sprung up and is on sale here – maps, books, DVDs, T-shirts, baseball caps, coasters, badges and, of course, fridge magnets.

In the 1992 *Wainwright in the Valleys of Lakeland*, published by Michael Joseph, AW posthumously states that he has a soft spot for Patterdale post office, as it was the first shop to sell his first *Pictorial Guide, The Eastern Fells*. He came here in 1955 and the shop's proprietor, a Mr Dawson, agreed to sell the book, following it up with an order for six more copies a week later.

Towards the end of this stage, both the walk and the Coast to Coast route cross the A591 trunk road between Grasmere and Keswick. Flash back to any weekend on this road in the 1950s and 1960s and there is a good chance the Ribble red bus would have motored by with Kendal's Borough Treasurer sitting on board. As the main highway through the Lake District, the A591 acted as the central spine, linking bus stations at Kendal, Ambleside and Keswick, and enabling AW to travel the length and breadth of Cumberland and Westmorland. The Kendal–Keswick road was AW's gateway to the fells and he could not avoid travelling along it, even when he was researching sections of the Far Eastern Fells and needed to get off the bus at Troutbeck and Ambleside. When it came to exploring the remoter Northern, North-Western and Western Fells, the Keswick bus service was certainly AW's lifeline.

THE ROUTE

Patterdale Post Office to Grisedale Tarn (4½ miles)

Start at the driveway between the White Lion Inn car park and the whitewashed cottages to the left of the village post office.

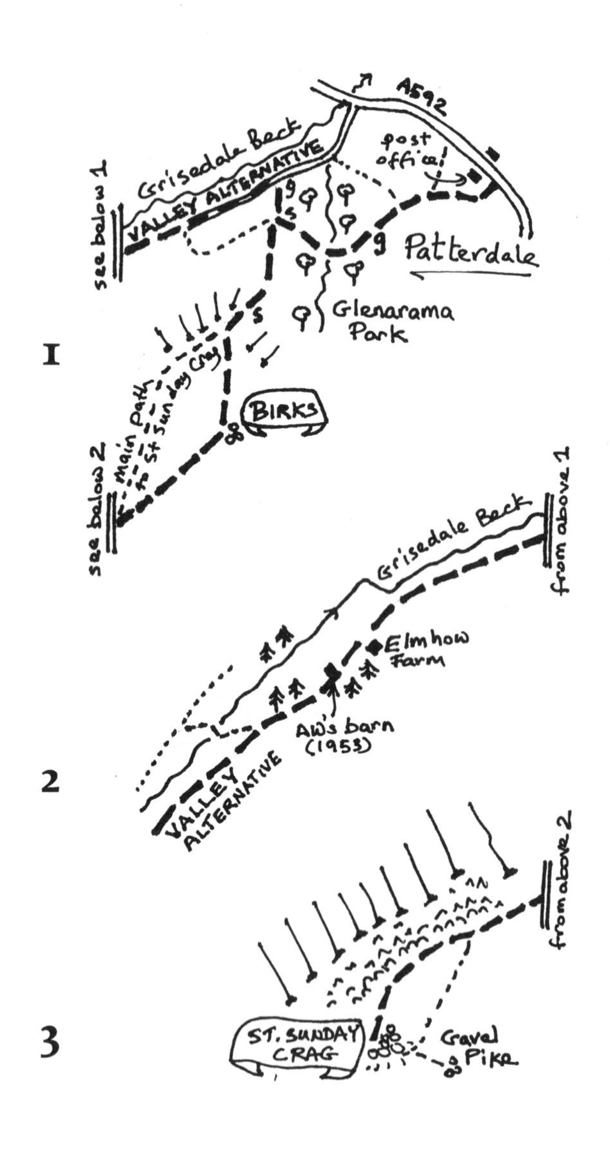
A592
post office
Grisedale Beck
VALLEY ALTERNATIVE
see below 1
Patterdale
Glenarama Park
I
St Sunday Crag
Main path to St Sunday Crag
BIRKS
see below 2
from above 1
Grisedale Beck
Elmhow Farm
AW's barn (1953)
VALLEY ALTERNATIVE
2
VALLEY ALTERNATIVE
from above 2
ST. SUNDAY CRAG
Gavel Pike
3

As Patterdale post office markets itself as the first shop to buy AW's fledgling *Pictorial Guide, The Eastern Fells*, then it surely deserves a visit. This may be the last chance to buy AW souvenirs or parcel up some no-longer-needed smelly socks and post them back home. Do not forget to check the Coast to Coast wipe board outside the shop in case someone has left a message. When I passed through in August 2011, someone had written, 'Don't do Helvellyn in the dark!'

The driveway swings right around the back of the buildings and continues straight ahead as a track through scrubby woodland to reach the bracken of the open fell. The path keeps a wall to the right and passes through a gate in a stone wall to enter Glenamara Park. Beyond the gate it stays on the lower slopes of the parkland, again keeping a wall boundary to the right. Hag Beck is forded and as the path skirts around the foot of Thornhow End, it reaches a junction of paths.

On old maps Glenamara Park is recorded as Glemara Park and this is the name AW used, even in his 1970s Coast to Coast guide. In AW's day this medieval deer park with its high walls was not in the ownership of the National Trust but it has been since 2002, thanks to a private bequest. It is grazed ancient woodland with remnants of a prehistoric settlement and charcoal burning.

At the path junction in Glenamara Park a decision needs to be made. Weather conditions and aching limbs (you will have nearly 100 miles under your belt since leaving Blackburn) will dictate the route from here to Grisedale Tarn. The alternatives are either the less demanding valley route through Grisedale or the mountain route taking in two 'Wainwrights' – Birks and St Sunday Crag. Both routes are spectacular and AW offered both options (as well as the much tougher Helvellyn ridge alternative) in *A Coast to Coast Walk*.

The Grisedale Valley route to Grisedale Tarn is a distance of 4 miles. If following this, turn right at the path junction and cross a stile in the fence. Drop down to a gate and reach a lane on the south side of wooded Grisedale Beck. Turn left along the lane, which soon becomes a bridleway track, keeping the beck on the right until after about 2 miles upstream a bridge crosses it. This is the higher of two bridges in the upper valley: ignore the first one, which leads to a sheepfold, and cross the second. The stony path climbs steeply to Ruthwaite Lodge climbing hut. From here it is a steady climb for another mile to reach the lofty pass by the stream outlet of Grisedale Tarn.

The stone barn where AW spent an uneasy Coronation Day night in June 1953 is passed on the right beyond Elmhow. Around about the same time, the derelict Victorian shooting hut of Ruthwaite Lodge, further up the valley, was being restored by its new owners, Sheffield University Mountaineering Club. A sketch of the lodge appears in AW's Coast to Coast guide, though the present plaque on the wall was not placed here until 1993,

when the building was restored by Outward Bound Ullswater after a fire. The plaque is dedicated to two local instructors who died on Mount Cook in 1988.

The original Ruthwaite Lodge, behind which are the industrial scars of old lead mines, was built by the Whig MP William Marshall (1796–1872). He was the Yorkshire-born son of a Leeds textile baron who was apparently given the Patterdale Hall estate, which included Grisedale, as a twenty-eighth birthday present in 1824. Prior to this the area had been largely ruled for over 250 years by the Mounsey family, the self-styled 'Kings of Patterdale'.

The St Sunday Crag route to Grisedale Tarn is a distance of 3½ miles. If following this, turn left at the path junction and leave the boundary of Glenamara Park to begin a very stiff climb along a well-used path, straight up the hillside towards a wall and crags at Thornhow End. Cross the stile in the wall and continue straight up along a grooved path. The more popular path for walkers eager to bypass Birks and get to the top of St Sunday Crag is clearly visible, following the edge of the ridge. But to 'bag' Birks, bear left along a fainter path, which begins a short distance up from the wall. Continue climbing for about half a mile to reach the grassy top of Birks.

Birks, 2,040 feet high, the twenty-fourth highest of thirty-five Eastern Fells, may appear merely a spur on the path up to St Sunday Crag, but it has its own summit. It is one of those featureless summits, a little cairn on top of grass, that AW could never get excited about. Still, he liked the ascent along the Thornhow End path and there are good views across the Ullswater Valley to the High Street range. AW bypassed the top of Birks on his Coast to Coast walk.

To reach the top of St Sunday Crag, just over a mile away, continue in the same direction, dropping slightly from the summit of Birks to the col between the two hills. The path then climbs again and will

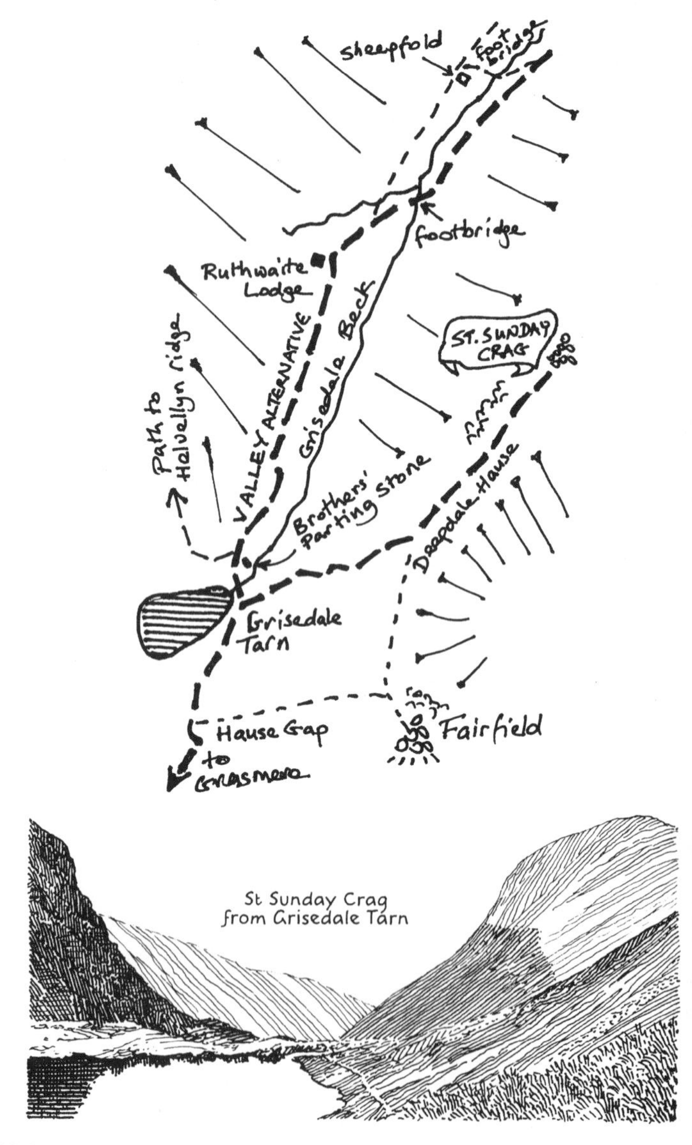

St Sunday Crag from Grisedale Tarn

be clearly seen forking into two straight ahead. At the fork you have a choice. To the left is an easier path which heads more directly to the summit of St Sunday Crag, aiming for the saddle between the summit and the distinct peak of Gavel Pike to the left. The steeper and more popular path forking right follows the north-east ridge and has the better view down to Ullswater. This path is not advisable in misty conditions, as it runs close to the edge of vertical crags.

St Sunday Crag, 2,756 feet high, the tenth highest of the Eastern Fells, squeezes into the top ten in terms of height, although the view from the top looking north, south and particularly west is dominated by bigger peaks – Raise, Catstycam, Helvellyn, Nethermost Pike, Dollywaggon Pike and Fairfield. AW liked the classic mountain profile of St Sunday Crag with its steep approaches, referring to it as a 'noble fell'. Its slender shape, together with the view it afforded to Lakeland's loveliest lake, is perhaps why AW decided to sketch the young Blackburn beauty Betty Ditchfield, sitting on its north-east ridge, in *The Eastern Fells.*

Continue in the same general south-west direction to descend St Sunday Crag along the obvious path heading for Deepdale Hause. This is the pass separating St Sunday Crag from its higher neighbour (by 107 feet), Fairfield. The pass between the two mountains is reached after about a mile. Do not start climbing again, and fork right along a path descending the hillside very steeply to Grisedale Tarn. At the eastern end of the tarn, you join the path that has climbed up from Grisedale.

St Sunday Crag, cairn

Grisedale Tarn to Grasmere Church (4 miles)

Just below the outlet of Grisedale Tarn, between the infant beck and the junction where the path to Dollywaggon Pike meets the path coming up from Grisedale, it is worth searching out the Brothers' Parting Stone, marked on OS maps and sketched by AW in *A Coast to Coast Walk*. This is a natural rock slab overlooking the valley, marked by an old metal signpost, on which are inscribed lines from Wordsworth's 'Elegiac Stanzas'. The inscription was placed here in the 1880s by the Wordsworth Society as a memorial to a point on the nearby Grisedale Pass where the poet said farewell to his younger brother John Wordsworth (1772–1805). The parting of the two brothers, on 29 September 1800, turned out to be their last, as John was later drowned at sea.

The death of Captain John Wordsworth has all the classic ingredients of a Victorian melodrama. A storm at sea, a ship heavily laden with valuable cargo crashing on to rocks, helpless onlookers in a nearby harbour, four hundred stricken passengers and crew bound for a voyage of discovery to Bengal and China on a ship that sank a few miles off the coast of Weymouth when a storm blew it on to rocks in the English Channel. John Wordsworth, the master of the *Earl of Abergavenny*, a trading vessel of the East India Company, had all his fortune tied up in the 1805 sea voyage.

Back in Grasmere the death of John, who had been living at Dove Cottage between sea voyages, was a devastating blow to William and his sister Dorothy. The Brothers' Parting Stone is a reminder that Wordsworth and his brother frequently

Cascades, Tongue Gill

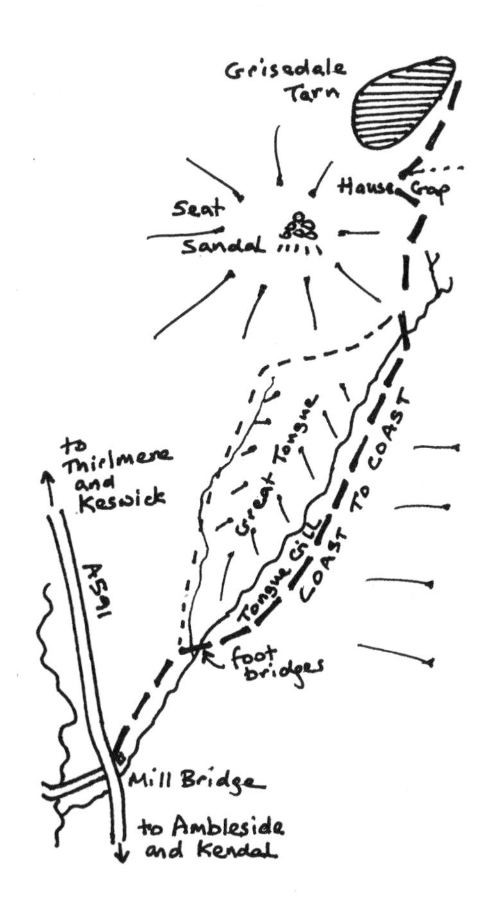

wandered over the passes and through the valleys of Lakeland for simple pleasure. The member of the Wordsworth Society who came up with the idea of this memorial was Reverend Hardwicke Rawnsley (1851–1920), the Vicar of Wray, who was later a founder of the National Trust.

From the stream outlet, follow the left-hand side of Grisedale Tarn along a rising path to the top of the Grisedale Pass.

The mountain pass and its tarn are enclosed almost on all sides by the Eastern Fells: Dollywaggon Pike, St Sunday Crag, Fairfield and Seat Sandal. The packhorse road linking Patterdale and the Vale of Grasmere made use of the natural breach in the mountains on either side of the pass – the valleys formed by Grisedale Beck and Tongue Gill. At Hause Gap you cross from Patterdale parish into the old parish of Grasmere; the boundary is marked by the wall that runs across the path and climbs up the slopes of both Fairfield and Seat Sandal. The parish boundary also runs across the summits of both these fells.

Continue straight ahead along the path that now drops steeply downhill to a flat boggy area known as Hause Moss. Beyond this, the path soon forks and you can choose either of the paths that skirt around the sides of Great Tongue, an elongated bracken-covered finger of land pointing downhill to Grasmere. The path running down the left-hand side, keeping above Tongue Gill, is the quickest and most popular descent. The path crosses the stream at a cascading waterfall and then heads straight downhill along the left-hand side of the beck. After about 1 mile the path swings right to cross the two

Vale of Grasmere

streams that converge at the foot of Great Tongue. Continue downhill along the track, now following the right-hand side of the wooded valley. The track soon meets the A591 Grasmere–Keswick road at cottages adjacent to Mill Bridge.

The Keswick road, heading north to Dunmail Raise through a gap in the fells, gave AW the perfect boundary in classifying the fells for his *Pictorial Guides*. Crossing the A591 road you leave the Eastern Fells of Book One behind and enter the territory of Book

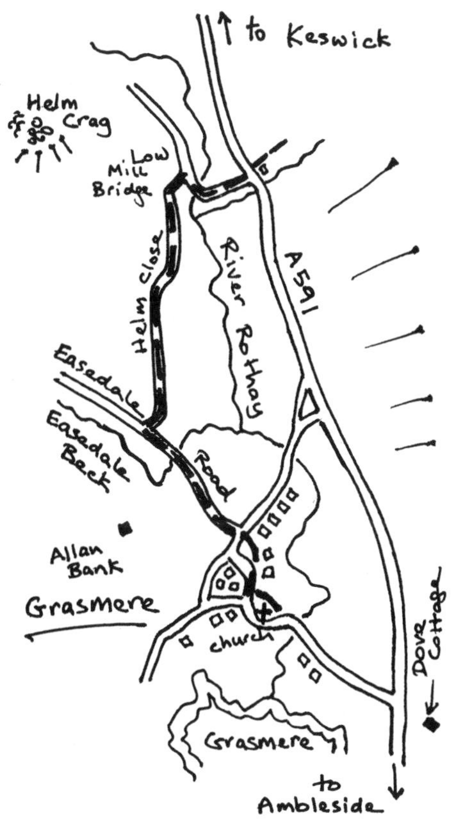

Three, *The Central Fells*. Helm Crag, a fine example of a Central Fell which AW also traversed on the Coast to Coast, can be seen straight ahead.

Walk straight across the main road with care and continue along the lane, Helm Close, directly opposite. You now follow this pleasant walled back lane for the next 1½ miles into Grasmere village. When it soon crosses the infant River Rothay at Low Mill Bridge, turn immediately left along the continuation of the lane, which winds around the bottom of Helm Crag.

The river accompanying you into Grasmere is the River Rothay, which rises close by where two streams, Raise Beck and Green Burn, converge just south of the old Cumberland–Westmorland border on Dunmail Raise. In the shadow of the busy Keswick road the little Rothay has an almost urban start to life and, in fact, it never quite shakes off the traffic of the A591 for its entire length. Still, it does at least manage to soothe itself in the calm waters of Grasmere and Rydal Water before, following a sedate passage past the Roman fort at Galava, it completely loses itself in Windermere.

The lane eventually reaches a junction with Easedale Road. Turn left along this to reach the village centre at a crossroads by shops. To the right is the Heaton Cooper Studio. To reach the parish church, walk straight ahead at the crossroads along College Street, running between Sam Read's bookshop and the village green.

The father of the landscape artist William Heaton Cooper (1903–95), was Alfred Heaton Cooper (1863–1929) who made the 'Wainwrightian' journey – from Lancashire to the Lakes – in late Victorian times. He had been brought up in Bolton and his parents were mill workers. This Alfred, like his later namesake AW, was inspired by Lakeland's dramatic scenery, which he captured in watercolour.

At the next junction, by the Wordsworth Hotel, turn left and at the bend in the road a gate on the left-hand side, next to the Gingerbread Shop, leads into the churchyard. As a chief tourist attraction of the village, the graves of the Wordsworth family are easy to find.

The pretty parish church of St Oswald has medieval origins and was built near the site of a seventh-century church established by Oswald, the King of Northumbria. The present church serves Grasmere, Rydal and Langdale, and each of the three townships has its own gate into the churchyard as well as its own part of the graveyard and even its own separate part of the church. You have entered via Grasmere's gate. William Heaton Cooper and his sculptor wife, Ophelia Bell (1915–75), were married in the church and also buried here.

There is little space in this book to provide much insight into the fascinating life and times of the Wordsworths. If you have finished this stage of the walk at lightning speed and have a few hours to spare, the excellent Dove Cottage and Wordsworth Museum, on the outskirts of the village, are the places to visit.

Grasmere village, some 38 miles from St Bees, is where we leave AW's Coast to Coast route, but only for the time being. It is the perfect overnight stop before the penultimate stage of the walk. AW's final resting place is only two days walk away. A crawl through the hostelries and hotel bars of Grasmere may well lead to interesting encounters with Coast to Coast walkers. AW is still bringing people into the Lakes and so is Wordsworth.

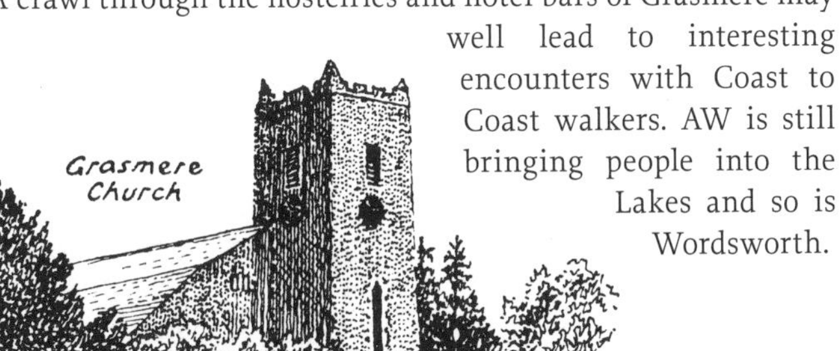

Stage Nine
GRASMERE CHURCH TO ROSTHWAITE BRIDGE
(12 miles)

'If I was heading for the hills, and not the office, I could set forth singing, not audibly, heaven forbid; just in my heart.'
Fellwanderer

This stage of the walk makes up for missed 'Wainwrights' by bagging no fewer than five summits in its first half. This is a journey through Book Three of AW's Pictorial Guides, *The Central Fells*, and it follows an upland traverse between Grasmere and Langdale, taking in the summits of the Langdale Pikes, two of AW's favourite mountains. An alternative lower-level route through the Langdale Valley is also outlined. The route passes from Westmorland into Cumberland and the second half of this stage is all downhill into Borrowdale, through the dramatic and lonely valley of Langstrath Beck. It is very much a walk of two halves.

A Free Man on Sundays

The thirteen years in which AW wrote his first seven books, the *Pictorial Guides to the Lakeland Fells,* are the period that really defined him. The years 1952 to 1965 were the classic Wainwright years, in which all the images of AW that later inhabited the public's imagination were moulded.

In these years his fellwalking had a definite purpose. He walked alone, avoided company, used the bus to get everywhere, hid himself away from his wife and spent every waking hour when he was not in the office working on his books.

This period saw the municipal accountant at the very height of his powers, producing seven finely crafted, meticulously detailed hand-written volumes to the fells. These became indispensable to walkers at a time when, after the trauma of the Second World War, recreation in the countryside was really taking off and visitors were flocking to the newly created Lake District National Park.

As each of the *Pictorial Guides* took AW two years to research and write in his spare time, no subsequent AW publication could match both the effort and passion he put in to his survey of 214 Lakeland fells. The only books that came close were *Westmorland Heritage* and *Kendal in the Nineteenth Century*; these were written in AW's retirement, when he had a lot more time. As was *A Coast to Coast Walk*, which was something of a jolly jaunt for AW and Betty.

AW's life changed during the writing of the *Pictorial Guides*. He had always been a man of letters but now he had to cope with fan mail and readers' queries (he replied to everything) on top of all his official council correspondence. Members of the public whom he didn't even know wanted to meet him; he was even harassed on the fells by walkers who recognized him. In *Fellwanderer* he recounts the tale of being asked if he was Wainwright by a woman with a small boy on the summit of High Stile in July 1964. Despite her insistence that he was, AW denied he was Wainwright, twice! By the time he had finished *The Western Fells* in autumn 1965 AW was approaching retirement and his hair had turned white. On the completion of his mammoth Lakeland project it wasn't crooner Al Martino storming up the pop charts but the Beatles and the Rolling Stones.

Stage nine of this walk wanders into the very heart of Lakeland, the area that AW progressed through with zeal in late 1956 and 1957 as he researched Book Three, *The Central Fells*. During the writing of this book, AW turned fifty. He was still not even halfway through his seven-volume mission. He had the success of *The Eastern Fells* behind him – it had already been reprinted – and *The Far Eastern Fells* was ready for publication. Despite a few worries about getting old and failing eyesight, AW had a plan and he was sticking to it.

AW's plan was one he relished. Having split Lakeland up into seven neatly defined sections, he spent around eighteen months using all his available free time at weekends, annual leave and summer evenings concentrating his walking in each particular area. He spent the evenings, particularly in autumn and winter, sketching and writing each book at home. AW would walk exclusively in the area he was working on. As he climbed each fell, he knew it would be many years before he would go back to it, if at all. That is why he got a lot of pleasure out of corresponding with readers who reminded him (and updated him on any changes to cairns) of fells he hadn't visited for years.

AW worked his way methodically around the National Park. After Books One, Two and Three came Book Four, *The Southern Fells*, published in 1960. This was the weightiest of the seven volumes, covering the popular Scafell and Coniston ranges. In the early 1960s AW had to spend a bit more time sitting on the bus, as he ventured out on connecting services from Keswick bus station to survey the areas he covered in the remaining three volumes – *The Northern Fells*, which included Blencathra and Skiddaw, *The North Western Fells*, covering the hills between Buttermere and Derwentwater, and *The Western Fells*, dominated by Great Gable and Pillar. These books were published in 1962, 1964 and 1966 respectively.

The Central Fells were easily accessible to AW in 1957, their boundaries defined by roads with bus routes – Grasmere to Keswick, Keswick to Borrowdale, and Ambleside to the Dungeon Ghyll terminus in Langdale. Book Three was dedicated to 'The Dogs of Lakeland' and in it AW continues with themes already established in his two earlier volumes. Man's intrusion into the landscape is unwelcome. He criticizes Manchester Corporation again, this time for its gloomy artificial conifer plantations and the despoliation of Thirlmere. He blames walkers for creating ugly short-cut paths that have caused erosion on Pike O' Stickle. He goes out of his way to avoid motorists and the Sunday afternoon and Bank Holiday traffic around Loughrigg Fell.

AW also ignores the 'Trespassers Will Be Prosecuted' notices on Armboth Fell. He took the view that where fells were privately owned with no rights of way across them, he still needed to record their summits and possible routes up and down them. This was part of his mission and people were paying good money for his books so he didn't want to short change them. A few 'private' signs were not going to stop AW.

The Central Fells records a total of twenty-seven fells, unusually not the highest in the Lake District, the loftiest peak being High Raise (2,500 feet). This stage of the walk takes in five 'Wainwrights' on the south side of High Raise, all part of a broad upland plateau stretching south-east towards Grasmere and south to a more abrupt end at the distinctive summits of the Langdale Pikes. In the order in which they are climbed, it takes in the following peaks: Silver How, Blea Rigg, Pavey Ark, Harrison Stickle and Pike O' Stickle.

AW had certainly visited the Central Fells south of High Raise on his early expeditions to the Lakes between the wars. His Whitsuntide holiday with three Town Hall colleagues in 1931 included as its final day's itinerary a 15-mile walk from Langdale to Ambleside, from where the group had to regretfully get the bus home to Blackburn. The peaks they visited on this last day were Pike of Stickle, Harrison Stickle, Pavey Ark, Sergeant Man, High Raise, Calf Crag, Gibson Knott and Helm Crag.

AW had explored Great Langdale in the 1930s and 1940s when it was still unspoilt by traffic and tourists. Much of his writing about this valley looks back wistfully to those halcyon days for the walker and regrets the post-war invasion of motor cars and caravans clogging up the narrow lanes, the noise of holiday crowds, and the felling of trees for new car parks. To a lesser extent AW had the same view of his favourite valley in the whole of Lakeland, Borrowdale. Travelling on the bus through these two dales in 1957, AW was, in a sense, looking back nostalgically to the days when he had the valleys to himself.

The lost world of the Lake District before car parks was embodied in the enigmatic figure of Millican Dalton (1867–1947), the 'Professor of Adventure', who was still to be found spending his summers in a cave beneath Castle Crag when AW wandered through Borrowdale before the war. AW later sketched the cave and mentions Dalton in the chapter on Castle Crag in Book Six, *The North Western Fells*. AW's Kendal friend Harry Griffin personally knew Dalton, a man who, at the dawn of the Edwardian era, forsook a respectable job and the London rat race to live a simple life in the mountains. In Tyrolean hat and shorts, Dalton – camper, climber and sailor – became a guide to the fells and in his rocky hermitage baked bread, ate berries and recycled everything.

AW used all the beautiful adjectives for Borrowdale: it was exquisite, delightful, heavenly and lovely. It was the place where 'all things blend in perfect harmony', a land of 'emerald pastures' and 'translucent streams', a 'rich tangle of tree and rock'. In *The North Western Fells* he states that the square mile of countryside around the Jaws of Borrowdale, just downstream from Rosthwaite village, is 'the loveliest square mile in Lakeland'. On the same page he lists other lovely square miles, including the adjacent Stonethwaite Valley (two of which this journey also passes through – the head of Ullswater and the Buttermere Valley).

This stage of the walk also takes you to the top of one (well, two really) of AW's favourite mountains, as listed in the conclusion to his final *Pictorial Guide, The Western Fells*: the Langdale Pikes – Harrison Stickle and Pike O' Stickle – which did not make AW's top six mountains but are mentioned as one (well, two really) of the mountains that just missed out on this very exclusive list which readers had been waiting years for AW to reveal.

The Langdale Pikes have everything AW liked about mountains. They have a classic mountain profile, dramatically rising from the valley floor to craggy summits that appear inaccessible. They have interesting ascents of infinite variety, with paths meandering up through ghylls and ravines, and past waterfalls, tarns and rock outcrops. They even have the added interest of prehistoric man's legacy in the form of Pike O' Stickle's stone axe factory.

AW sketched the Langdale Pikes from every conceivable angle. He devotes forty-four pages of *The Central Fells* to Harrison Stickle, Pike O'Stickle, Loft Crag (the third Langdale Pike) and Pavey Ark.

Pavey Ark

2288'

from the western slopes of Blea Rigg

With Thorn Crag, which never made it as a 'Wainwright', AW lumped these peaks together as the Langdales Pikes group, all five of them actually being prominent outcrops at the southern end of the boggy plateau continuing northwards over Thunacar Knott to High Raise. Only a sharp-eyed municipal accountant could dissect the confusing and erratic nature of the Langdale Pikes down to their basic component parts. There was so much intricate detail to record on these peaks that AW drew maps to the larger scale of 6 inches to 1 mile in his chapters on Harrison Stickle, Loft Crag and Pavey Ark.

In 1931 AW set out from the Old Dungeon Ghyll Hotel, on the last day of his week's holiday, with Jim, Eric and Harry his co-workers from Blackburn Town Hall. After climbing the Langdale Pikes they headed north over High Raise before following the Helm Crag ridge down into Grasmere. These hills certainly had a lot of memories for AW. In his twilight years, he recalled the time he had spent the night with his khaki blanket on Harrison Stickle (another uneasy night spent chain-smoking) and watched a fox at play. AW was not a natural wild camper but he considered it worth it, for it allowed him to set off at dawn for another day's exploring and to have the mountain sunrise all to himself.

Langdales is the last of the old Westmorland parishes our walk takes us through before joining the Stake Pass. When you reach the highest point of the Stake Pass you finally say farewell to AW's adopted county and enter Borrowdale in what was Cumberland. Like Patterdale and Grasmere before it, the Langdales was a huge rural parish, stretching from the villages and farmsteads in the valley floor to the ridge summits of the fells on either side of the valley. Langdales is the last outpost of Westmorland, as it had a border to the south with that part of Lancashire 'beyond the sands', while to the north and west, the border was with Cumberland.

AW knew Cumberland almost as well as he knew Westmorland. The majority of the Lakeland fells were within the bounds of this twelfth-century border county, including England's highest mountain, Scafell Pike. The only *Pictorial Guide* entirely outside this county was Book Two, *The Far Eastern Fells*.

The Cumberland town AW knew best was Keswick. This was the setting, in the late 1960s, for clandestine meetings in cafés with Betty; it was also the place where he would get off the Sunday morning bus and, more often than not, get on another one bound for Borrowdale, Threlkeld, Buttermere, Cockermouth or Bassenthwaite. Returning to Keswick AW would enjoy his Sunday tea in a café before getting on the 6.30 p.m. bus back to Kendal, hoping it would go very slowly – he wanted to enjoy the view and was in no hurry to get home.

The Ribble bus service that brought him to Keswick didn't extend into rural west Cumberland, concentrating on express services to Keswick, Carlisle, Penrith and Scotland. It was the jolly fleet of the Cumberland Motor Services, based in Whitehaven, that carried AW from here. The company, formed in 1921, had its heyday in the 1950s, which was fortunate for AW. In summer months the two bus companies, Ribble and Cumberland operated jointly, providing excursions for tourists. In 1961, a full day's Lakes Tour would have cost 17/6, return fare.

If AW had attempted to research his *Pictorial Guides* by bus any later than he did, he might have found it difficult. Many Cumberland bus services were seasonal but in the 1970s even summer routes began to be withdrawn, especially to places like the Newlands Valley. The situation got worse with deregulation in the 1980s, when unprofitable rural bus services were axed. AW's old nemesis, the motor car, was ultimately to blame. By 1988 both Ribble and Cumberland Motor Services had become part of the operator Stagecoach Northwest. The halcyon days of bus travel were well and truly over. Thank the heavens AW found Betty and her little Volkswagen Beetle.

The quirkiness of AW's *Pictorial Guides*, even when they first appeared, is perhaps one of the reasons they were so successful. Aside from being immensely practical to hill walkers, they were written by a man born in the Edwardian era who wrote like a Victorian. AW had an old-fashioned turn of phrase. Car drivers were 'motorists', trig points were 'triangulation stations' and AW referred to 'Ordnance Survey', not 'O.S.'. With his numerous references to trespassers, stalkers and the lurking threat of gamekeepers and the Manchester Corporation, AW conjured up a lost pre-war world.

Other contemporary guidebooks to Lakeland invariably looked more 'modern'. AW admired the work of the mountain photographer and climber W.A. Poucher (1891–1988), who had his first book on the Lake District published in 1940. When Poucher brought out his own walkers' guide to the fells, *The Lakeland Peaks*, in 1960, it was a rather glossy affair for a London publisher (Constable), brimming with photos and annotated extracts from Bartholomew's 1-inch maps. The Surrey-based Mr Poucher, like AW, was also in a day job, although it was far removed from the world of municipal accountancy: he worked as a research chemist for the Yardley cosmetics company.

AW's *Pictorial Guides* harked back to an age before television and cars but were largely read by an audience who owned both. A browse through the *Westmorland Gazette* in 1955, the year Book One was published, reveals reams of enticing advertisements for home entertainments and labour-saving machines. All the latest TV sets and record players from Ferguson, Pye and Bush were available on 'easy terms', with 'no callers', from stores like Whitesides of Stramongate, Kendal. AW, or rather his wife Ruth, could 'banish that kitchen drudgery' with a range of new cookers, boilers and washers.

Fast forward a decade to 1965, the year AW finished writing Book Seven, and the *Westmorland Gazette* has pages and pages of car adverts – the Morris 1000, Fords Cortina, Anglia and Zephyr, the Vauxhall Victor, Hillman Imp, Austin Mini and the new Singer Gazelle. Meanwhile Rediffusion of Highgate, Kendal, was offering a brand-new 22-inch wired TV set to rent at 7/9 a week or buy for £56.

AW's guidebooks appeared just at the right time, when the Lake District had been designated a National Park and motoring visitors were being encouraged to come and experience it. AW was, in many ways, a post-war version of the Victorian writer M.J. Baddeley, whose popular guidebook to the Lakes met the demands of the earlier wave of day trippers who arrived at Windermere by steam train.

Bizarrely, both television and cars, the powerful shapers of modern society, came to help AW in his retirement years. TV exposure in the 1980s and Betty driving him around to research his sketchbooks helped sustain AW's writing career for another twenty-five years. In AW's personal conclusion to his final volume *The Western Fells,* he records that the very last fell he surveyed was Starling Dodd, on 10 September 1965. With fell number 214 climbed, AW's thirteen-year masterpiece was almost complete.

THE ROUTE

Grasmere Church to Stake Pass (7 miles)

The walk aims for the top of the Stake Pass, from where it is a 5-mile valley route downhill to Borrowdale. The main route described here to the Stake Pass follows a westerly course along the broad upland plateau between Grasmere and Langdale and takes in five 'Wainwright' peaks. The steepest climb is the ascent of Pavey Ark and the highest point reached is the summit of Harrison Stickle (2,403 feet).

There is an easier route which just takes in one 'Wainwright' – Silver How above Grasmere. This route is described below as the Langdale Valley alternative. If conditions are really bad, you can even avoid Silver How and simply follow the tarmac of Red Bank Road around the south side of the lake at Grasmere and walk over the hill to Great Langdale via Elterwater. This route is easy to follow using the OS Explorer Map OL7. Even if you follow the road route or the Langdale Valley alternative there is a still a steep ascent from the head of Great Langdale at Mickleden to the top of Stake Pass at approximately 1,600 feet.

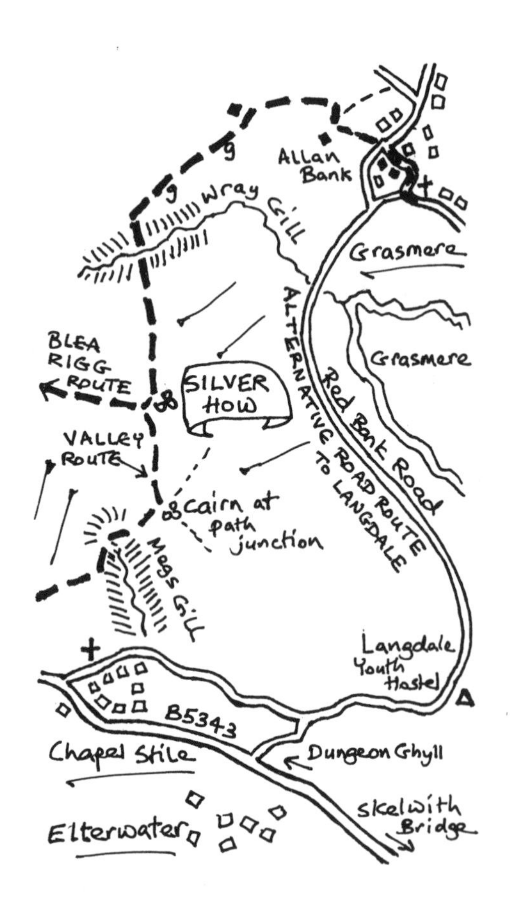

To join the well-used path to Silver How, start at the gate by the church entrance and turn right along the main street back towards the village centre. Bear left at the Wordsworth Hotel and pass the Red Lion Hotel on the left to reach a crossroads. Go straight ahead along the dead-end road to the left of the café, which forms the driveway to Allan Bank, a National Trust property.

When AW came past here surveying his route up Silver How in 1957, the Georgian residence of Allan Bank was still being lived in by Eleanor Rawnsley, the widow of Canon Hardwicke Rawnsley, co-founder of the National Trust. The campaigning Victorian vicar had bought the house in 1915 for his pending retirement but died five years later, bequeathing the property to the Trust with his wife as tenant. Eleanor was known for writing plays in Grasmere dialect, performed in the grounds of Allan Bank; she also wrote a biography of her husband and books about Wordsworth's Grasmere.

Allan Bank's most famous resident was, of course, Wordsworth and he was the first tenant. He lived here for three years, from 1808 to 1811, having moved out of cramped Dove Cottage with his wife, Mary, their extended family, their three children and those habitual hangers-on Coleridge and de Quincey. During their tenancy of Allan Bank, William and Mary had two more babies. Allan Bank had been built in 1805 as a retirement home for a Liverpool merchant, John Crump, one of Grasmere's many wealthy 'offcomers', who came to the Lakes to build villas. Wordsworth had considered the house a bit of an eyesore when it was first built. An AW sketch of Allan Bank can be seen in *Westmorland Heritage*.

Allan Bank, Grasmere

As you reach Allan Bank turn right along the signed footpath which follows a driveway around the hillside with a good view across to Helm Crag. This winds around to farm buildings at Score Crag. Take the track forking left in front of the farm, signed to Silver How and Langdale. This passes through a gate and becomes a stony track climbing uphill to pass through another gate and reach the open fellside. Bear left here along the well-used path, which now climbs more steeply, keeping boundary walls to the left. The path passes through dense juniper shrubs and after a prominent cairn go straight ahead and drop down to the deep cleft of Wray Gill. A little rocky scramble is required on the far side of the gill. From there follow a distinct path to the top of Silver How.

Silver How, 1,292 feet high, is the twenty-fourth highest fell out of the twenty-seven recorded by AW in *The Central Fells.*

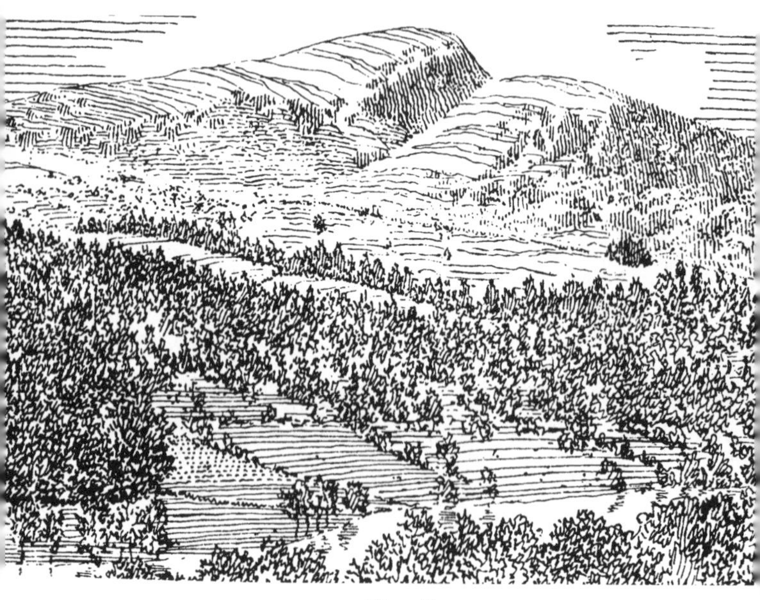

Silver How

Despite its relative insignificance, AW was a big fan and loved the hill for its great variety, unexpected delights and views to the Vale of Grasmere. On Silver How, AW saw 'landscape artistry at its best'. For similar reasons, he also loved the meandering walk from here along the broad ridge to Blea Rigg. He recorded the route of ascent up Silver How not just from Grasmere but also from Elterwater and Chapel Stile.

The Langdale Pikes route: 5½ miles from Silver How to Stake Pass. Hopefully it will be clear enough to see the way ahead, with the bristly ridge of Blea Rigg, together with Pavey Ark and Harrison Stickle visible beyond the craggy shoulder of Great Castle Howe. Drop down from the summit of Silver How in the direction of Langdale and turn immediately right, continuing straight ahead along the hummocky plateau. The path is indistinct in places and there is a confusion of tracks. The distance between Silver How and Blea Rigg is 2 miles and the path goes up and down over hummocks across

Blea Rigg

gradually rising land. The path passes a sprinkling of tarns, after which it climbs more steeply over crags and passes more tarns before reaching the cairn on the bristly summit of Blea Rigg.

Blea Rigg, 1,776 feet high, is the fourteenth highest of the Central Fells. It is an elongated rocky ridge above marshy ground, which continues to rise north-westwards to the two highest summits in the Central Fells, Sergeant Man and High Raise. The ridge separates the two prominent tarns seen from the summit cairn, Easedale Tarn on the Grasmere side and Stickle Tarn on the Langdale side. Pavey Ark and Harrison Stickle, next on the 'Wainwright' bagging list, dominate the view from here.

The Blea Rigg ridge also formed the old parish boundary between the parishes of Grasmere and Langdales. Dropping down from here towards Stickle Tarn, you enter the latter, Langdales, the last Westmorland parish to be visited on this walk.

In good weather conditions, the path from Blea Rigg to Stickle Tarn is easy to make out. From the summit continue in the direction of Sergeant Man but very soon take the path forking left, leaving the main ridge and descending to Stickle Tarn, with the overwhelming rock face of Pavey Ark behind it directly below.

At Stickle Tarn, faced with the prospect of climbing around the side of Pavey Ark, you have the option of joining the alternative route through Great Langdale valley. To do this, simply follow the left shoreline of the tarn to the stream outlet and pick up what AW would have considered the tourists' path, which descends steeply alongside Stickle Ghyll towards the National Trust car park below. The route from this car park to the top of the Stake Pass is outlined below.

AW records four ascents up Pavey Ark from Stickle Tarn alone. You will be pleased to hear this walk does not take the extreme Jack's Rake route and this is not recommended. We take 'a surprisingly easier way to the summit', a route AW called

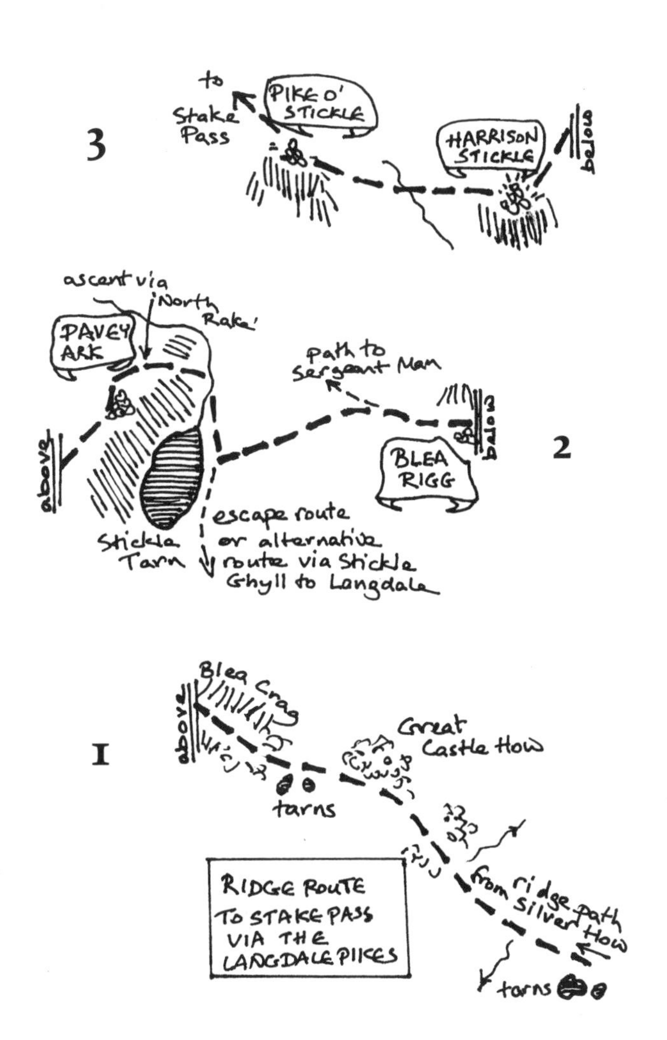
3
to
Stake
Pass
PIKE O' STICKLE
HARRISON STICKLE
below
ascent via
'North Rake'
PAVEY ARK
path to
Sergeant Man
above
below
2
BLEA RIGG
Stickle
Tarn
escape route
or alternative
route via Stickle
Ghyll to Langdale
Blea Crag
above
I
Great
Castle How
tarns
RIDGE ROUTE
TO STAKE PASS
VIA THE
LANGDALE PIKES
from ridge path
Silver How
tarns

the North Rake ascent. He recommended his readers try it sometime – and a lot of them have.

The Shelter Stone on the top of Blea Rigg

To climb Pavey Ark via AW's North Rake route, turn right at the tarn and follow it to its stream inlet. Follow the right-hand side of this stream, Bright Beck. The path soon crosses over it and heads to the right of Pavey Ark's East Buttress aiming towards a scree gully. Climb a well-used steep path uphill through an obvious gap between crags. Keep above the buttresses and gullies to the left. The slopes of the North Rake ease off near the top and a boggy plateau is reached. Turn left to reach the summit of Pavey Ark.

In good weather the continuation of the path to the top of Harrison Stickle is easy to see. Simply drop down to the depression behind the latter peak, which joins a path on the ridge from Thunacar Knott. Bear left along this and you will reach the top of Harrison Stickle after a short rocky scramble.

Continue along the path that drops down from the summit, heading straight towards the distinctive sugarloaf of Pike O' Stickle. The peak between them, over to the left, is another 'Wainwright', Loft Crag. The ridge path crosses the upper reaches of the beck flowing into Dungeon Ghyll. Paths on the left here lead to the summit of Loft Crag. Take one of these if you wish to 'bag' another 'Wainwright'. Otherwise just follow the main path, which soon reaches the summit of Pike O' Stickle after yet another steep rocky scramble.

In AW's list of Central Fells, Pavey Ark (2,288 feet) is the seventh highest, Harrison Stickle (2,403 feet) the third highest, Loft Crag (2,270 feet) the eighth highest and Pike O' Stickle (2,323 feet) the sixth highest. AW also included Thorn Crag in his five summits of the Langdale Pikes, although he considers this a subsidiary of Loft Crag. AW certainly had his work cut out putting the complex physical geography of the Langdale Pikes down on paper but he does it with aplomb. The chapters for each of these peaks in *The Central Fells* suggest that when he wandered up here in the late 1950s he left no stone unturned.

Facing the broad plateau at the back of the summit rocks, drop down from the bell-shaped top of Pike O' Stickle and bear left along a path aiming towards the upper reaches of the Stake Beck valley, which heads north. The path drops steeply to the boggy shelf of Martcrag Moor with Stake Beck over to the right. After about a mile of walking you reach the summit of Stake Pass at a cairn by a junction of paths.

Pike o'Stickle summit cairn

The Great Langdale valley alternative route: 6½ miles from Silver How to Stake Pass. Drop down from the summit of Silver How towards the Langdale side and bear left to pick up a distinct path that descends very gradually to a large cairn at a crossroads of paths above the steep-sided ravine of Meg's Gill. Turn right at the path junction and head for Meg's Gill, which looks down to Chapel Stile and its quarries. At the top of the gill the path turns right and skirts around the steep-sided hill to continue downhill along the right-hand side of the ravine and reach a grassy shelf overlooking Langdale. Bear right here along a path that descends the hillside. This path meets the B5343 road close to Harry Place Farm.

Follow the road up the valley for only a short distance before joining the byway on the left, which runs along the north side of Great Langdale Beck and meets the road again by the Stickle Tarn car park. Walk to the rear of the car park and go through the gates, turning left off the popular path to the tarn, following the stony track which continues up the valley, following the edge of the hillside, to pass behind the Old Dungeon Ghyll Hotel. The track continues straight ahead for almost 2 miles to cross a footbridge over Stake Gill. Ignore the path forking left (the start of the route path up Rosset Gill) and continue straight up the steep zigzag path following the left-hand side of the beck. A climb of almost a mile leads to the cairn at the top of the Stake Pass.

The unspoilt Langdale Valley that AW had wandered through in the 1930s before cars came en masse had, of course, attracted tourists since Wordsworth's day. In Victorian times horse-drawn charabancs of visitors would disembark at the Old Dungeon Ghyll Hotel, just as AW did when he came here on the bus from Ambleside. The Old Dungeon Ghyll Hotel was given to the National Trust in 1929 by the historian G.M. Trevelyan (1876–1962). He was the first president of the Youth Hostels Association and is buried in the churchyard at Chapel Stile.

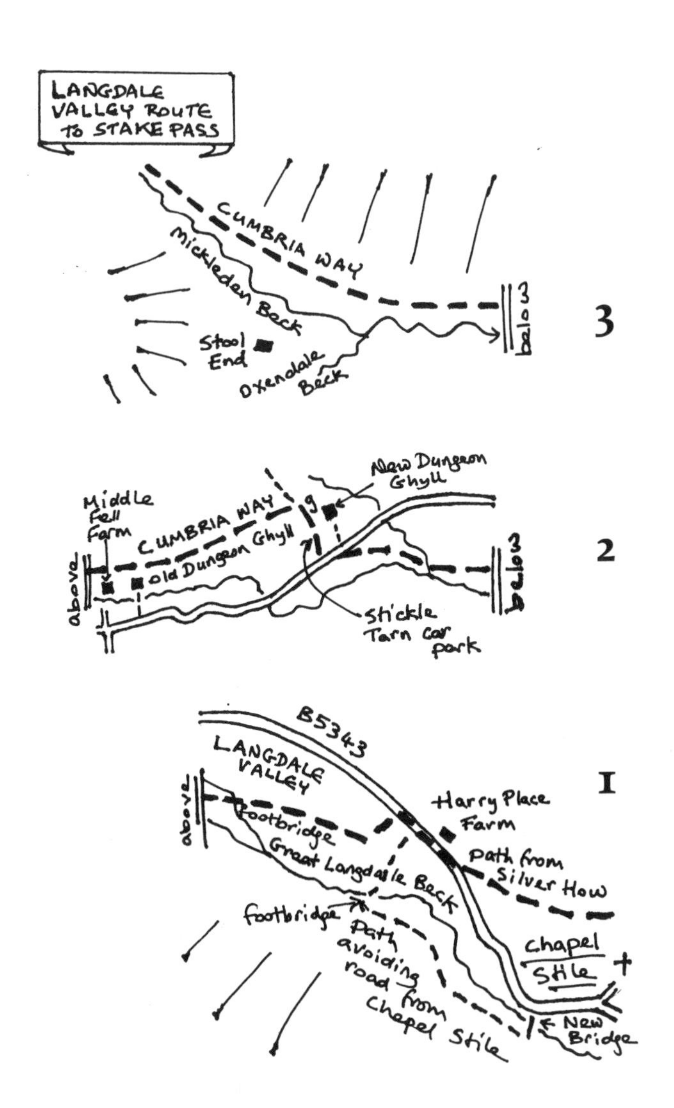
LANGDALE VALLEY ROUTE TO STAKE PASS
CUMBRIA WAY
Mickleden Beck
Stool End
Oxendale Beck
below
3
New Dungeon Ghyll
Middle Fell Farm
CUMBRIA WAY
Old Dungeon Ghyll
above
below
Stickle Tarn car park
2
B5343
LANGDALE VALLEY
above
footbridge
Great Langdale Beck
Harry Place Farm
Path from Silver How
footbridge
Path avoiding road from Chapel Stile
Chapel Stile
New Bridge
1

Stake Pass to Rosthwaite Bridge (5 miles)

You have now finally arrived in Cumberland, entering this old county at the parish of Borrowdale. The Stake Pass and Langstrath Beck below it also mark the boundary between AW's Central Fells and the northern end of his Southern Fells. The Stake Pass bridleway coming up from Langdale also forms part of the 70-mile route known as the Cumbria Way. This route, from Ulverston to Carlisle, was devised in the 1970s when creating long-distance paths was all the rage. Our walk now follows the Cumbria Way to Rosthwaite Bridge. It is virtually downhill all the way.

By the cairn at the top of the Stake Pass the correct route for Borrowdale is to continue downhill along the right-hand side of a little tarn. Beyond the little tarn the path bears right towards the Stake Beck valley. It keeps on a high slope above the stream, which is down to the right, and soon reveals a breathtaking view of Langstrathdale. Follow the recently restored original zigzag path steeply downhill to a footbridge crossing of Stake Beck in the valley below.

The glistening silvery line of Langstrath Beck meanders its way through a steep-sided glacial valley straight out of a geography textbook. It is enclosed by walls of high crags on both sides, above which rise the lofty heights of Glaramara to the west and High Raise to the east. With his fear of Lakeland valleys being developed by man for reservoirs, roads and forests, AW particularly enjoyed unspoilt Langstrathdale, perfectly free from any such interference and no cars.

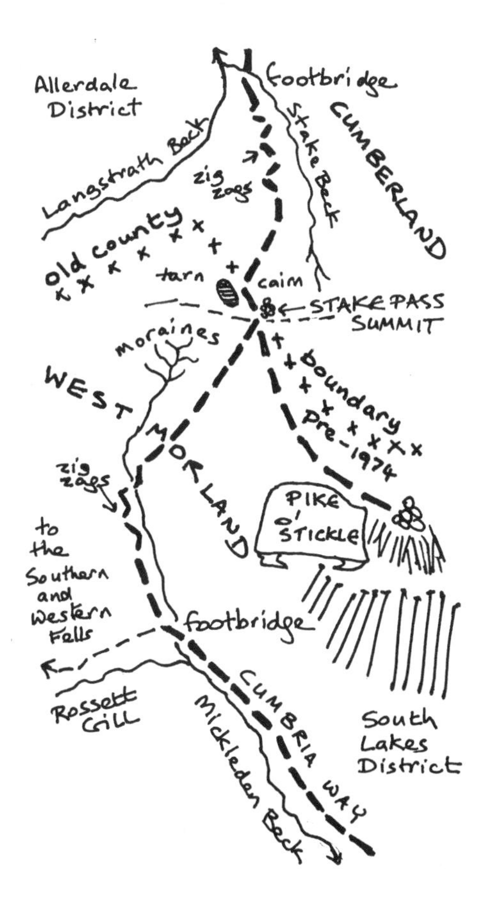

A reminder that AW's Lakeland legacy continues to this day is the beautifully restored section of the Stake Pass bridleway where it zigzags steeply down the western flank of Stake Beck. This route has been reinstated by the 'Fix the Fells' Project, aimed at tackling path erosion problems, and this particular path was part funded through sales of a 2010 calendar by the Wainwright Society. AW was never one for taking short cuts just to save time and criticized walkers for doing this.

The original route of the Stake Pass, the packhorse road between the valleys of Langdale and Borrowdale, followed a zigzag pattern on its steepest sections either side of the top of the pass, to ease the gradient. For those who lay the weight of the Lake District's path erosion problems at AW's door, it is worth noting that there were complaints by travellers about the poor state of the Stake Pass even in the nineteenth century.

Beyond the footbridge walk straight ahead down the valley, keeping Langstrath Beck on the left. The route follows the bridleway for nearly 2 miles to its confluence with Greenup Gill in a spectacular setting in trees below Eagle Crag. It passes Blea Rock, crosses a ladder stile and passes through gates, ignoring a footbridge on the left but continuing straight ahead to a memorial footbridge over Greenup Gill. Cross this and go up the steps to meet the adjoining track coming down the side valley.

View of Langstrath from Eagle Crag

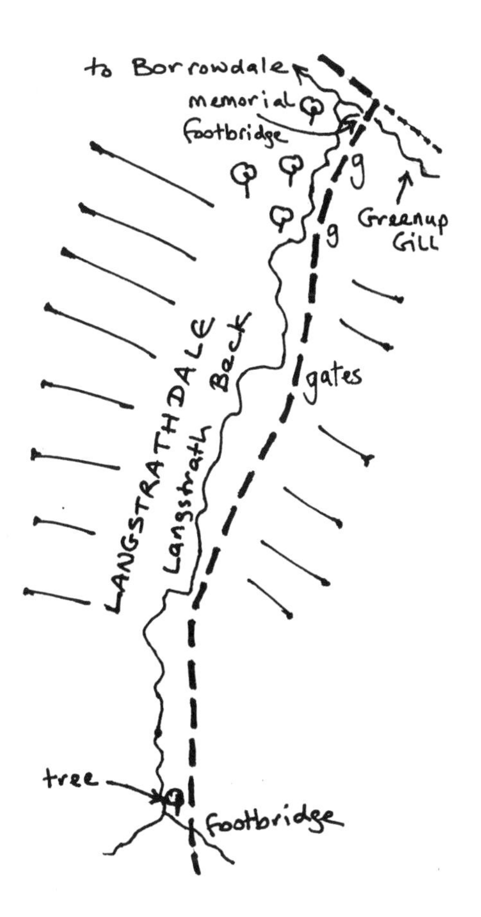

The plaque on the footbridge recalls the tragic tale of Gordon Hallworth, a member of Manchester University Mountaineering Club, who died of exhaustion while taking shelter below Lining Crag in January 1939. He was only twenty-one years old. A second memorial plaque recording the same event can be found on a rock by the side of the path climbing up Greenup Gill.

Beyond the bridge you join the track running down the

Stonethwaite Valley, which forms a perfectly sedate ending to this stage of the walk. Here you also rejoin the Coast to Coast path, which takes a different route between Borrowdale and Grasmere via Greenup Edge and Helm Crag.

Downstream of the bridge, Greenup Gill meets Langstrath Beck in a tranquil spot and together they form the crystal-clear Stonethwaite Beck, which flows north through the hamlets of Borrowdale. The beck is a major tributary of the River Derwent,

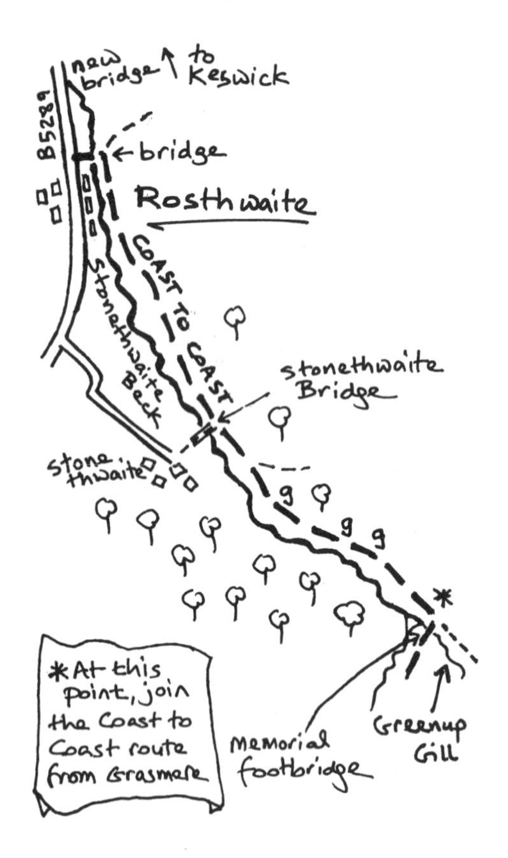

which continues northwards to the Irish Sea through Derwent Water and Bassenthwaite Lake.

In the Middle Ages, Borrowdale, forming the upper reaches of the River Derwent, was carved up by the great Cistercian monasteries of Furness and Fountains. From the sixteenth century onwards the rise of yeoman farmers and the mining of both slate and graphite on the fells nearby led to the development of the present-day farms and the principal village communities of Rosthwaite, Seathwaite, Stonethwaite and Grange. Tourism came here in Victorian times after the opening of Keswick railway station in 1865.

AW loved this part of Lakeland, as the grand scenery of crags, lakes, waterfalls and woodland is condensed into a compact area of exquisite loveliness. In his lifetime Borrowdale attracted its fair share of eccentrics. Millican Dalton's cave is now owned by the National Trust, while in the 1970s and 1980s, the film director Ken Russell lived appropriately in the 'Jaws of Borrowdale', inviting celebrities to his cottage below Shepherd's Crag.

Turn left along the valley path and follow it downstream for 1½ miles until you reach Rosthwaite village. Keep Stonethwaite Beck on the left all the way; the track passes through several gates between the stream and the hillside. The first bridge passed on the left leads to Stonethwaite: ignore this unless you are planning to stay overnight in this part of the dale. Continue about ¾ mile past this bridge to meet the next stone bridge on the left. Cross this and follow it to the B5289 Honister–Keswick road. Turn left for the Longlands Youth Hostel and the amenities of Rosthwaite.

Stage Ten
ROSTHWAITE BRIDGE TO BUTTERMERE CHURCH
(10 miles)

'There may be an opportunity for a pictorial guidebook to heaven. I may be permitted to come down occasionally and flap my wings over Haystacks.'
Ex-Fellwanderer

This stage of the walk re-enacts AW's very last journey, the walk up from Honister Pass to scatter his ashes by Innominate Tarn. The very last peak climbed is his beloved Haystacks, in the heart of the mountains recorded in his last *Pictorial Guide, The Western Fells*. It is uphill virtually all the way to the dramatic rocky viewpoint on Haystacks, and then you go downhill to walk along the lake shore of Buttermere and end at the little roadside church with its memorial window to Wainwright.

The Fitting Finale

On Sunday, 20 January 1991 the world sat anxiously by the telly. Breaking news: Iraqi SCUD rockets fire at Saudi Arabia, US Patriot missiles intercept them. More breaking news: Saddam Hussein parades seven captured Allied airmen on Iraqi television, possible human shields in his 'mother of all battles' with the West. Even more breaking news: General 'Stormin'' Norman Schwarzkopf, commander of Operation Desert Storm, blusters on to TV screens boasting that the 'coalition of the willing' has destroyed all Iraq's fixed SCUD launchers. Meanwhile, in a side ward of Westmorland County Hospital, author and fellwalker Alfred Wainwright draws his last breath.

The fireworks in the Persian Gulf overshadowed the quiet passing of AW, who had been born in an age of colonial wars and increasing militarism, as the naval arms race between the

British and German empires escalated in the run-up to the Great War. Despite all the massive social, technological and scientific revolutions that occurred during AW's life over the course of the twentieth century, in one sense nothing much had changed: man was still slaughtering man.

Although newsprint and air time were dominated by the global heavyweights of Saddam Hussein and Stormin' Norman, reports of AW's death, three days after his eighty-fourth birthday, did make the national papers, TV and radio. Thanks to his having a London publisher, several BBC TV series under his belt and an appearance on Radio 4's *Desert Island Discs* with Sue Lawley, AW's public profile was, at the time of his death, at its zenith.

It was all relative, of course. He wasn't an A-list TV celebrity of the day like Wogan, Jimmy Nail and the cast of Eastenders. His first TV programmes walking in the company of Eric Robson were shown in the spring of 1986 on BBC2 around 7.30 p.m. But even though they were often up against AW's favourite *Coronation Street*, the Wainwright programmes pulled in big audiences. Not bad for a man who had shunned publicity for over thirty years.

In the days following his death, newspapers ran obituaries, largely on the theme of the Lancastrian who fell in love with the Lakes. Stories were accompanied by the now familiar image of a homely AW in his twilight years – in his hand-knitted cardigan sitting at work at his desk, or in his armchair with a cat flopped over him, or with flat cap, sitting on the fells puffing his pipe, a thoughtful white-haired old man in a shabby coat. These were, after all, the only images the press had of AW. Fame certainly came too late in life for AW to exploit the potential of being a walking advert for outdoor gear. He was never to be seen in a Berghaus fleece. In photos, he was more like a character from *Last of the Summer Wine*.

In the newspapers of the Monday and Tuesday following his death, AW's genial mutton-chopped visage contrasted sharply with the front-page images of night-time missile fire over Baghdad, tank convoys in the Arabian Desert and the shell-shocked faces of captured airmen. On Monday 21 January, the Blackburn newspaper the *Lancashire Evening Telegraph* included a brief write-up on AW's death under the strapline 'Legend of the Lakes dies', next to the main headline 'Missile Alert'. The back pages reported that the day before the Rovers had lost again; it was their fourth home defeat in a row, losing 1–0 to Ipswich, as they continued to struggle in Division Two.

The Tuesday edition of the Telegraph had a more fitting two-page tribute to AW, 'Legacy of Love for the Lakes', by Geoffrey Rumney. In this the reporter boasts that the *Lancashire Evening Telegraph* was the first to get the scoop of a rare interview with AW, as he was persuaded in 1984 to talk to the paper's feature writer, Jean Alcorn, in the days when he was still a recluse. The tribute also included the kind words of Clifford Singleton, former Blackburn Council Chief Executive, who had been the office junior in the Borough Treasurer's office when AW, twice his age, had worked there.

The weekly *Westmorland Gazette* could not report on AW's demise until it next came out on the Friday after his death on 25 January, by which time everyone in Kendal had heard the news. Almost as if the company was waiting for AW to die before it could get away with it, his death shared the front page with a lead story about Cumberland Motor Services increasing their bus fares in south Lakeland. The details of AW's private funeral and cremation (the previous day) were recorded under the article title 'Wainwright Remembered', accompanied by the familiar photo of him working at his desk and puffing on his pipe.

Inside this edition of the *Westmorland Gazette* was an article by its news editor, Richard North, entitled 'At Peace with his Fells'. This was accompanied by tributes from the BBC producer Richard Else, Percy Duff, Hunter Davies and Andrew Nichol, the Gazette's Book Publishing Manager. Richard Else recounted the story of how when one of the Wainwright TV series clashed with *Coronation Street*, AW gave in to Betty's demands to purchase a video recorder. There were also readers' tributes – from a Barbara Swire of Arnside, a Derrick Stott from Essex – and a poem entitled 'A Tribute to Wainwright', submitted by N. Brason of Northumberland.

The same edition included the following notice in the Births, Deaths, Marriages section:

> WAINWRIGHT On January 20, peacefully at Westmorland County Hospital, ALFRED WAINWRIGHT MBE, aged 84 years, the dearly loved husband of Betty and dear father of Peter and Doreen. Private cremation took place at Lancaster on January 24. If desired, donations for Animal Rescue (Cumbria) c/o Fred Ruxton, Funeral Director, 1 Wildman Street, Kendal.

AW's body crossed the county boundary back into Lancashire because of the lack of facilities in South Lakeland. Doreen was Peter's wife and Westmorland County Hospital is the hospital now known as Westmorland General, situated on the southern edge of Kendal. AW spent the last two weeks of his life here in a semi-conscious state after suffering heart failure in his Kendal Green home. Although he had been a smoker since his later teenage years, AW had enjoyed a life free of any major illness until then. In later years it was only his eyes that packed up.

In the weeks following AW's death, the BBC repeated several episodes of the Wainwright TV series with Eric Robson, covering Lakeland and the Coast to Coast. The scheduled repeats were, of course, subject to events in the Gulf.

This stage of the walk ends fittingly in the mountains that feature in AW's last *Pictorial Guide. The Western Fells* was completed in the autumn of 1965 and published in 1966. This seventh volume was dedicated to 'All Who Have Helped Me', with a special thank-you to his unnamed wife 'for not standing in my way'. This is the closest AW gets to acknowledging the role Ruth played in the story of the Pictorial Guides. If AW and Ruth had operated as a normal married couple and spent time at weekends together then AW might never have written his seven volumes describing the Lakeland fells.

Ruth Wainwright walked out of the marital home for good in September 1966, the year *The Western Fells* was published. She lived in a rented cottage in Kentmere before moving to a house in Windermere. Hunter Davies notes that she died in 1985 and her ashes were scattered on Loughrigg Terrace.

The Western Fells is a survey of 33 peaks between Buttermere and Wastwater, the highest points being the summits of Great Gable and Pillar. In his conclusion, AW starts to look back on his thirteen-year odyssey, noting that the scenery of south and west Lakeland is the finest of all in his opinion. Part of the appeal of the Western Fells to AW was that it was an area, a bit like the Far Eastern Fells, largely free of the plague of summer tourists arriving by motor car. AW then goes on to list various favourites – mountains, summits, ridge walks and 'exciting situations'. After listing his six best mountains – Scafell Pike, Bowfell, Pillar, Great Gable, Blencathra and Crinkle Crags – he goes on to list half a dozen more he was sorry to omit – Scafell, the two Langdale Pikes, Place Fell, Carrock Fell and, 'most of all', Haystacks. In the case of Haystacks, his only excuse for omitting it from his top six fells was that it wasn't high enough.

When did AW's love affair with Haystacks begin? If he did not climb it on his first visit to the Lakes in 1930 then he certainly climbed it on his return in May 1931 during his Whitsuntide tour. The itinerary for day four of that trip was (yet another gruelling day) from Buttermere to Wasdale along the High Stile ridge to Haystacks, followed by Great Gable, Pillar and a range of other peaks before descending to Wastwater. It was, therefore, a romance that began in his twenties.

In *The Western Fells*, AW dedicates twelve pages to Haystacks, despite its lowly altitude, approximately 1,900 feet, just over 100 feet higher than Pendle Hill in Lancashire. AW recommended Haystacks as a cure for all ills, from toothache to persistent worries, and he vividly describes the hill, surrounded by much grander fells, as 'a shaggy terrier in the company of foxhounds'. His affection for Haystacks is clear. He loved exploring its surprises around every corner, its infinite variety of tarns and tors, its immense beauty and individuality.

On page ten of the chapter on Haystacks, hidden in small print describing the summit, AW reveals, 'There are fierce crags and rough screes and outcrops that will be grittier still when the author's ashes are scattered here.' In that sentence, written in 1965, AW's destiny became inextricably linked with Haystacks. A year later, AW elaborated further in *Fellwanderer*, the story behind the *Pictorial Guides*, stating that his last resting place was to be by the side of Innominate Tarn. The very last sentences in *Fellwanderer*, the first of AW's publications not to be handwritten, are probably his most famous of all: 'And if you, dear reader, should get a bit of grit in your boot as you are crossing Haystacks in the years to come, please treat it with respect. It might be me.'

AW paid a tribute to Haystacks by routing his Coast to Coast walk over it in the 1970s. And in the mid-1980s he was on the mountain again for the last time in the company of Eric Robson and a TV film crew as part of one of the original BBC Wainwright programmes, and the pleasure AW gets from being back in the fells, despite the foul rainy weather, is clear for viewers to see. The bit the magic of television does not show is AW being driven most of the way up the hill in a truck, but despite being in his late seventies, he walked up the last part himself. In the documentary AW chats to Eric Robson and says he will be in good company in his last resting place by Innominate Tarn as a woman had already scattered her husband's ashes there.

In the same programme, AW and Eric Robson walked around the abandoned Honister slate mine, and AW recalled the days when the quarry was still active. It was still open in the mid-1960s when AW was surveying various routes of ascent from the Honister Pass for *The Western Fells*. AW recalls his final filmed visit to Haystacks in Ex-*Fellwanderer*, published in 1987, remembering the problems he had slipping and stumbling as his failing eyesight made it difficult for him to identify the rough ground. As he says, the fells 'shed tears for me that day'.

So it came to pass that in 1991 AW's final wish, expressed in *Fellwanderer*, was fulfilled: to be carried up Haystacks in a little box, emptied out and left there alone. The final journey of Alfred Wainwright took place on Friday, 22 March 1991. His ashes were driven from Kendal to the old slate quarry at the top of the Honister Pass, then carried by a party of four – his widow, Betty, Percy Duff and Percy's two sons – up to Innominate Tarn, where AW's ashes were scattered.

In the edition of the *Westmorland Gazette* that came out on the same day as the scattering of the ashes, AW again made front-page news. Under the headline 'We'll set 'em up' was the story of the Gazette continuing to pick up the tab for the half pint AW had promised (back in 1968) for every walker completing the Pennine Way who arrived at the Border Hotel, Kirk Yetholm. Perhaps this generous offer was why AW's A *Pennine Way Companion* had sold so well. In the same day's edition, there was also a story about Allerdale District Council Technical Services Committee turning down a suggestion that Innominate Tarn on Haystacks be renamed Wainwright Tarn (nothing ever came of this proposal).

This stage of our walk ends in the Buttermere Valley, the natural dividing line between AW's North Western Fells and Western Fells. For the last two volumes of his *Pictorial Guides* AW spent a lot of time in this valley in the early 1960s, arriving by the Cumberland Bus summer service from Keswick over the Newlands Pass. In the conclusion to Book Six, *The North Western Fells,* AW already has a sense of regret that his thirteen-year love affair with the fells is coming to an end. He had timed his project to perfection, as at exactly the same time the axe was beginning to fall on rural bus services as more and more people took to the car.

AW liked Buttermere, both valley and village, because the area, 'a foretaste of heaven', was still largely unspoilt by mass tourism. It was the gateway particularly to the Western Fells and the High Stile ridge. In *Wainwright in the Valleys of Lakeland* AW recounts the story of Wainwright's Rowan, the young tree

The Buttermere Valley

clinging steadfastly to a crag by the side of Hassnesshow Beck on the north side of Buttermere. AW had first mentioned this rowan in his chapter on Robinson in *The North Western Fells* and asked readers to keep him informed of its development. They did, of course, and before his death he was quite pleased that walkers had started to name this tree after him. It was a natural, unassuming memorial to AW, seen only by walkers and certainly more appropriate than Wainwright's name on a shopping development.

The memorial to AW in Buttermere's little church on the rock against the backdrop of the placid lake and the towering Western

Fells is also a fitting tribute and forms the perfect end to this journey. The Church of St James the Great is dedicated to the patron saint of pilgrims and labourers – appropriately, for AW came to worship the fells and spent his whole life engaged in hard work, which inspired countless others to follow in his footsteps. The church was built of stones taken from Sour Milk Ghyll and the slopes of Red Pike. Its south window looks out towards the dark bristling crags of Haystacks. Below it is an inscribed tablet which reads:

PAUSE AND REMEMBER
ALFRED WAINWRIGHT
FELLWALKER, GUIDE BOOK AUTHOR
AND ILLUSTRATOR
WHO LOVED THIS VALLEY
LIFT YOUR EYES TO HAYSTACKS
HIS FAVOURITE PLACE
1907–91

The memorial, placed here in 1994, bookends this walk, which started 126 miles away, not far from the blue plaque outside AW's birthplace at 331 Audley Range, Blackburn.

In January 2007 a thanksgiving service was held in Blackburn Cathedral to celebrate the centenary of AW's birth. In February 2009 it was the turn of the little church at Buttermere to hold a memorial service, this time for both Alfred and Betty Wainwright, who had passed away on 20 August 2008, aged eighty-six, seventeen years after scattering her husband's ashes on the fells.

Buttermere village has a long association with writers. The story of the Maid of Buttermere has been recounted in literature for over two centuries. She was Mary Robinson (1778–1837), the landlord's daughter at what is now the Fish Inn; her beauty was so beguiling that she was mentioned in one of the earliest tourist guidebooks to the Lakes, *A Fortnight's Ramble to the Lakes in Westmoreland, Lancashire and Cumberland*, published in 1792.

Intriguingly the author of this book kept his identity a secret. He was, in fact, a journalist, Joseph Palmer (1756–1815), and his book made Mary Robinson something of a tourist attraction. In 1802 she fell for and married a cad and a bounder, Colonel Hope, a supposed MP, gentleman and brother of an earl, who ended up being exposed as a bigamist and fraudster and was hanged at Carlisle the following year. The tale was a sensation in the London papers and became something that fascinated the Lake poets.

When AW first started his excursions into Lakeland the eighteenth-century Bridge Hotel was owned by a writer, Nicholas Size (1866–1953), who had something in common with AW in that he was born a Lancastrian, moved to the Lakes and has a resting place in the Buttermere Valley. He was fascinated by the Norse heritage of this part of Cumberland and had a few historical novels published, including *The Secret Valley*, the tale of the Cumbrian's defence of Rannerdale against eleventh-century Norman invaders.

The similarities with AW end there, as Nicholas Size was an entrepreneurial hotelier, keen to attract the new wave of tourists arriving by motor car to his establishment, which he had reopened in 1920, when it was known as the Victoria Hotel. Size opened a golf course for his guests on the shores of Crummock Water and even had plans for a chair lift to the summit of High Crag. One of the hotel's old guest books records AW's signature, showing that he stayed here, on a trip with his cousin from Penistone, on 14 October 1946, when he was living in Castle Grove, Kendal. AW may well have met Nicholas Size, a larger-than-life personality whose ambitious plans seemed to be upsetting traditional Lakeland farmers.

As this journey through northern England now ends in Buttermere churchyard, walkers can enjoy the view to Haystacks and the High Stile ridge and take a moment for both personal reflection and consideration of AW's achievements and his legacy.

AW started life with nothing and managed to jump off the relentless never-ending cycle of mill-town life through a combination of sheer hard work and a few strokes of luck. His successful local government career was a major achievement in itself but was eclipsed by his talents as an author and illustrator, which he used to create the unique *Pictorial Guides*. He sold millions of books as well as devising the Coast to Coast Walk. The *Pictorial Guides* still sell and have now been meticulously updated by cartographer Chris Jesty. In essence, AW's journey was a life of both hard work and great works.

AW gave his royalties to the charity Animal Rescue Cumbria, and his donations enabled the building of the permanent dog and cat refuge, Kapellan. He left half a pint on the bar for walkers who successfully complete the Pennine Way. AW always wrote back, often at great length, to people he had never met. Born a working-class man in the age of Mitchell and Kenyon's silent films, he ended up a TV celebrity in his late seventies.

On 9 November 2002, fifty years to the day after AW sat down to write the first page of his first *Pictorial Guide*, over 100 people met in Ambleside Youth Hostel to form the Wainwright Society. Now with over a thousand members, the society has ensured that AW's legacy is not forgotten and it is actively involved in projects raising money for charity and promoting AW's work.

The most pleasing thing about looking back on AW's body of work for the north of England is that the places and views he sketched remain largely the same today. The National Parks, the AONBs and the local authority planning departments have largely done their job. The great age of reservoir building and blankets of conifer forests, a constant worry to AW, has passed.

But there is still no need for complacency. New threats to the countryside remain – wind farms, major road schemes, relaxing planning laws in favour of development – and perhaps the biggest tribute any walker can pay to AW is to ensure that the countryside of the north of England, captured in his countless sketches, remains free from inappropriate intrusions by man in the future. Otherwise his work will no longer be relevant, just nostalgic.

Rosthwaite Bridge to Innominate Tarn (5½ miles)

Turn left along the B5289 road into Rosthwaite village. Directly opposite the Royal Oak Hotel turn right down a narrow walled lane leading to cottages. Follow this as it swings left; then leave it on the right next to a cottage to join a field path on the left to Longthwaite Youth Hostel and Seatoller. The path follows a wall side on the right

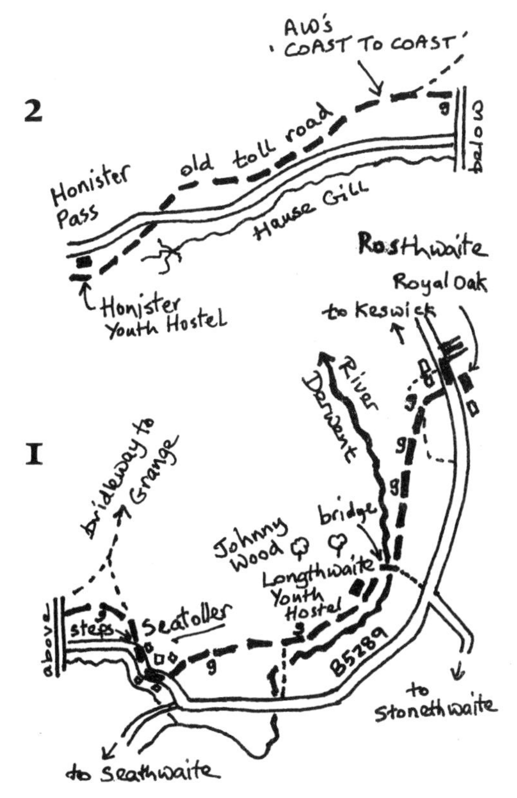

at first, passing through gates at more field boundaries heading for Peat Howe farm. The path joins a track to the left of a bridge over the River Derwent. Cross this bridge and then turn left, following the path in front of the hostel.

Longthwaite is the name of the tiny hamlet on the banks of the River Derwent. The youth hostel was not here on AW's earliest excursions into Borrowdale; it was purpose built and opened in 1939.

From Rosthwaite to Scarth Gap, below Haystacks summit, the route rejoins AW's Coast to Coast Walk. This may be the final day for walkers on our journey but for hikers on the Coast to Coast Walk going in the opposite direction, this will be day two of their expedition.

Keep the river on the left and follow the waymarked path to Seatoller, which passes through Johnny Wood. The path clings to the water's edge, and you will have to scramble over mossy boulders and tree roots (a chain set in the rock helps at one point); it then follows a woodland track through several gates and wall gaps. When the path emerges from the wood do not take the path forking left down to a footbridge. Instead continue through the edge of the wood, passing behind the Glaramara outdoor centre. The path soon reaches the corner of the car park by the toilets in Seatoller.

Much of Borrowdale, its valley farm and high fells, is in the ownership of the National Trust. Formed in 1895, the Trust acquired its first property in the valley, the woodlands of Brandlehow on the western shore of Derwent Water, as early as 1902. By the time AW was surveying the fells for his guidebooks in the 1950s and 1960s the Trust had acquired most of the major valley heads in the Lake District. Today it manages some 735 sites in Borrowdale alone, including extensive semi-natural woodlands of which Johnny Wood, a sessile oak forest rich in mosses and liverworts, is a part.

Go through the car park and turn right along the B5289 road leading through the hamlet at the bottom of the Honister Pass.

The former Yew Tree Inn, passed on the left, dates from the 1620s and was once cottages that housed German miners working the pure graphite 'wad' seams in nearby Seathwaite. Germans brought their mining techniques to Borrowdale as early as the mid-fifteenth century, when graphite was extracted to be used in casting moulds for cannon and musket balls. The upper valley directly west from here has a rich industrial legacy and you are about to follow the old toll road leading to the green slate mines below Honister Crag.

Follow the road uphill through Seatoller only as far as the sharp left-hand bend. Leave it here by the footpath sign indicating 'Honister Pass 1½ miles' and climb the stone steps to a gate. The steps continue steeply uphill alongside a wall to the right. The path swings left away from the wall and at a junction of paths fork left and continue uphill,

heading for a gate in the lower wall. Turn left along the track and pass through another gate at the next boundary. The path follows an old toll road here and is soon joined on the right by a higher track, a bridleway, coming up the valley from Grange. Continue straight ahead along the gated old road, which becomes a wide stone track heading towards the cluster of buildings at the top of the Honister Pass. The track crosses the tarmac road and continues on the opposite side, passing behind Honister Youth Hostel and going through a gate to reach the slate works.

The old toll route follows the original perilous line of the road from Honister to Buttermere built by the quarry company. The Honister Mine, shut in the mid-1980s, reopened as a tourist attraction and working slate mine in 1997. It had its heyday in the eighteenth and nineteenth centuries, culminating in the creation of several late Victorian tramways and inclines to extract roofing slate from Honister Crag, Yew Crag and Dubs Quarry. The top of the pass, Honister Hause, became the central hub of operations and the present youth hostel was formerly mine workers' accommodation.

Honister Hause is a watershed between the becks flowing east into Borrowdale and the River Derwent and the becks flowing west into Buttermere and the River Cocker. The top of the pass also forms a parish boundary. On the road summit you leave Borrowdale behind and in the car park adjacent to the mine finally enter the last parish visited on this journey, Buttermere.

Honister Crag

Join the bridleway that starts in the mine car park, signed 'Gatesgarth via Dubs 2½ miles'. This heads left out of the car park along a quarry track towards the high crags overlooking the road but soon reaches a path junction with a wooden fingerpost on the left signed to Great Gable and Haystacks. Join this steep stony path, which follows the line of an old tramway. The path diverts to the right of the incline but soon rejoins it and follows it straight uphill to the wall remains of a Drum House. From here, keep to the dismantled tramway, which

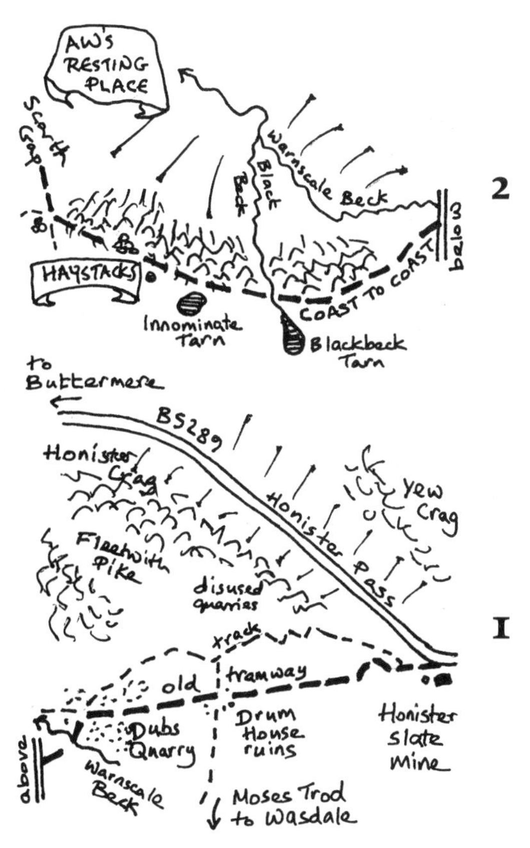

Remains of the Drum House

descends to join a zigzag track running through the disused Dubs Quarry.

The Drum House was where the winding gear was sited: this regulated the trucks carrying slate going up and down the inclines between Dubs Quarry and Honister Hause. The tramway was completed in 1891, but this quarry was closed in 1932. The highest point of the incline by the Drum House ruins provides the first view of Haystacks straight ahead.

The path crossing the tramway at the ruins of the Drum House heads towards Brandreth and Great Gable, and is thought to be the start of an old route used to transport slate on sleds from the quarries below Fleetwith Pike to Wasdale and the coast at Ravenglass. This curious route, following the contours below mountain summits, was used before 1850 and is known as Moses Trod, thought to be named after a quarryman who distilled whisky on the hillside. AW devotes a whole page to Moses Trod in his chapter on Great Gable in *The Western Fells.*

Drop down from the ruined hut in the quarry, following the zigzag track to cross Warnscale Beck. The distinct path starts to ascend again from here, going over and around little crags to descend stone steps and reach the outlet of the tear-shaped Blackbeck Tarn, from where there is a classic view down the Buttermere Valley. The path climbs gradually from here to reach the northern end of Innominate Tarn.

There is no need to say anything more about the final resting place of AW and no doubt countless others. The dramatic scenery speaks for itself and passing by the tarn should not be rushed. Hopefully the weather will be kind enough for you to enjoy a long lunch stop in the company of AW and his kindred spirits.

Innominate Tarn to Buttermere Church (4½ miles)

Continue along the right-hand shoreline of Innominate Tarn. The path starts to climb again to another little tarn sheltering below the stacked rock columns that form the summit of Haystacks. Some scrambling is required to reach the twin cairns on the top which face each other across a rocky ridge.

Haystacks, approximately 1,900 feet high, appears in the list of fells ordered by height in *The Western Fells* as summit number 22 out of a total of 33. All the hills surrounding it are bigger and it is part of a long ridge of lofty peaks between Ennerdale and Buttermere that includes Red Pike, High Stile and High Crag, and rises to the head of Ennerdale Valley, where sits the king of the Western Fells, Great Gable. On its north-east side, Haystacks looks across the deep cleft of Warnscale Beck to Fleetwith Pike,

The north crags of Haystacks

and on its south-west side it looks across to mighty Pillar, rising from the forests blanketing the valley of the River Liza.

Great care must be taken when descending the rocky summit ridge in the direction of the High Stile ridge to reach a cairn at a crossroads of paths at Scarth Gap. Do not climb any more but take the path descending right from the cairn in the direction of Buttermere.

You leave the Coast to Coast route for the last time here, as AW's long-distance trail heads downhill to the forests of Ennerdale. The descent to Buttermere is via the bridleway known as the Scarth Gap Pass, an old packhorse route that crossed over into Ennerdale and linked with the Black Sail Pass, which climbed over to Wasdale. The route is now popular with walkers as the easiest route from Buttermere to Black Sail Youth Hostel.

The summit of Haystacks

Join the Scarth Gap Pass and follow it downhill for the next mile to the head of Buttermere. The track starts very stony but soon improves, descending quickly, passing through two gates and zigzagging steeply down the side of a conifer wood to join a farm track. Go straight ahead through a gate, crossing Peggy's Bridge over Warnscale Beck, going through another gate and following the track to Gatesgarth Farm. Approaching the farmyard, go through

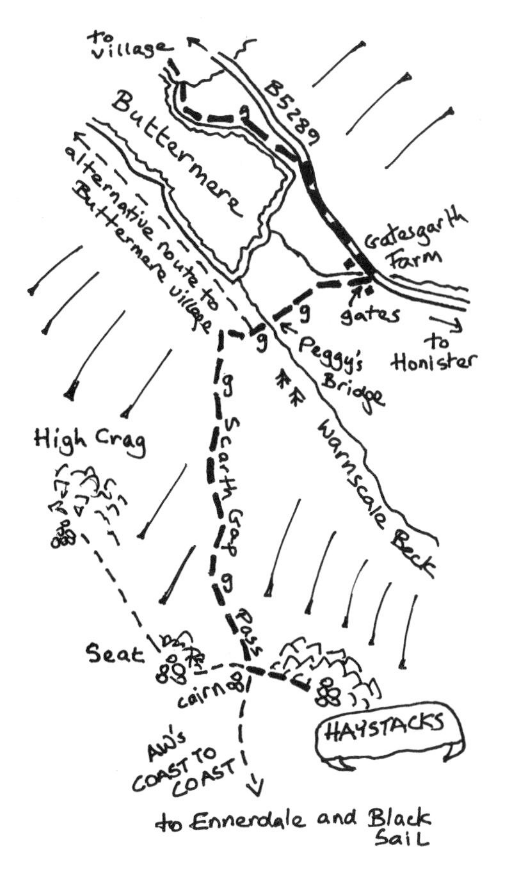

a gate on the left and the fenced path runs between a beck and the yard. Join the B5289 road coming down from Honister where it crosses the beck.

Warnscale Beck and Gatescarthdale Beck form inlets to Buttermere; the former rises in Blackbeck Tarn and the crags between Haystacks and Fleetwith Pike, and the latter rises near the top of the Honister Pass, its valley now used by the B road. The last 2 miles of our route are a gentle stroll along the shore of Buttermere. The outlet of the lake passes through Crummock Water and then forms the River Cocker, which joins the River Derwent at Cockermouth, some 10 miles south of Gatesgarth.

Turn left and follow the road down the valley towards the lake. After about ¼ mile on the road, join the permissive footpath on the left, which goes through a gate and clings closely to the lake shore. The path skirts Crag Wood and crosses a footbridge over Hassnesshow Beck. Beyond this, the lake hits a rocky shoreline and the path goes through a curious rock tunnel.

Approximately ½ mile upstream along Hassnesshow Beck is the crag on the steep slopes of Robinson where Wainwright's Rowan grows. The estate of Hassness was owned by a Manchester mill owner, George Benson, in the nineteenth century and he had his workers blast open the rock tunnel in the 1880s so that he could enjoy a complete walking circuit around the lake.

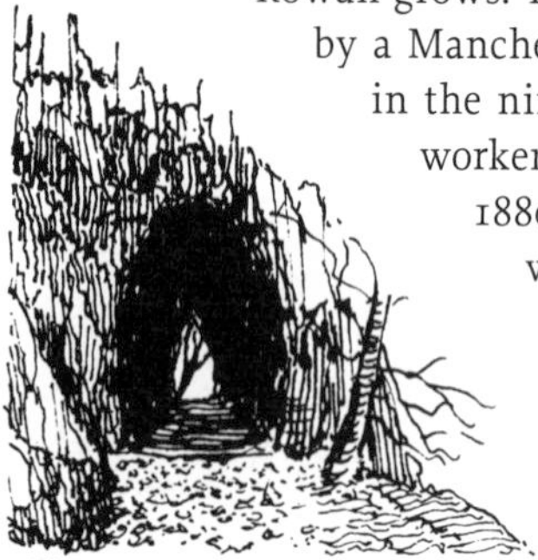

Continue along the shore beyond the tunnel through the lovely woodland of Pike Rigg. At the top right-hand

The lakeside path passes through a 30-yard tunnel cut out of the rock below Hassness. These grounds were formerly private.

corner of the lake leave the shoreline and continue straight ahead along the gated track that crosses a footbridge, swings sharp right and then left, and reaches the B road in the village through the cluster of buildings at Wilkinsyke Farm. Turn right uphill along the road to visit the little church of St James with its Wainwright memorial window. Turn left to enjoy well-earned refreshment in the village's hostelries and cafés and work out how on earth you are going to get home from here.

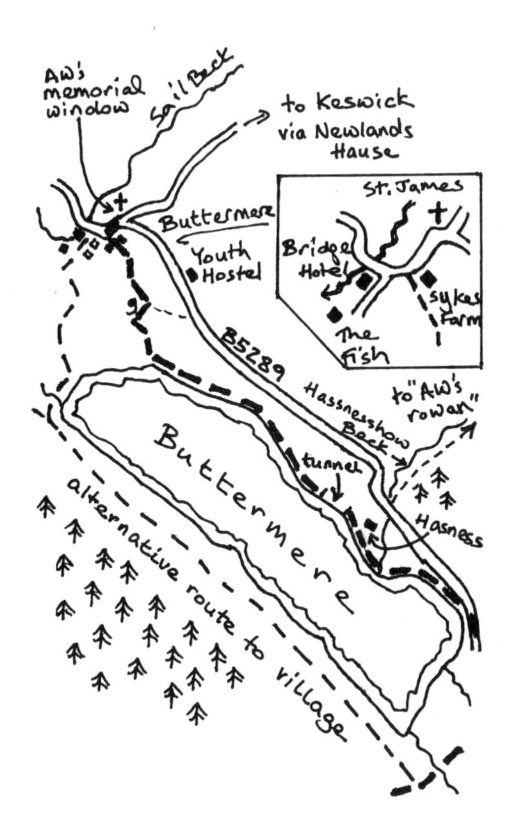

On the hillside above the little church of St James is the walled burial plot of Nicholas Size, the former owner of the Victoria Hotel, now the Bridge Hotel. There is no graveyard in Buttermere and he is reputed to be the only person buried in this part of the valley. He looks up to AW and AW looks down on him.

The present St James's Church was built in 1840, close to the site of an earlier chapel, and in its earliest days it was still part of the Diocese of Chester. Within the confines of this atmospheric church there are reminders of life journeys, some less fortunate than Wainwright's, including a poignant bronze memorial to Alan Edmond Catherall, who was born in Buttermere in 1921 and died serving in the RAF in the South Pacific in 1943. At the age of just twenty-two, his life was cut short in the same freshness of youth in which the young Alfred Wainwright discovered the Lakes.

I apologize at this late stage for not leaving a free half pint at the bar of one of Buttermere's hostelries for walkers who have successfully completed the 126 miles of this journey. Unfortunately I write in a time of austerity and bar bills cannot be met. Do not be disappointed: drinking in the bountiful natural wonders of Buttermere will be reward enough.

Innominate Tarn

Bibliography

The following books, directories, newspapers and websites were an invaluable source of information in the preparation of this book.

Books by and about Wainwright

Davies, Hunter, *Wainwright: The Biography* (Michael Joseph, 1995)

Davies , Hunter, (ed.), *The Wainwright Letters* (Frances Lincoln, 2011)

Wainwright, Alfred, *Wainwright's Tour in the Lake District: Whitsuntide 1931* (Michael Joseph, 1993)

____, *Pictorial Guides to the Lakeland Fells*, Books One to Seven (2nd editions, revised by Chris Jesty, Frances Lincoln, 2005–9)

____, *The Outlying Fells of Lakeland* (2nd edition, revised by Chris Jesty, Frances Lincoln, 2011)

____, *Westmorland Heritage* (Frances Lincoln, 2004)

____, *Pennine Way Companion* (2nd edition, revised by Chris Jesty, Frances Lincoln, 2012)

____, *A Coast to Coast Walk* (2nd edition, revised by Chris Jesty, Frances Lincoln, 2010)

____, *Fellwanderer* (Westmorland Gazette, 1966)

____, *Walks in Limestone Country* (Frances Lincoln, 2003)

____, *Kendal in the Nineteenth Century* (Westmorland Gazette, 1977)

____, *Three Westmorland Rivers* (Westmorland Gazette, 1979)

____, *A Ribble Sketchbook* (Westmorland Gazette, 1980)

____, *A Lune Sketchbook* (Westmorland Gazette, 1980)

____, *A Bowland Sketchbook* (Westmorland Gazette, 1981)

____, *Ex-Fellwanderer* (Westmorland Gazette, 1987)

____, *Wainwright's Favourite Lakeland Mountains* (Michael Joseph, 1991)

____, *Memoirs of a Fellwanderer* (Michael Joseph, 1992)

____, *Wainwright in the Valleys of Lakeland* (Michael Joseph, 1992)

Books about Blackburn and Lancashire

Beattie, Derek, *Blackburn: A History* (Carnegie, 2007)

Cole, Matthew, *Blackburn's Shops at the Turn of the Century* (Landy Publishing, 1996)

Graystone, Philip, *Walking Roman Roads in the Fylde and the Ribble Valley* (University of Lancaster, 1996)

____, *Walking Roman Roads in Bowland* (University of Lancaster, 1992)

Green, Harry, *Rambles by Highway, Lane and Field-path* (Blackburn Weekly Telegraph, 1920)

Holliday, Andrew, *Blackburn in Retrospect* (Blackburn Public Libraries Department, 1974)

Lofthouse, Jessica, *Three Rivers* (Robert Hale, 1946)

____, *Lancashire Countrygoer* (Robert Hale, 1962)

Miller, George, C., *Bygone Blackburn* (Miller, 1950)

Mitchell, W.R., *The Walker's Guide to Bowland and Pendle* (Smith Settle, 1993)

____, *Bowland and Pendle Hill* (Phillimore, 2004)

Shaw, J.G., *Notes on the Blackburn Waterworks* (Blackburn Times, 1891)

Swain, Robert, *A Walker's Guide to the Lancaster Canal* (Cicerone, 1990)

Timmins, Geoffrey, *Blackburn: A Pictorial History* (Phillimore, 1993)

Wake, Jehanne, *Thwaites: The Life and Times of Daniel Thwaites Brewery 1807–2007* (Scotforth Books, 2007)

Books about Kendal and Cumbria

Baddeley's The Lake District (Ward, Lock & Co., seventeenth edition)

Berry, Geoffrey, & Beard, Geoffrey, *The Lake District: A Century of Conservation* (John Bartholomew, 1980)

Bingham, Roger, *Kendal: A Social History* (Cicerone, 1995)

Coopey, John & Jean, *Kendal Green: A Georgian Wasteland Transformed* (Helm Press, 2002)

Duff, Margaret & Percy, *Kendal in Old Photographs* (Alan Sutton, 1992)

Ffinch, Michael, *Kendal and the Kent Valley* (Robert Hale, 1983)

Griffin, A. Harry (ed. Martin Wainwright), *A Lifetime of Mountains* (Aurum Press, 2005)

Hayhurst, Kath, & Hyelman, Anne, *Burton and Holme in Times Past* (Countryside Publications, 1987)
Hayhurst, Kath, *Burton in Kendal, Clawthorpe and Dalton: Photographic Memories* (Holme & District Local History Society, 2003)
Hindle, Brian Paul, *Roads and Trackways of the Lake District* (Moorland, 1984)
Satchell, John, *Kendal's Canal: History, Industry and People* (Kendal Civic Society, 2001)

Miscellaneous

Maund, T.B., *Ribble Motor Services: Volume 1* (Venture Publications, 1993)
Ogden, Eric, *British Bus Systems No. 2: Ribble* (Transport Publishing, 1983)
Stephenson, Tom (ed. A. Holt), *Forbidden Land: The Struggle for Access to Mountain and Moorland* (Manchester University Press, 1989)

Other Sources

Barrett's Directory of Blackburn
Bingham, Roger K., 'Heversham: A Website History' (www.heversham.org)
Blackburn Council minute books
The Blackburn Times
Blackburn with Darwen Council (www.cottontown.org)
Kelly's Directory of Westmorland
Kendal and District Directory
Lancashire Evening Telegraph
Wainwright Society (www.wainwright.org.uk)
Westmorland Gazette

List of Illustrations

Abbreviations

ABS: *A Bowland Sketchbook* (1981)
ALS: *A Lune Sketchbook* (1980)
ARS: *A Ribble Sketchbook* (1980)
CCW: *A Coast to Coast Walk* (1973)
MEM: *Memoirs of a Fellwanderer* (1992)
OFL: *The Outlying Fells of Lakeland* (1974)
PG1: *A Pictorial Guide to the Lakeland Fells, Book 1: The Eastern Fells* (1955)
PG2: *A Pictorial Guide to the Lakeland Fells, Book 2: The Far Eastern Fells* (1957)
PG3: *A Pictorial Guide to the Lakeland Fells, Book 3: The Central Fells* (1958)
PG6: *A Pictorial Guide to the Lakeland Fells, Book 6: The North Western Fells* (1964)
PG7: *A Pictorial Guide to the Lakeland Fells, Book 7: The Western Fells* (1966)
TWR: *Three Westmorland Rivers* (1979)
WH: *Westmorland Heritage* (1974)

Index

Acknowledgments

The biggest thank-you goes to my wife, Claire, and children, Billy and Bethan, who have endured my all-consuming Wainwright project for over a year. The kids finally have their dad back to play with them and at least they now know what Alfred Wainwright looks like. Also to the other members of my family who have helped me free up time to complete the book, namely Rachel and Ossie. Not forgetting my dad, Roy, for his unwavering enthusiasm for all my projects.

A big thanks must go to Paul Holden, who provided the original inspiration for this book by introducing me to Harry Green's *Rambles by Highway, Lane and Field-path*, the guidebook that Wainwright and Lawrence Wolstenholme followed on their youthful excursions in the Ribble Valley. Paul's excellent knowledge of Blackburn's history together with the memories of his father-in-law Lawrence have proved invaluable in filling the gaps in my research into Wainwright's early life.

I am indebted, of course, to Hunter Davies, who wrote a brilliant biography of Wainwright and has brought much of his personal correspondence into the public domain. Hunter's work has brought Wainwright to life and greatly deepened our understanding of him. It has proved an outstanding source of reference.

Thanks also to staff at Blackburn, Kendal and Clitheroe libraries and at the Lancashire Public Records Office, who have helped me access reference material; to Peter Linney and John Burland of the Wainwright Society for answering my queries; to all those involved in the collaborative effort of transforming my manuscript into its final form – and that includes Andrew Dunn, Michael Brunström, Anne Askwith and everyone at Frances Lincoln; to the Wainwright Estate for allowing use of original text and sketches; and to Derry Brabbs for his cover photo.

I acknowledge the support of all the walkers who take part in the Blackburn with Darwen health walks project and who have shown interest in the project as we have rambled through the countryside of Wainwright's youth.

Finally, apart from Dolly the dog who has been with me every step of the way, I would like to thank the two lifelong friends who have accompanied me on sections of the walk: Mark Abbott, who got very wet on the Langdales, and Andy Watmough, who climbed Scot Rake and realized his backpack was actually too heavy to walk with. Their company is always welcome on my own life journey.

This book is dedicated to the memory of
RICHARD FORSYTH
(1950–2005)
who loved walking in the British countryside